Dennis [illegible]

Oswald Chambers:
Abandoned to God

Oswald Chambers: *Abandoned to God*

The Life Story of the Author of My Utmost for His Highest

David McCasland

Oswald Chambers: Abandoned to God

Discovery House Publishers is affiliated with Radio Bible Class, Grand Rapids, Michigan

Discovery House books are distributed to the trade by Thomas Nelson Publishers, Nashville, Tennessee 37214

Library of Congress Cataloging-in-Publication Data

McCasland, David.
Oswald Chambers : abandoned to God / David McCasland.
p. cm.
ISBN 0–929239–75–X
1. Chambers, Oswald, 1874–1917. 2. Clergy—Great Britain—Biography. 3. Evangelists—Great Britain—Biography. 4. Christian poetry, English. I. Title.
BR1725.C43M33 1993
269′.2′092—dc20
[B] 93–9528
CIP

Printed in the United States of America

94 95 96 97 98 / DP / 10 9 8 7 6 5 4 3

Editor's Note: All of Oswald Chambers' letters, diary entries, and prayer journal entries are represented here exactly as they appear in the their original form. Mr. Chambers' poems, while not substantially altered, have been punctuated and typeset according to the standard conventions of poetry.

Once again,
To Kathleen

CONTENTS

1
A KERNEL OF WHEAT

Cairo, Egypt—November 16, 1917

Biddy Chambers glanced beyond the straight rows of thin wooden crosses toward the tall, iron gates of the British military cemetery in Old Cairo. She knew the funeral cortege must be nearing, but the high stone walls surrounding the burial ground where she stood shielded her from the familiar street sounds so close, yet so distant from her mind today.

Beside her stood four-year-old Kathleen, quiet and uncomprehending. She knew that her Daddy had gone to be with Jesus, and that was wonderful. But Daddy had gone lots of places before—to Alexandria, to Fayoum, to Ismailia, or to Suez—and no doubt he would be home again soon.

Biddy glanced down at the little girl she and Oswald called their "flower of God." Their eyes met and Kathleen's face broke into a smile. Biddy wished she knew her daughter's thoughts. Perhaps she understood perfectly that her Daddy was now helping the soldiers in heaven and wouldn't be coming back at all. Because of her childlike trust in God, she might be able to accept that awful finality better than all the grown-ups around her. Kathleen did know that something had made her mother very sad. The day before, Biddy had wept as she wrapped her arms around her carefree daughter and said, "Your Daddy has gone to heaven." That was the first time Kathleen had ever seen her mother cry.

A glimpse of horses on the street drew Biddy's eyes back to the gate. She squinted a bit—her characteristic reaction to something with which she didn't completely agree. She was uncomfortable with the extent of this military funeral for Oswald. She had consented to it only because of the men he had served and loved. This was their way of honoring him and saying good-bye.

The funeral cortege had started at 4:00 p.m. from Gizeh Red Cross Hospital, a mile away on the west bank of the Nile. The casket, draped with the Union Jack and covered with a spray of white chrysanthemums, rested on a gun carriage drawn by a team of four black horses. Six officers marched alongside the casket while an escort of a hundred soldiers followed, with rifles reversed—the traditional sign of respect for a fallen comrade in arms.

Under a cloudless sky the procession had moved eastward across the bridge spanning the murky, green waters of the Nile. Donkey carts and vegetable vendors stood silently in the dusty streets as the soldiers and the gun carriage moved slowly past. Barefoot children gazed in wonder.

In the west the glowing sun, revered and worshipped by the ancient Egyptians, dropped toward the Sphinx and the towering pyramids of Gizeh. Beyond them the Great Western Desert stretched silently into a shimmering horizon.

By November 1917, World War I had slogged into its fourth murderous year, and death was a frequent visitor to the hospitals and convalescent homes of Egypt. Military funerals were common in Cairo, but this one was unusual, containing elements reserved for a high ranking officer or government official. It was extraordinary that the man so honored was neither officer nor official but the Rev. Oswald Chambers, Y.M.C.A. secretary at nearby Zeitoun.

A large contingent of civilians, including women and Egyptians, awaited the procession at the burial site. Even the native servants from Zeitoun had come in solemn grief. One eyewitness later recalled that "almost everyone Chambers knew in Cairo found their way quietly and simply to the place."

Affectionately known among the troops as "the O.C." (an abbreviation for the Officer in Charge), Chambers had died the day before of complications following surgery for a ruptured appendix. As the word of his passing traveled up the line, from Cairo to Palestine, hundreds of men received the news in stunned disbelief. Surely there was some mistake, a garbled message, a misunderstanding. Why would God take Chambers when He had so few men like him? And why at the age of forty-three? It made no sense at all.

Many soldiers stole away to quiet places to face their loss in private and give thanks for the now-completed life of this young, dynamic man of God. How many times he had said to them, "Nothing that happens can upset God or the Almighty Reality of Redemption." On the front lines near Beersheba, the news struck Peter Kay like a bullet in the chest. His mind wandered back to the days at Zeitoun with his little friend, Kathleen Chambers, and her father. How easily they had slipped past his guard against religious people. Oswald had been the first chaplain to penetrate Kay's tough exterior through simple friendship and genuine respect. Peter's only religion had been wine, women, and song when he listened to Chambers talk about Jesus Christ and His atonement. He pictured the night he stood outside the Devotional Hut and claimed Christ as his Savior and Lord. And now Chambers was dead? Peter Kay bowed his head and wept uncontrollably when he heard the news. None of his mates from the Australian outback could understand what had reduced the battle-hardened soldier to such tears.

Biddy watched the officers gently carry her husband's casket into the peaceful quiet of the cemetery. Throughout the long days and nights beside him in the hospital, she had been so sure that Oswald would make it. The word from the Bible to her own heart during that time had seemed so clear, "This sickness is not unto death, but for the glory of God."

Gladys Ingram and Eva Spink held hands tightly, trying to hold back the tears they knew Oswald would have smiled away. At the Bible Training College in London, he had spoken so confidently of a loving God who never makes mistakes. When the war came, hadn't God led them all to Egypt in His service? Hadn't He promised to watch over them and keep them in His care? Hadn't He?

Rev. Samuel Zwemer, a noted American missionary, spoke briefly, along with Padre William Watson, a Scottish chaplain. Their message was of Jesus Christ, of His work through His servant Oswald Chambers, and of every Christian's eternal hope in Him.

Then, those assembled sang Psalm 121 from the Scottish Psalter:

I to the hills will lift mine eyes
from whence doth come mine aid.
My safety cometh from the Lord,
who heav'n and earth hath made.
Thy foot he'll not let slide, nor will
he slumber that thee keeps.
Behold, he that keeps Israel,
he slumbers not, nor sleeps.
The Lord thee keeps, the Lord thy shade
on thy right hand doth stay:
The moon by night thee shall not smite,
nor yet the sun by day.
The Lord shall keep thy soul; he shall
preserve thee from all ill
Henceforth thy going out and in
God keep for ever will.

After a prayer of thanksgiving and committal, they sang a final hymn, "For All the Saints Who from Their Labours Rest."

Stanley Barling, William Jessop, and Lord Radstock of the Y.M.C.A. sang with the mingled sense of loss and hope that Christians know in the face of death. With voices struggling through a flood of emotions, they remembered the optimism and irrepressible confidence in God that had endeared Chambers to them all. On the final verses, their voices, along with the others, rang out toward the twilight settling over the distant Mokattam Hills.

But lo! there breaks a yet more glorious day;
The saints triumphant rise in bright array;
The King of glory passes on His way.
Alleluia! Alleluia!
From earth's wide bounds, from ocean's farthest coast,
Through gates of pearl streams in the countless host
Singing to Father, Son, and Holy Ghost,
Alleluia! Alleluia!

A firing party from the Northumberland Fusiliers discharged three rifle volleys into the evening sky. The reports echoed into the distance as a bugler sounded the "Last Post."

Stanley Barling plucked a white chrysanthemum from the spray standing next to the grave, knelt down, and handed it to Kathleen with a smile. The words he wanted to say stuck in his throat as she sniffed the flower and returned his smile. He took her hand in both of his, gave it a gentle squeeze, then rose to his feet. How could she understand how much he was going to miss her father?

The crowd dispersed, talking, dabbing at eyes, and, yes, even smiling. For some, there was only a deep sense of loss. But for those who knew Oswald and his Savior, the sense of Christ's triumph overpowered the greatest pain. Biddy gently grasped Kathleen's hand and walked toward a waiting car. As they drove toward the Zwemer's house in central Cairo, she closed her eyes and saw Oswald, a few months before, polishing his boots in the Bungalow at Zeitoun. They had just visited their friend Gertrude Ballinger, suffering from typhoid fever and lying near death in a hospital.

Biddy had said, "I wonder what God is going to do."

Between brushstrokes, Oswald had replied, "I don't care what God *does*. It's what God *is* that I care about."

Biddy managed a smile. She knew the heart of love and concern from which her husband had spoken what might seem a callous remark. He cared deeply what happened to Miss Ballinger, but he knew that God's actions could be very confusing, while the Lord Himself never was.

She and Oswald had been married for just over seven years, and now, humanly speaking, the worst had happened. She was a widow at thirty-four, with a young daughter, no financial resources, and no means of support. If that were not enough, she was living away from the care of home and family in an inhospitable desert region of a foreign land during a time of war.

Already people were asking questions for which she had no answers: "Are you going to go back to England? What will this do to Kathleen? How will you manage without Oswald?"

Biddy closed her eyes, pulled Kathleen close to her, and softly began to sing the hymn that welled up in her heart: "Praise My Soul, the King of Heaven, to His Feet Thy Tribute Bring."

It would not be the last time she sang those words when all seemed lost and her only hope lay in the grace of Almighty God.

2
THE SEED OF GREATER THINGS

The cable from Cairo arrived around mid-day at the stately London home of Mrs. Reader Harris, head of the Pentecostal League of Prayer. Hoping it contained good news, Mrs. Harris slit the envelope and quickly removed the thin paper inside. The message left her stunned.

OSWALD IN HIS PRESENCE

Her mind raced to link the words with the reality they conveyed. Oswald gone from this life? But when, why, and how? People would want to know. But this was wartime, and everyone understood that letters posted that day in Egypt could take three weeks to arrive in England—providing the ship convoy eluded the German submarines. Perhaps she could cable the Y.M.C.A. to request more information.

Mrs. Harris gazed out the window at the fog-shrouded, barren trees on Clapham Common. Chambers had loved to walk the grassy fields of the common with his students from the Bible Training College, formerly located not fifty yards from where she stood. Now she must send the news of his passing throughout the League.

Four miles away in East Dulwich, Oswald's sister, Gertrude, answered the door of the Chambers' home at 11 Tintagel Crescent.

"A cable? Yes, thank you."

She returned to the small kitchen where Oswald's parents, Clarence and Hannah, sat at the table. Gertrude handed the envelope to her bearded, white-haired father, three weeks before his eightieth birthday. Clarence read the words aloud, "OSWALD IN HIS PRESENCE."

No details. No explanation of why their youngest son was dead. This was the way of news in the war. Almost without comprehending the fact themselves, the three began writing to family members and friends. ". . . Cable just received from Cairo . . . Oswald with the Lord . . . will send more as we know." If the letters caught the early post, they would reach the others in England and Scotland by the next morning.

At the time of Chambers' death, American troops had been in Europe only five months. War fervor still throbbed in the United States as people sang "I'm a Yankee Doodle Dandy" and "We won't come back till it's over, over there." Charlie Chaplin, Mary Pickford, and other movie stars promoted liberty bonds, and families prayed for a quick end to the war.

By the end of 1917, nearly every household in Britain had lost a husband, father, or son in the war. During the Battle of the Somme in July, 600,000 Allied soldiers had been killed. The Germans had lost half a million men. People who could not absorb the tragedy on an international scale found themselves torn again and again by the pain of personal grief. Britain was weary of rationed food, financial hardships, and broken lives but was still determined to fight on. The conflict some had predicted would end in a few months approached its fourth Christmas with no sign of "peace on earth, good will toward men." The only bright spot was General Allenby's advance in Palestine. Chambers had been expecting orders to that front when his call came to "higher service."

Word of Chambers' death reached the Rev. David Lambert in Sunderland on Saturday, November 17. "Received the astounding news that Rev. Oswald Chambers has passed away in Egypt," he wrote in a diary letter to his son in France. "I cannot take it in. Dead e're his prime. Of all the men I have known, none have influenced me more. I loved him as my own soul. I have not felt any blow so much since little Normie died in 1908. It is not hopeless sorrow or resentment, but sheer staggerment."

Just over nine years before, Lambert and his wife, Emma, had met Chambers shortly after losing their youngest son. They had buried Norman on a bank holiday weekend when the bright sunshine and happy crowds seemed to mock their sorrow. A month later, when Chambers came to Sunderland for a League of Prayer Convention, the grieving young couple longed for a word and a healing touch from God.

Out of curiosity, Lambert looked in on one of the afternoon League meetings and was "arrested by the vigorous style and virile message of a young minister with a Scottish accent." Oswald's subject, Regeneration, "fell like a lightning-stroke upon the artificiality and man-made activities of much of the religion of that time."

Chambers became a guest in their home, a favorite friend of their children, and the source of lasting spiritual encouragement.

Lambert paused in the letter to his son and took a yellowed envelope from his desk drawer. From it, he removed a typical piece of hurried but succinct correspondence, received from Oswald in 1909:

> *My dear Bro. Lambert,*
>
> *Praise God for your report that the Devil is paying attention to you—so long as he keeps firing at us you may depend he thinks that we are worth watching. My hearty greetings to your wife and bairns.*
>
> *The 'plague of flies' was not peculiar to Egypt—you will find them in the shape of busy little people that try to get over the window of your soul and irritate your outlook. God bless you.*
>
> *Yours, Oswald Chambers*

On November 18, 1917, the day after receiving news of Oswald's death, Lambert continued his diary: "The one thing with me most is the passing of O.C. I recall many scenes of the past when he first came to Wesley Hall, those marvellous Bible Readings he gave us. And now he has gone. And yet I realise him alive in a remarkable way. Not through any sense contact, but as I realise that Paul and Luther and Spurgeon and Moody and Reader Harris and the great saints are living. They are. So is O.C., in the radiance of His Presence."

On December 5, 1917, the League of Prayer's Wednesday evening meeting at Caxton Hall, Westminster, was set apart as a memorial service for Chambers. After tributes from League members and friends, Oswald's eldest brother, Arthur, took the podium.

He described Oswald as a "young hero of the Cross" and likened him to Barnabas—"a good man, and full of the Holy Ghost and of faith" (Acts 11:24).

"Oswald was a man with an energetic, inspiring personality," Arthur said. "Once started in any direction, he quickly outpaced his teachers. I persuaded him to pray his first prayer in a prayer meeting, but he soon passed me by and became a master in intercession.

"He was full of the Holy Ghost and that was the secret of his happy service. He was absolutely free from worry, living what he liked to call a 'restlessly restful life.'

"Oswald was a good man with no value for mere money or personal advantage. He would give away to all who asked. He had no use for those who sought to make much of him instead of the message he had to bring.

"He was full of faith. How well I remember his return in 1907 from a round-the-world trip on which he felt called to go. He threw down half-a-crown and said, 'There, I've been round the world, all found, on no-pence a week, and have half-a-crown left.' On the first leg of that voyage, aboard the *S.S. Baltic*, he told me he had spoken on spiritual things to every one of the 1,300 people on board, from the captain to the boy in the stokehold.

" 'Much people was added to the Lord' sums up the result of his life. His one aim was to be 'broken bread and poured out wine' for the Master. Throughout his life, his early mornings were given to prayer for others and receiving the daily anointing which gave him such a skillful touch with souls both here in England and finally in Egypt."

The service closed with the singing of one of Oswald's favorite hymns, "O Love That Wilt Not Let Me Go."

Ten days later, at another memorial service in Manchester, the Rev. David Lambert brought the tribute to O.C., outlining the teaching of the man whose life he called "the finest commentary on the Sermon on the Mount I know." All of the hundreds there who knew the man being remembered could have added an unforgettable phrase uttered by him, or recalled an act of kindness, indelibly imprinted on their memory.

Lambert summed up the impact of this life lived so fully for the Lord: "The most precious thing that has come to many of us through the message of God's beloved servant, Oswald Chambers, is that for the lowliest, least promising, and most insignificant person, the Great Life is possible. The mightiest things are made available for ordinary persons in and through Christ Jesus our Lord.

"God help us to follow him as he followed Christ."

* * * * *

That should have been the end of it. Oswald Chambers was only one of hundreds of thousands of British men who died during the Great War. We could expect his contemporaries to speak of him from time to time for months or even years, and then the references would fade with the passing of time and his generation. Instead, exactly the opposite has happened. Today, more people know his name and writings than when he was alive.

Long years after Chambers' death, his words are still in the hearts and on the lips of people around the world. The books that bear his name are read daily by literally millions of people in scores of languages. His messages can be found in print, on audio tapes, calendars, bookmarks, and even refrigerator magnets.

Why the continued interest in the words of a man who was born before automobiles, telephones, and electric lights? Why do his statements sound as if they were written right after he read today's newspaper?

The answer lies both in the message and the man. The two are inseparable. This is the story of their merging into the unique individual whom the world has refused to forget.

It is also the story of the woman standing at his grave in Old Cairo, wondering how she could go on without him.

Her given name was Gertrude, but Oswald always called her Biddy, an affectionate nickname. After Oswald's death, she spent the rest of her life giving his words to the world. The result of her self-sacrificing work under very difficult conditions was some fifty books bearing his name, but never mentioning her own.

"When the heart sees what God wants," Oswald used to say, "the body must be willing to spend and be spent for that cause alone."

Both of them saw, they were willing, and they were spent. What follows is the story of *their* utmost for God's highest.

PART 1

"A child's life has no dates; it is free, silent, dateless. A child's life ought to be a child's life, full of simplicity."
—Bringing Sons Into Glory

3
A SCOTTISH BOYHOOD

(1874–1889)

Aberdeen, Scotland—Sunday, June 14, 1874

At 7:30 in the morning, a large group of domestic servants arrived at the Aberdeen Music Hall, hoping to gain entrance to Dwight L. Moody's 9:00 meeting. Although admission was by ticket only, the servants sang hymns in the street for more than an hour until they were finally allowed inside. Moody preached a powerful evangelistic message from the text "Here am I, send me."

Later that same afternoon, a crowd estimated at 20,000 filled the grassy slope of the Broadhill in Aberdeen for an outdoor meeting. Laborers from Aberdeen's renowned granite quarries sat beside herring fishermen, bankers, and university professors. Women and children also took their places in the swelling crowd. The atmosphere was electric with anticipation.

All had come to hear an uneducated American named Dwight L. Moody speak about God. While a few critics complained that Moody's rapid-fire delivery and Yankee mannerisms made him difficult to understand, his meetings were thronged in Aberdeen, just as they had been in the larger cities of Glasgow and Edinburgh. His unique blend of Scripture and stories held the attention of his listeners in a remarkable way.

The thirty-six-year-old Rev. Clarence Chambers surveyed the immense crowd on the Broadhill. The church he pastored, Crown Terrace Baptist, was considered healthy and growing, but if every seat were filled, he would preach to no more than 300 on a Sunday morning. This sight was staggering for Clarence, who was born in the same year as Moody.

At 3:00 p.m., Moody and his associate, Ira Sankey, mounted the platform erected on a knoll at the base of the hill. Sankey, a gifted soloist and song writer, was changing the face of church music in America and Britain with his popular book of hymns. Accompanying himself on a harmonium, Sankey cast his strong baritone voice across the hillside, singing the words of a poem he had recently found in a newspaper and set to music: "There were ninety and nine that safely lay in the shelter of the fold." Many in the audience wept openly as he sang.

After several solos, Sankey led the choir and the assembly in a rousing version of "Hold the Fort." Moody then preached for twenty minutes on "The wages of sin is death," and the entire service was over in an hour.

That same afternoon, in the modest Chambers' home on Bon Accord Terrace, Hannah Chambers kept one ear open to her brood of six children. Arthur–13, Bertha–11, Ernest–7, Edith–5, Franklin–3, and Gertrude–2, were enjoying a quiet, Lord's Day afternoon.

Hannah winced only slightly as the child within her gave a sudden kick. Whether boy or girl, it was an active soul. A month more and, by God's grace, their children would number seven. How she wished it had been eight. Her thoughts wandered back to little Eva Mary, born on their fifth wedding anniversary, July 16, 1865. If she had lived she would be almost nine now. She had died at seven months, and the pain of losing her was still in Hannah's heart.

Hannah greeted all the talk of the Moody meetings with an approving smile. Nearly twenty years before, she had been converted to Christ under the preaching of the great London Baptist minister, Charles Haddon Spurgeon. Both Clarence and Hannah had been baptized by Spurgeon, with the event confirming their mutual resolve to serve Christ completely. Clarence abandoned his plans to be a hairdresser and became one of the first students at Spurgeon's Pastor's College at the Metropolitan Tabernacle in London. Following his ordination, Clarence served a church in Romsey for two years then came to Aberdeen in 1866 to be the pastor of Crown Terrace Baptist.

Clarence Chambers was a man of strong purpose and stern appearance. Tall and long-whiskered with bushy eyebrows, he swept his brown hair straight back from a line that had retreated halfway toward the back of his scalp. His eyes peered through small, round, wire-rim glasses, and his thin lips rarely broke into a smile.

Hannah, on the other hand, overflowed with warmth and good-natured fun. Born in the London suburb of Homerton in 1840, she graced each day with the charm of a brook rippling through a Scottish Highland meadow. The two were like many Victorian couples, with Clarence providing the strictness and Hannah tempering that with tender affection.

Clarence Chambers returned from the Broadhill gathering long enough for afternoon tea before returning to Moody's evening service scheduled for 8:00 p.m. in the Music Hall. By 7:00 p.m., the hall was jammed and thousands had been turned away, so the meeting began an hour ahead of schedule. Moody spoke on "The Prodigal Son," and so many people responded to his invitation to stay for "private conversation about their souls" that nearby churches, including Crown Terrace, were opened for evangelistic services and personal counseling. A few days later, Moody and Sankey left Aberdeen with revival fires still blazing.

A month after their departure, Hannah Chambers awakened her husband in the early darkness of Friday, July 24, 1874. "It's time," she said with a note of urgency in her voice. Clarence sent their house girl to summon the midwife while he remained by Hannah's side. At 2:30 a.m., not long before the first signs of the far northern dawn appeared in the sky, Oswald Chambers was born. Unlike all his brothers and sisters, he was given no middle name. He was, and would always be to those who knew him, just Oswald.

While the campaign of Moody and Sankey brought great spiritual renewal to the people of Aberdeen, it created challenges for Clarence Chambers and the other ministers in town. The *Aberdeen Journal* of June 24, 1874, said, "Laying aside the spiritual and moral aspects of the movement, we should say that the chief object which may be served by Messrs. Moody and Sankey's visit may be to import more life into our religious services; to elevate to a more sanctified place in the services of the sanctuary the divine gift of song; and to shorten the oratorical part of the service. The meetings of our American friends have been well attended by ministers of various denominations, and it will be for them to take the lead in instituting such reforms as will lead to a deeper personal interest on the part of Church members."

By the time Oswald was eighteen months old, rumblings of discontent with the ministry of Clarence Chambers were being heard at Crown Terrace. The complaints seemed to center on style rather than doctrine—"Sermons lack energy and life; aimless in character; not practically useful . . . ." Most criticisms were not specific but reflected a collective desire for change. After an initial airing of feelings in February 1876, a clear call for Clarence's resignation came in November of that year.

He agreed to seek another position and asked the congregation to allow him to continue as pastor until he could find another church. With Oswald, now two, and little Florence, the last of the Chambers children, only two months old, it was a difficult time to move. Grudgingly, the congregation promised its "cooperation," but only until the next March. Three months after the March deadline, without another call in view, Clarence yielded to the mounting tension and resigned his post in June 1877.

Not long afterward, the North Staffordshire Baptist Association in England appointed him Home Missions Evangelist in the famous china-making area of the Potteries. Soon the family exchanged the fresh North Sea breezes of Aberdeen for the smoky kilns of Stoke-on-Trent and the beginnings of a small church in the nearby town of Fenton.

While Clarence had a new job, little had changed for Hannah except their location. She had four children in school each day and four younger ones, including Oswald, at home. Her budget was meager and money was scarce, but none of her brood ever suspected that anything less than the abundance of the Almighty was theirs. She greeted each day with joy and each crisis with the assurance that the Lord would provide.

Oswald, like many children reared in a Christian home, learned to pray at a young age. But because of his earnest faith in God, his prayers seemed to go beyond mere form. His brother

Franklin described Oswald's prayers at the age of five as "very original" and recalled times when the older children, along with their mother, would tiptoe up the stairs at night and sit quietly to hear him pray as he knelt by his bed.

After setting his heart on having two guinea pigs, Oswald prayed each night for them and inspected the chicken run the next morning to see if they had arrived. He believed they would come because he had asked God. When the morning came that they were there, he never wondered if a family member had provided them. He simply thanked God.

"This childlike confidence in God, enlarged and enriched in wonderful ways," said Franklin in later years, "was the same in essence and simplicity whether he asked for guinea pigs or railway fares or passage money to Japan." When Oswald was seven, his father accepted a call to the Baptist Chapel in Perth, and the family returned to Scotland. There, along the banks of the beautiful River Tay, Oswald spent his formative boyhood years.

Often called the Fair City, Perth was a paradise for an active young person who loved the outdoors. Along with his brother Franklin, who was three years older, Oswald loved to climb the steep slopes of Kinnoul Hill, an extinct volcano rising from the banks of the Tay just east of town. From the seven-hundred-foot summit the boys could see a beautiful panorama of rugged mountains and cultivated fields. Then they could explore the dangerous cliffs, looking for agates. In the gully known as Windy Ghoull, their shouts would echo back as many as nine times.

Huge salmon lurked in the River Tay, and Woody Island could easily become Stevenson's "Treasure Island" for a boy of vivid imagination. While Oswald managed to escape the prevalent childhood diseases of the time, Oswald's explorations produced a number of accidents, including sprained ankles, a broken arm, and a hip thrown out of joint.

Friends and family members described ten-year-old Oswald as a boy of "characteristic quietness combined with rollicking fun." Merry and irresponsible, he showed little trace of the intense mental concentration that distinguished his character in later life. If there was a childhood trait that foreshadowed his gift and passion as a young man, it appeared in the realm of art.

Classes in drawing were required for even the youngest students at Sharp's Institution, a private school Oswald attended for seven years. At an early age, he displayed unusual aptitude. A large chalk drawing of a golden eagle, which he made on a blackboard, was preserved and proudly displayed to school visitors for some time. His other classes included Oral Bible Instruction, Reading and Spelling, Singing, Physical Exercises, and Musical Drill.

During Oswald's years at Sharp's, the school boasted an enrollment of some 450 students in an expanding program of classical and practical instruction. Latin, French, and German took their place alongside courses in mathematics, the sciences, religious instruction, and repetition of poetry of literary merit. The broad and rigorous curriculum was designed to prepare students to enter either the work force or continue toward a university degree.

From the Chambers' home at 27 Queen Street, a brisk fifteen-minute walk across the public meadow known as the South Inch took Oswald into the town center. He loved the smell of shortbread from Fenwick's Bakery and never tired of peering through the windows into Henderson's Game Butchers, where the heads of antlered deer were mounted outside. Oswald's sympathies lay with the animals, not the hunters.

The Baptist Chapel, with pews for two hundred, occupied the second story of a building on South Street. Here the Chambers family came each Sunday morning and evening while Oswald's father preached and Franklin played the organ. Self-taught and highly skilled, Franklin began his career as a church organist at the age of nine. Oswald, too, became an accomplished musician, equally adept at organ and piano.

Franklin later described their family life in Perth as a very united one: "Each evening, after the home-lessons were done, was given up to games of various kinds. We found our enjoyment and entertainment in our own home. No outside amusements could possibly compare with the fun and happiness to be found there. We never had any desire to be out playing or walking about with chums."

The only record of Oswald's education at Sharp's Institution lies in Franklin's observation that "the intense brain power of later life was not evident in those early days, and he never won a prize while at school." In all likelihood, Clarence's 1889 resignation from his pastorate in Perth prevented fifteen-year-old Oswald from earning the coveted Leaving Certificate, a key element for anyone interested in pursuing a full university education.

After Clarence was appointed Traveling Secretary of the Baptist Total Abstinence Association in June of 1889, the family remained in Perth for three months while their future home was determined. Most of the children were already on their own. Only Gertrude, Oswald, and Florence were still at home.

Oswald was elated when he learned that they were moving to London. The thought of life in that great city stirred him with excitement. More than anything he wanted to pursue his training in art. As he thought of the museums and galleries and stunning architecture in London, the possibilities for learning seemed endless.

The problem, as usual, was money. The family had never had any surplus to speak of, and Oswald's father felt that a healthy fifteen-year-old boy with a good education should go to work and contribute to the family's support. As soon as they could move to London, Clarence wanted his youngest son to look for a job.

Oswald loved his father but could not accept his ever-practical, ever-economizing approach to life. Money meant nothing to the aspiring artist whose dreams had nothing to do with monetary success. In September of 1889, Oswald took a long, final walk beside the River Tay and said good-bye to his boyhood. He looked forward to his next walks along the banks of the mighty Thames.

4
LONDON

(1889–1895)

The River Thames springs to life in the Cotswold Hills of south-central England. From there it winds through picturesque countryside, passing through Eton, Oxford, and Windsor. By the time it flows under London Bridge, it is two hundred and fifty yards wide and filled with boats and barges of every description. Forty miles east of London, it slips past Gravesend and completes the two hundred mile journey from its source to the North Sea. Since London's founding in A.D. 43, the river has been the city's gateway to the world.

When fifteen-year-old Oswald Chambers arrived in London, fifty working wharves lined the city waterfront along the Thames. Upper and Lower Thames Streets bulged with enormous warehouses, filled with goods from around the world—fruit, tea, and wine; furs, teakwood, and wool.

During the 1890s, London traffic grew increasingly more dense and chaotic. On the streets of the world's most populous city double-decker buses, electric trams, push carts, and horse-drawn wagons fought for space. Far below the bustling thoroughfares, underground electric trains rumbled through the darkness, crowded with their portion of London's four million inhabitants.

Oswald couldn't turn his head quickly enough to take it all in. The Industrial Revolution of the nineteenth century brought rapid and continuous technological change into every aspect of daily life, from locomotives to tea kettles. Inventions leapfrogged each other, creating a feeling of unlimited potential for human achievement and better living.

But for all its verve and promise, the London in which Chambers grew toward manhood was marked by vast extremes. The plush Savoy Hotel boasted electricity in every room and twenty-four-hour service. In the fashionable West End, mansions lined the quiet streets of Mayfair and Chelsea. But beyond Aldgate, people subsisted in the East End slums surrounded by filth, squalor, and disease. One observer said that the "human wretchedness" in London "is made to look still more wretched simply from the fact of its being associated with the most abundant comfort in the world."

The contrasts were everywhere. On the streets, 60,000 costermongers sold fish, fruit, and vegetables from their pushcarts by day. At night, ladies and gentlemen in evening attire stepped out of fine carriages into lavishly appointed theaters. The curtains rose on the early plays of the iconoclastic George Bernard Shaw and the biting satire of Oscar Wilde.

Chambers explored the city with delight, taking every opportunity to visit places that before had been only names in a book. He loved the cavernous silence of St. Paul's Cathedral, where he could ponder the astounding blend of art, architecture, and worship created by the legendary Christopher Wren. Stepping outside, his senses were immediately assaulted by the noise and rush of commerce that passed by in a never-ending rush to make a shilling. Behind all the noise and activity, the poetic mind of Chambers viewed the scene in terms of people. He wrote:

LONDONERS
(April 4, 1894)

Busy, driving, rushing Londoners,
Driven, palefaced, wiry blunderers,
Striving ever,
Praying never,
Busy, driving, rushing Londoners.

Thoughtless, flippant, godless Londoners,
Tricky, grasping, cruel plunderers,
"Doing" ever,
"Done by" never,
Thoughtless, flippant, godless Londoners.

Tired out, weary, haggard Londoners,
Beer-sopped, feeble, worn-out conjurers,
Struggling ever,
Resting never,
Tired out, weary, haggard Londoners.

Silent, lifeless, buried Londoners,
Death and Time have proved true sunderers,
Gone for ever,
Remembered never,
Silent, lifeless, buried Londoners.

In September of 1889, the Chambers family settled into a two-story, Victorian row house in Peckham, four miles southeast of the heart of London. The house at 114 Crofton Road sat near the top of a hill rising southward from the busy High Street on which buses, trams, and horse-drawn conveyances passed by from morning till night. In the frenetic pace of greater London, Oswald soon found himself missing the pastoral serenity of Perth.

Before the furniture was properly arranged, Oswald's father was away on his duties for the Baptist Total Abstinence Association. As one of two traveling secretaries, Clarence Chambers' job required a grueling schedule of visiting churches throughout the length and breadth of England, Scotland, and Wales. For the next two years he would scarcely be home long enough to repack his bag before leaving again. During Oswald's important teenage years, his mother provided his closest parental friendship and strongest influence.

Hannah used their limited financial resources to create a home where gracious hospitality welcomed all who came. Her diligence, ingenuity, and happy disposition produced an environment in which no one felt any lack. Bertha, unmarried at twenty-six, moved to London from Dundee to sell ladies' formal evening wear. Gertrude, seventeen, still struggled with poor health after a childhood illness that had almost taken her life. Oswald, fifteen, and Florence, thirteen, continued in school.

Little more than half a mile from the Chambers' house stood Rye Lane Baptist Chapel. Under the leadership of the Rev. J. T. Briscoe since 1877, the church had quadrupled in size, becoming a thriving congregation of eight hundred members, with more than a thousand people gathering for Sunday morning worship. Hannah led the way in the family's involvement, joining the church along with Bertha early in 1890.

The Rev. Briscoe was a forceful preacher whose sermons were described as "interesting and eloquent." With a heart for evangelism and an interest in individuals, the Rev. Briscoe led his congregation by example. During the Sunday evening service he scanned the pews for eager, attentive faces. A keen young person who was present for several weeks in a row would often be singled out by the pastor after the service and asked, "Why are you here instead of out doing evangelism at one of the missions?" Mr. Briscoe was interested in developing workers for God's Kingdom, not gathering a crowd for himself.

These were days of growing spiritual awareness and commitment for Oswald. Not long after the family arrived in London, he accompanied his father to hear Spurgeon preach at the great Metropolitan Tabernacle. On the way home Oswald remarked that if there had been an opportunity to give himself to the Lord at the service, he would have done so. His father was quick to respond, "You can do it now, my boy."

There in the street, the young man gave himself to God. In later years Oswald would speak of "being born again as a lad," and his brother Arthur would identify this night as the time when he "quietly, but decidedly, surrendered to Jesus Christ as his Saviour." In the days that followed, Oswald's life confirmed the authenticity of his spiritual birth.

On December 2, 1890, sixteen-year-old Oswald and his sister Gertrude were baptized by the Rev. Briscoe and were received as members into Rye Lane Baptist Chapel. Very soon, Oswald's spiritual commitment and intensity began to show.

Robert Flaherty, known to many as "Uncle Bob," often stood at the back of Rye Lane Chapel to welcome visitors to Sunday services. During the days of required pew rents, he shielded newcomers from possible embarrassment by his smiling invitation, "Turn to the right when you enter the chapel and come and sit in my pew, just inside on the right."

Flaherty was athletic and alert, a lover of tennis in summer, ice skating in winter, and walking all year round. As leader of the

Young Men's Christian Workers' Association at Rye Lane, he was a magnet to Oswald Chambers and others who longed to serve the God they had come to know. He had been converted and baptized by the Rev. Briscoe in 1884, only six years before Oswald joined the church. Now, with an increasingly rich knowledge of the Scriptures and a deep interest in individuals, Flaherty could often be seen walking with one of the young men in the church, arms linked, talking earnestly of the Lord Jesus Christ.

Flaherty was immediately impressed by what he called "the deep spirituality" of the young Chambers. Oswald began attending the weekly prayer meetings regularly, but it was some time before he took part by praying aloud. "His prayers at first were crude, just a sentence or two, but they were expressions which laid hold of one," Flaherty said. "More than once I heard him say, 'O Lord, drench us with humility,' a great prayer for one so young."

In a Bible class for young men, Chambers delved into the Scriptures, always focusing on the application of the truth in daily life. In company with Flaherty, he participated in evangelistic meetings in local lodging houses where the very poorest people of London found a temporary home. In contrast with the freshly scrubbed Sunday morning congregation at Rye Lane, the lodging house crowd smelled of tobacco smoke and stale beer. Few had bathed recently and they presented a formidable audience for a youthful "preacher" who had not yet begun to shave. What could he say to these people who had been down so many detours and dead ends on the road of life?

Chambers came to them not only with a strong dose of youthful idealism, but with the gospel of Jesus Christ. In spite of the self-inflicted nature of many of their problems, his heart went out to them in genuine concern. Robert Flaherty said of young Oswald: "He was always an ardent worker among the down and out. These men always appealed to him, and perhaps gave him a deeper insight into the power of sin to degrade, and also the greater power of the grace of God to break the power of cancelled sin and to redeem men to Himself."

For the first time in his life, Oswald was part of a church where his father was not the pastor. In concert with a flourishing group of at least a hundred young Christians his own age, Chambers was free to be himself, expressing the spiritual vitality springing out of His growing relationship with Christ.

One of his closest friends of these days was George Oxer, who recalled their comradeship in these words: "I was Oswald Chambers' chum, as far as his somewhat unique soul could have a chum, for some years when both of us were in the late teens and early twenties. At that time his soul was dining most happily and somewhat voraciously at the table of the poet Browning, and his 'tidbits' of Robert were constantly passed on to me for my delectation, but I fear that my felicity was sometimes more assumed than factual.

"The fact that he espied angels where I saw only a fence did not militate against a real friendship. Each to the other was a fellow-flounderer in wayside bogs not unfamiliar to travelers along the road of the great 'Quest.' I used to run my doubts full tilt at him, and can even now feel his arm grip mine and hear the urge of his spirit in the Scotch of his voice, 'Courage, lad.' "

It was customary in churches of that day for persons desiring to become members to be visited by elders or deacons who questioned them concerning their personal faith in Christ. Church minutes reveal that young George Oxer received not only the two regularly assigned visitors, but also a third sent to ascertain the exact nature of his beliefs.

"How easy it was in those early days," Oxer continued, "to detect the brave soul beating behind the brain in turmoil, battling with the 'tugs.' The impress of his spirit upon my own is ineradicable."

The rapidly growing circle of young people at Rye Lane Chapel included one son and four daughters of a local grocer and tea merchant named Benjamin Brain. All five made their public declaration of faith in Christ and were baptized during 1889 and 1890. Louisa Brain, known as "Louie," became the object of George Oxer's attentions, while her younger sister, Chrissie, captured the interest of Oswald Chambers. Every Sunday morning they all attended worship in the spacious but crowded sanctuary of Rye Lane Chapel. Every pew was filled to capacity including those in the U-shaped balcony, looking down on the raised pulpit platform with its highly polished wooden rail. When the Rev. Briscoe rose to preach, his warmth melted every barrier of position and distance between him and the congregation. It was "Pa" Briscoe speaking fervent, unforgettable words of encouragement from God. Sunday evenings found Chambers and many other young people involved in open air meetings or holding services in the nearby Sumner Road Mission.

By the standards of the day, most young people socialized in chaperoned groups, instead of moving more freely as unescorted couples. In a way, this made the courtship process more subtle and challenging, and perhaps more interesting. When Oswald Chambers played the piano at a church social or hymn sing, there was no rule that said Chrissie Brain couldn't stand close beside him and turn pages in the hymnal. And her presence awakened feelings in him he had never known before.

Oswald was only a year older than Chrissie, and the two soon became close friends. By the age of fifteen, with her formal education ended, she worked full-time in her father's grocery store. She cherished Oswald's sense of humor, so uniquely blended with his spiritual intensity and vision for the future. He, in turn, found in Chrissie a sympathetic listener who felt no need to give pat answers to his spiritual struggles. Over a period of months, they became true soul-mates, eventually treasuring the glow of first-love and a growing relationship in which they could share their deepest hopes and dreams.

Chrissie admired Oswald for his deep commitment to Christ and his courageous preaching in street meetings, often to antagonistic crowds. "I heard many of his youthful addresses," she said. "His first open-air address was given in a crowded thoroughfare in Peckham; he spoke on 'Ho, every one that thirsteth, come ye to the waters.' It was a glorious message, the giving of which cost him so much that he was ill the next day. Many other addresses followed, and when only eighteen he gave an address to parents at a Sunday School social. It was the best address to parents I ever heard, but its precocity was somewhat staggering! It ended with 'Home should be heaven, and Heaven should be home.' "

Oswald shared his poems, written during days of spiritual growth and doubt, almost exclusively with Chrissie, who understood and cared.

FRAGMENTS
(London, November 10, 1893)

Undone. Great deeds, precious principles and true,
Fallen far, far short of, striving, struggling,
Battling. Almost — — gone!
Heartsick and weary. Undone. Undone!

Wasted time! Bitter torturing memory!
Work, overwork, and work again after
Drowneth not the bitterness of wasted time
Unrecallable and unforgettable.

FRAGMENTS
(London, December 16, 1893)

Unappreciated! Great thoughts,
Greater imaginings, Music—all executed,.
Patience waits—dies—unappreciated.

Myself. Pure, terrible, high,
Vile, sensual, devilish,
God-like, Devil-like—A man!

While Oswald's spiritual development was accelerating at Rye Lane Chapel, his artistic nature was experiencing a great deal of frustration. Although he was clearly gifted in music and art, his practical father could not conceive of his youngest son finding a life-work in either endeavor. Art, his father thought, was a luxury, and earning a living was a necessity. Music was an enhancement of life and a pleasure, but not a secure source of income for a man.

The pragmatic approach of the Rev. Clarence Chambers, no doubt, led to Oswald's being apprenticed to an engraver. By working under a skilled master for a prescribed time, Oswald could earn a small wage and become certified as a journeyman in the trade. The course of Oswald's life might have been much different had he not carelessly stepped off a tram one day and injured himself to such an extent that the newly begun apprenticeship had to be canceled.

Oswald longed for further art training, but his father expressed a serious moral objection in addition to his practical concerns. At the National Art Training School (later renamed the Royal College of Art), students were expected to draw the human figure from nude models. Seeing this as an abomination to God, Clarence could not approve of such a venture. Oswald loved his father, but did not agree with his view of art. To him, art was God's gift to make life on earth bearable. Poetry and music were not luxuries, but necessities.

INSANE
(December 26, 1893)

Insane!
Thus man proclaimeth the poetic—
Rhymes, jingles of all words, may not be sane,
But Poetry? those motions of the soul
Expressed inadequately in words—never!
That dew descending on the heart—insanity?

Music—insanity?
Only if sanity be that hard, dry,
Mechanical monotony of so-called fact.
But if that mechanical monotony of fact
Be but as the organ case, what then?
The appreciation of the music insanity?

Man! who is man? there's One, his creator,
Who gave those divine essences we call
Music, Poetry, Art, through which God breathes
His Spirit of Peace into the soul.

Mechanical monotony of so-called fact
Whereby we in this clay do exist—
God gave this too, and lo! death and His judgment
Descends on him who ignores this means sent
For existence here
Whilst training for existence hereafter.

Likewise,
On him who calleth those divine breathings
Puny and unreal, God comes in judgment,
Shutting his eyes to all the beautiful,
His ears to the altogether lovely,
His mind to the pure and noble.

Man, beware!
God is a Spirit,
And they that worship Him must worship Him
In Spirit.

It is uncertain whether reason or Hannah eventually prevailed. Perhaps it was the fact that an Art Master's Certificate would enable Oswald to teach art in school and thus earn a living. Whatever the reasons, Clarence eventually relented, and Oswald enthusiastically seized the opportunity to continue his studies, reveling in the chance to train in his area of interest.

The National Art Training School existed primarily to train teachers for the United Kingdom and to instruct those who wished to work as artists and designers in industry. Located just south of Hyde Park and next to the Royal Albert Hall, it served some five hundred students in a variety of artistic disciplines. Five days a week for two years Oswald journeyed from Peckham to South Kensington, immersing himself in artistic technique and principles. He performed particularly well in "black and white," showing rare ability with pencil sketches. A large portrait of Beethoven done by him in 1893 portrays the deaf composer with a piercing eye and determined set of jaw suffused with a kindness rarely seen in other depictions of him.

Although not a National Art Scholar with all fees paid, Chambers may have received some financial help through "Studentships" that provided a weekly allowance toward the payment of school expenses. His older brothers very likely contributed financially to this phase of his education.

Oswald received his Art Master's Certificate early in 1895 and was awarded a two-year scholarship to study in the great art centers of Europe. However, he startled the art faculty and his friends by turning the scholarship down. The decision was entirely his own, based on his observations of those who had suffered moral and spiritual ruin during similar courses of study.

His affection for Chrissie continued to grow and they carried on a lively correspondence, even while living near each other in London. After a difficult time of unemployment and struggle to find God's will for the way ahead, Oswald felt gripped by a sense of calling. He wrote to Chrissie on April 22, 1895:

'Whom shall I send to proclaim the salvation of the aesthetic kingdom, who will go for us?' Then through all my weakness, my sinfulness and my frailty my soul cried, 'Here am I, send me.' I would as soon drown myself as undertake such a work unless He was with me, unless He called me, unless He sent me. Jesus Christ is my Saviour, my Master, He is the hot coal from off the altar that has touched my soul, my eyes, my ears, my mouth—and I must. Pray for me. I do not know how this is to be done—but there is something wrong somewhere, else Christians and art, music and poetry would not in their training be so opposed to Christ, mark you. It is the training that is wrong, not the visible works of music and art and poetry. Again I say, I do not know how this is to be accomplished, but if God calls, God will guide and I know that this kingdom shall become the kingdom of His Son. I said I had begun, the outlook is almost too much, but for Jesus sake, I plunge into arduous hard study to prepare me, that men must listen, because of the double authority which I must have—of the knowledge and of God, in His strength there shall be both.

Ruskin struck the sin of the spirit of immorality with the sledgehammer of a champion, fired by the Spirit of Christ, and the kingdom of art trembled, that champion is growing feeble now, and art is settling to the sensually reposeful position of previous ages. Our Saviour, as far as my limited knowledge goes, has no representative to teach, to reprove, to exhort—and Oh Spirit of God, Thou knowest, an ambition, a longing, a love has seized me powerfully, and has convinced me of the lack. I know my life work is in the Almighty strength of Jehovah to strike for the redemption, or rather proving Christ's redemption for the aesthetic kingdom. There is much in all these already bowed to the Kingship of Christ, but the spirit of art is to so sad an extent, the spirit of immorality.

The kingdom of the aesthetics lies in a groveling quagmire, half fine, half impure; there is a crying need for a fearless preacher of Christ

> *in the midst of that kingdom, for a fearless writer, writing with the blood of Christ, proclaiming His claims in the midst of that kingdom, for a fearless lecturer above pandering to popular taste, to warn and exhort that all the kingdoms of this world are to become Christ's—that artists, poets and musicians be good and fearless Christians. The preacher, lecturer, writer must be a man of God first, then a soulful student, that he may preach, lecture and write with authority.*
>
> *Methinks I have heard that cry and have seen the beseeching look of Christ towards that kingdom, longing for it to be His own. It may be said that the ordinary minister can do this, only a few can, the majority know not the love of beauty as an artist knows it, and artists as a rule will not heed ministers. The duty of ministers is to instruct the people out of the bigoted notions against art. It is for the man of God artist to enter this aesthetic kingdom and live and struggle and strain for its salvation and exaltation.*

In June he decided to enroll in a two-year arts course at the University of Edinburgh. The rigorous program would provide valuable training, but leave him without a full university degree.

He wrote to Chrissie on June 27, 1895: "Do not be too sorry that I cannot go in for a University curriculum, maybe I shall be best without it. 'Seekest thou great things for thyself? Seek them not.' But although I cannot give myself a University training, I will to the limit of my power educate myself for His sake. Oh how much weaning it will take, how much discipline! before my life shines forth with the deep passion of my soul 'for the sake of Jesus Christ.' Perhaps I shall not be worthy until He has weaned me by a great sorrow. What the great sorrow will be, I do not know; perhaps it won't be at all."

As much as Chambers anticipated studying in Edinburgh, he felt the emotional pain of leaving his home, church, and friends. There would be no more evenings around the piano in Chrissie's home with George Oxer, Louie Brain, and the others from Rye Lane Chapel. His long talks with Chrissie would have to give way to long letters, a poor substitute for companionship and the sound of her voice.

Before his departure for the university Oswald and Chrissie spent a summer evening together in her home. Just for her he played the slow movement of Beethoven's "Moonlight Sonata," and then read Tennyson's "Maud." Chrissie, now twenty years old, was sure she loved Oswald, and was willing to wait as long as she had to for him. He held strong feelings for her too and felt a part of him torn away when they parted.

On July 24, his twenty-first birthday, Oswald paused to make an emotional diary entry before leaving London:

> I'm going away from my home now, like a bird leaving the old nest, and I'm fond of home. This room with its four plain walls has opened out into Heaven. Here have I drunk in God, here have I prayed, here have I wept, here have I worked, here have I agonized, and now, Farewell Home! I smile, because all you know and have seen, God has known and seen too. How grand, you'll never tell the secrets whispered by me in the ear of God, and God's whispered words in mine. No, you'll be secret. Dear room, good-bye!
>
> And Father and Mother and Gertrude, Oh God, be great and kind and ever present to them. And all the rest, but they are most away, and these are most at home, these know me in my nature as I am, they have been to me quiet and kind and steadfast and I love them. . . .
>
> Scotland, all hail! How my soul beats and strains and yearns for you, Scotland, Bonnie, bonnie Scotland, how I love you! It'll not be long now afore I'll be among yer hills and braes and woods, Scotland. Ye'll give me the steadfastness of yer everlasting hills, the strength of yer storm-torn firs, the power of yer mountain streams, the tenderness of yer bluebells, and the faithfulness of yer noble pride.

Six years had passed since the boy of fifteen had come with his family from Perth to the city of London, so filled with devils and dreams. His heart, always tender toward God, had unreservedly embraced Christ as Savior, Master, and Lord.

Now, after years of uncertainty, the way ahead seemed clear. The young man sped northward by train, alone, following what he felt was the unmistakable call from God. Mixed with that sense of calling was his own youthful idealism and a longing to accomplish something great, something profoundly important for God.

After years of spiritual anguish and wrestling, the dreams had won, the devils were vanquished, and joy reigned supreme. At least for a time.

PART 2

"It takes me a long while to realize that God has no respect for anything I bring Him. All He wants from me is unconditional surrender."

—My Utmost For His Highest

5
EDINBURGH

(1895–1897)

As the train from London puffed its way past the luxuriant gardens of Princes Street and came to a stop in Waverley Station, Oswald felt he had come "home." He treasured Scotland, the land of his birth, and was always careful to list his nationality as Scottish, never British or English.

Edinburgh! How Oswald loved this city with its dark, sometimes brooding, look and its grand monuments to men and God. During past visits he had stood on Calton Hill and gazed for hours at the city skyline. The graceful Memorial to Sir Walter Scott towered two hundred fifty feet above the bustling shoppers and horse-drawn trams of Princes Street. Beyond it, on a high crag of volcanic rock, stood the imposing medieval Castle. Looking left, down the Royal Mile, the spire of St. Giles Cathedral, the mother church of Presbyterianism, towered over tenement roofs.

Chambers had begun life in the Granite City of Aberdeen and had savored his boyhood in the Fair City of Perth. Now he ventured to the Queen City of Edinburgh to study in answer to God's call. He prayed that here, the clay of his calling to serve God through art could be shaped and fired into a radiant, finished piece.

Edinburgh had nurtured a host of artists who left their marks on the world. Many of them, however, had paid dearly for their success. Sir Walter Scott reached the pinnacle of literary fame early in life, but his later years were marred by broken health and the struggle to rise from bankruptcy. The acclaimed Robert Louis Stevenson, in the grave less than a year, had gained the world in a literary sense while turning from the spiritual heritage of his youth. Chambers had ample evidence that artistic endeavor, life-giving in its own right, could ferment a heady emotional brew that was both intoxicating and potentially lethal.

Apart from the artistic and literary world, many courageous men of God had gone before Chambers here, and he was reminded of them at every turn. Foremost among Oswald's heroes of the faith were the Scottish Covenanters of three centuries before who paid with their blood for refusing to acknowledge the head of state as the head of the church. Chambers marveled at their unflinching commitment and zeal, from their bold signing of The National Covenant in Greyfriars Churchyard in 1638 to their courageous deaths during "the Killing Time" under James VII in 1685 and 1686. Their motto soon became his own: "For Christ's Crown and Covenant."

Franklin Chambers made the sixty-mile journey by train from Perth to help his younger brother find lodgings and settle in before the University term began. Oswald secured a room three flights up at 17 Livingstone Street in the home of a Christian couple, Mr. and Mrs. David Bell. In his room Mrs. Bell pointed out the favorite chair of the great preacher J. H. Jowett, who had lived there a few years before during his undergraduate days. With the room arranged and the door closed, the brothers knelt in prayer, asking as did Elisha of Elijah (2 Kings 2:9) that a portion of Jowett's spirit would come upon Oswald.

Half a mile from Oswald's room stood the stately Old Buildings of the University of Edinburgh. Founded in 1583, it now accommodated 2,700 students in its six faculties: Arts, Science, Divinity, Law, Medicine, and Music. Numerically the 1,500 prospective physicians dominated the student ranks, which included some 700 studying the arts and just over 400 in Law. Awaiting him each day were professors internationally respected as masters in their fields.

Professor David Masson's lectures on rhetoric and English literature were verbal works of art. Sir James Barrie, the Scottish playwright and author of *Peter Pan,* recalled seeing Masson clutch the gaslight bracket when struggling for just the right phrase. In Barrie's book, *An Edinburgh Eleven,* he wrote: "It was when his mind groped for an image that he clutched the bracket. He seemed to tear his good things out of it. Silence overcame the class. Some were fascinated by the man, others trembled for the bracket. It shook, groaned, and yielded. Masson said another of the things that made his lectures literature; the crisis was passed and everybody breathed again."

Professor Henry Calderwood left a flourishing career as a clergyman in Glasgow to take Edinburgh's chair of moral philosophy. His *Handbook of Moral Philosophy* provided university students in Britain and America with a basic textbook for twenty-five years. Above all Calderwood knew his students personally and took a genuine interest in each one.

Andrew Seth, professor of logic, psychology, and metaphysics lectured as if deep in thought. Every word was carefully weighed, avoiding useless repetition and inexact meanings. One student described his slow, labored style of lecturing as "itself, a valuable training in logic."

Undoubtedly the greatest academic influence on Chambers was Professor Gerard Baldwin Brown. Always called by his middle name, Baldwin Brown was in his twelfth year as chair of the department of fine art. In the autumn of 1895, every weekday at 3:00 p.m. Oswald Chambers and six other students assembled in the fine arts classroom for Brown's course on Classical Archaeology and the History of Ancient Art.

Baldwin Brown was an energetic, athletic man easily recognized in profile by his square chin, receding hairline, and thick, brush-like mustache. As an undergraduate, he had pulled his oar at Oriel College, Oxford, and played 'a straight bat' in cricket. Now, at 46, he played a strong game of tennis and loved outdoor exercise. Even on the harshest winter days, no one had ever seen him wear a topcoat.

On the first day of class, he outlined the course of study:

Before Christmas, they would survey the Greek world of art, including:

- Typical rites of special importance for religion and for art.
- Olympia, the Acropolis of Athens, Delphi, Corinth, and other citadels. The cemetery at Mycene and other sacred cemeteries.

• The ancient city, its plan, sacred and secular buildings, the theater, the private house.
• The place of art in the daily life of the ancients. Its many forms, especially in its application to things of use. The differing materials employed.
• The life of the craftsman and the technical methods and processes in use in the ancient world.

The students hastily scribbled notes, trying to comprehend how all this would be covered in so little time. From there, the professor said, they would move on to see "how the study of Artistic Monuments illustrates Classical and Biblical literature, and bears on historical investigation in general." Murray's *Greek Archaeology* should be read at once. Gardner's *Greek Sculpture* was to be read through before January.

Baldwin Brown's rigorous standards were exceeded only by his personal scholarship and his fascinating lectures. The University student magazine, typically critical and often irreverent, referred to Brown's lectures as "the most interesting course delivered in our university."

Professor Brown was well versed in the Scriptures, particularly the Old Testament. But he was as equally at home with Michelangelo and the Sistine Chapel as he was with Hiram of Tyre and the religious antiquities of the Jews. His lectures created a hunger to travel the world and see what he had seen. Brown infused the subject with vitality. To him, art was first and foremost the story of people. Architecture was an expression of form and function coming from within. If you wish to understand a people, Brown believed, you must study what they built and how they used it. Art, archaeology, and architecture were the study of life, not just an examination of canvas, stone, and timber.

From the beginning of the term in October 1895, Oswald plunged into his studies with vigor and delight. Letters to Chrissie Brain in London reveal his optimism:

> *I made very satisfactory progress last week, work is prosperous, my studies at the University most delightful, and my health of body and vigour of mind were never what they are now.*

> *I can study and work and think without fatigue, and that is most delightful.*

In another of his many letters to Chrissie he wrote:

> *My lodgings are really Home. I'm quite a son and am perfectly comfortable. It's grand because I can devote my time to study. I do not know any of the students, I live by myself, in myself, and to myself, that ultimately I may be all for others and my Master.*

Oswald's choice of a somewhat reclusive life indicates his seriousness of purpose and the introspective nature of his personality at this time. Yet while he could be intensely self-analytical, he was never self-absorbed, never a person who shunned other people.

"These people [Mr. and Mrs. Bell] will have a great influence on my life, I'm certain," he wrote. "Life here is splendid, so that I feel very grateful indeed. I can never doubt after this that God rules in the minutest affairs of the everyday life of the individual."

True to his word, Chambers never expressed doubt about God's rule, but he was entering a time when God's ways would cause him great anguish. Within a few months, his freelance work in art had all but dried up and he was facing severe financial strain. More than that, he struggled inwardly, with his own purpose of heart and sense of God's call.

Diary, 26 April 1896: The Holy Spirit must anoint me for the work, fire me, and so vividly convince me that such and such a way is mine to aim at, or I shall not go, I will not, I dare not; I shall just be content to earn my living—but, no, that cannot be. From my very childhood the persuasion has been that of a work, strange and great, an experience deep and peculiar, it has haunted me ever and ever. It spoke clearly to me about my coming here and I came, but now the mists have risen and chase and seethe up all through my soul and nothing is distinct.

There seems to be a great flood-tide bearing me out and all voices grow fainter. I am afraid I am too sordid and earthly for God to speak to and inspire; but I will wait for a heavenly vision in this matter. No man by mere high human wisdom would dare undertake a step for Jesus' sake unless he knows that the Holy Spirit has directly spoken to him; and until He comes, I shall not go.

Here is the lamb and the wood, but where is the fire? Nothing but the fire of the most Holy Spirit of God can make the offering holy and unblamable and acceptable in His sight.

During Oswald's months in Edinburgh, the city was known as "a veritable University of preaching, as well as of arts and sciences." A host of gifted preachers stood in their pulpits every Sunday, and Chambers listened eagerly to many of them. At St. Bernard's (Church of Scotland) he especially enjoyed Dr. George Matheson's first prayer. Some called it "the finest part of the service." Matheson, often called the blind poet-preacher, was well-known for his hymn "Oh Love That Wilt Not Let Me Go," a song that became Chambers' favorite.

At the Free High Church, another poet-preacher, Dr. Walter C. Smith, attracted a large congregation with his biblical, expository preaching, rich with illustrations. Dr. Smith preached "to win men and women from the world and from themselves for Christ." The magnificent hymn of praise "Immortal, Invisible, God Only Wise" came from his pen.

Undoubtedly the greatest influence on Chambers and countless other students was Dr. Alexander Whyte, pastor of Free St. George's Church. More than a great pulpit orator, Whyte was also a dedicated teacher of the Bible. Every Sunday, following the evening preaching service, five hundred young men gathered at 8:15 in Free St. George's for Dr. Whyte's Class. The venerated pastor came down from the pulpit, took off his clerical gown and spoke informally, but with great intensity, for forty-five minutes. Just before nine o'clock, he stated three or four questions for the men to consider as they read during the coming week.

During Chambers' first year in Edinburgh, Whyte focused on "The Mystics" during these Young Men's Classes. Each week he discussed the spiritual vitality and commitment of Tauler, Thomas à Kempis, Luther, Santa Teresa, St. John of the Cross, Madame Guyon, and Fenelon. Through books like *Vaughan's Hours With the Mystics* and *Theologica Germanica* he introduced his eager students to many of the spiritual and devotional writers of the seventeenth century. In 1896 the class began a series titled "The Great Autobiographies." Alexander Whyte loved great books and freely recommended them to his listeners. Many times Chambers saw him hold aloft a battered old volume with loving care as he urged his audience, "Sell your beds and buy it."

The weeks rolled by, filled with the spiritual and intellectual stimulation Oswald had long sought. Under Professor Calderwood, Chambers grappled with the psychology of ethics and the rival theories of Herbert Spencer, Hegel, and John Stuart Mill. To understand the history of moral philosophy, he immersed himself in Plato, Socrates, and Aristotle. Professor Seth introduced him to the place of psychology as a science and the writings of William James. David Masson gripped the gas jet near his lectern and swept through the literary history of the British Islands from their historical beginnings to the present, finally reaching Chambers' beloved Wordsworth, Scott, Tennyson, and Browning.

Oswald's diligent study during his first year paid off. He was named Third Prize man in fine arts by Baldwin Brown and received a First Class Certificate along with high commendation for his essays. His competence in painting and sketching as well as his intellectual achievements seemed to verify God's calling to influence the world of art.

Weekends and term breaks provided an opportunity for quick trips to Perth and encouraging times with Franklin. They hiked the hills of their boyhood, played and listened to music they loved, and talked long into the nights of how the Christian life could be lived out through the arts. Times with Franklin were always refreshing, but by the summer of 1896, Oswald's circumstances had taken a different turn. A continuing scarcity of art work had plunged him into severe financial straits. Only Chrissie knew how difficult his situation really was:

> *1 August 1896*
>
> *Writing is, I fear, to take the proportion of a big undertaking. It is one thing to think; it is another thing to express your thought in writing. However, I shall undertake it (a short story) calling it 'The Dreamer of S.K. (South Kensington)'. If I fail it will teach me much by the effort; if I am successful then I shall be deeply grateful. He knows our need of money to take a share in the privilege and duty of helping those who bore us into this life, and He will not neglect us or them.*
>
> *I will have faith in God while He shows me my ignorance, my mistakes, my weak-*

> *nesses, and takes away all my shallow credulities I used to call faith. I cry to Him strongly —will He not hear? I asked Him for patience, and one after another He takes away my prospects of success. By the means of the keen criticism of experts, He has lifted the veil and showed me how I have tried to express my thoughts before I knew my A B C. He shows me the necessity of long arduous study, and then places circumstances so pressing as to demand immediate money, yet all hopes of money help from the only possible source are dashed to the ground. I've reached the edge of human patience, and I gaze standing still, because I can go no farther, and cry—"How long, O Lord, how long?"*
>
> *12 August 1896*
> *Such revolutions and alterations in affairs, so suddenly coming, so suddenly going, leave me half dazed. I no sooner begin to feel grateful than the wilderness comes again, but I fear nothing. God is love. This will be the very best discipline I can have for patience.*
>
> *I am certainly conscious that success during the past few months might not have been good for me because of ambition and pride. The thwarting is good training in patience and consolidation of character.*

Through September of 1896, Oswald continued to meet more and more closed doors. His name did not appear in the Matriculation Book for the 1896–97 academic year, indicating his inability to register for the term, likely due to his lack of funds. A classmate with contacts in the publishing world sent Oswald's portfolio of artwork to the editor of *Black and White*, a prestigious London magazine, but nothing came of it.

Professor Baldwin Brown wrote to the principal of nearby Heriot Watt Ladies' College in Edinburgh, recommending Oswald for a position as instructor in art. As a letter to Chrissie shows, Oswald hoped it might be the solution to his needs:

> *Getting my position made [in the Ladies' College], I may slowly work on to higher mat-*

ters, and Oh! if in the infinite goodness of God, He would permit me to be of use to His great cause in Art, then how could I contain such an honour; but His is the future not mine.

I have of course been engaged in fragments of work such as book covers, designs, advertisements, but am waiting to see how matters will turn out in the good providence of God. Pray, fearing nothing, about this way of mine, for I am indeed most anxious to know God's will in the matter, as yet I do not remotely know what it is.

It is a year since I came to Edinburgh, and most truthfully I can say in spite of all its severe difficulties and discipline, it will ever be one of the most important and influential years of my life.

Nothing came of the Heriot Watt inquiry. While his professors and friends offered constant assurance of Oswald's gifts and abilities in art, door after door refused to open.

More troubling than his financial extremity was an inner stirring he had felt for some time—the idea of becoming a minister. Could God be leading him in that direction? He didn't see how it was possible. It would mean a complete turnaround from the call he had so confidently followed a year earlier. It would mean abandoning his art studies and leaving the university. Most of all, it would mean exchanging a lifework uniquely suited to his interests and gifts for something to which he had never aspired. With great finality he had recently written George Oxer, "I shall never go into the ministry until God takes me by the scruff of the neck and throws me in."

The matter was far from settled, however. In a letter to Chrissie, he related an unnerving event during an October visit with Franklin in Perth:

I went to see John MacDonald's father, he is a colporteur and a singular man of deep religious experience, the Holy Spirit being his constant theme of meditation and conversation. He astounded me by telling me that I was to be a minister. He said as soon as I came in with my brother he felt it impressed on him

> *that I was destined to be a minister, and on leaving he prayed for me most earnestly that God would open my way.*

The tug-of-war in Oswald's heart intensified as the days grew shorter and the leaves of autumn released their grip on the branches to which they had held so tightly. Was that what Oswald needed to do? Was he holding on to a vision that he must now release?

One evening in late autumn, unable to concentrate, Oswald left his room and walked eastward toward Queen's Park, the Sanctuary of Holyrood House. Having decided to spend the entire night in prayer, he could think of no better place to be alone than on Arthur's Seat, the highest hill overlooking Edinburgh. It took the long-legged, athletic young man less than half an hour to reach the top of the extinct volcano, which rose some eight hundred feet above the city.

It was a familiar pathway, one Oswald had followed many times along the Pipers Walk, past the clumps of ling heather, ascending to the top of the Dry Dam and then to the rocky summit. With every step, the world fell farther behind, both in sound and feeling. Chambers often sought the high places for solitude and communion with God.

In the fading light he could see the sails of ships on the wind-whipped Firth of Forth to the north. The university buildings and the surrounding Old Town lay at his feet. Wrapping a plaid around his shoulders to ward off the evening chill, Oswald walked down a few yards from the summit to a small indentation in the rock. There, shielded from the wind, he surveyed the twinkling lights of the city and poured his heart out to God.

While he prayed, the sounds below changed as evening drifted into night. The rumble of heavy wagons and trams gave way to the staccato hoofbeats of horses pulling carriages and cabs. The bells from half a dozen churches chimed eleven, accompanied by the drunken singing of some undergraduates reeling from a public house to their digs. By the stroke of midnight, quiet reigned as a fog rolled in from the firth and obscured the city.

Chambers prayed aloud, alternately thanking God and pleading with Him to make His way plain. He wanted to serve Him in art, to go where others could not or would not take the gospel of Jesus Christ. But the way seemed blocked and now, perhaps forbidden. "Oh God," he pleaded, "make Thy way plain to me."

As the hours wore on, his soul cried out in anguished silence. Sometime during the night, according to Chambers' account, he heard a voice that actually spoke these words, "I want you in My service—but I can do without you."

Was that the guidance he sought? Was this the answer to his struggle? Suddenly the call to the ministry seemed so clear. He was ready to obey, but how? What should he do? It was a call with no more guidance than he possessed before.

Returning to his lodgings the next morning, he found that his mail contained the annual report from Dunoon College, a small theological training school near Glasgow. He had no idea who sent it to him or why. Yet he felt it must be part of God's plan, having come totally unsolicited at this very time. He wrote the Principal, the Rev. Duncan MacGregor, introducing himself and asking for more information.

Near the end of November, with the way still uncertain, God's call was becoming progressively more sure. He wrote to Chrissie:

> *It seems tonight that the great Spirit of God is near and all the lower common-sense things have dwindled away down into their proper proportions, and the thought that is strongest in me is that of entering the ministry. How often have I hinted at it, how often have I stifled it back and down; but I cannot keep it hid any longer for it is perplexing me tremendously. It would be playing with the sacred touch of God to neglect or stifle again this strange yet deep conviction that some time I must be a minister.*
>
> *This inward conviction, the decided thwarting all along the art line, nay, the repeated and pointed shutting of doors that seemed just opening, as well as the confident opinion of many friends—all leads me to consider most earnestly before God what is his will. I am going to leave the opening of the way in His hands, nor am I going to try and enter the ministry until it is so startlingly clear that not to go*

would be to disobey, and this startling clearness has not come yet, but I feel it is coming. Let us not turn our eyes from Jesus Christ.

The same letter continued:

On Sunday I met Mr. George Stooke of the China Inland Mission and he wants me to go to China with him, he himself introduced the subject. He says he is certain that the ministry is my ultimate goal and he has promised to pray for guidance.

Brighter, clearer and more exquisite is the spiritual within becoming, and my whole being is ablaze and passionately on fire to preach Christ. All my art aims are swallowed up in this now. It is the almighty love of God that constrains me, and in the midst of a keen consciousness of complete unworthiness, my soul cries out within me—Here am I, send me. By the grace of God, when the way is clear, I will go, obstruct who may, laugh who will, scoff who can. It is Christ Who was crucified and Who rose again and it is God who suffered so inconceivably to redeem men, Who bids me go.

Oswald's family and friends frequently urged him to deal less with abstract ideas and more with the practical matters of life. Again, only Chrissie knew his struggle over how to face his financial realities without compromising his faith:

For three weeks now I have had no work—art, portrait painting—all my commissions are finished and I have no new ones. I have not been able to pay my landlady for sometime now and I have, as my sole money possession in this world, 1 shilling, 8 pence. This is certainly not an abstract matter, but one of immediate concern, everything I have tried has been hopelessly unsuccessful. This coming week brings no shadow of a prospect. I look at home and see a great need for money there, and yet I have tried and prayed to gain money sufficient to help them, and yet I am not afraid, I am not downcast, I am serious, fervently serious that I can face the whole unflinchingly be-

> *cause my faith and consolation is in the Lord my God.*
>
> *This is not the first time I have been in such straits. I have been through much worse times, with 6 pence as my sole possession, and all has been well because God is here. It will be alright, and never let my home folks know anything of this, they think I do well and so I do. I have stated all this because I know that 'a mind stayed upon God' is the only way to ennoble human life. You cannot live a noble life in this world without the assurance that God is there.*
>
> *I am not in the least disturbed about these hard times, night and day my soul is yearning and crying and my spirit waiting for a great absorbing work to come for me to engage in for His sake and it will come, and we will look up and be strong and of a good courage. God is not very far off.*

A November gathering of the Christian Union brought Hudson Taylor, founder of the China Inland Mission, to the University of Edinburgh. After attending the meeting Chambers wrote: "Hudson Taylor said last night that Our Lord's words 'Have faith in God' really mean 'Have faith in the faithfulness of God,' not in your own faithfulness."

"I am completely at rest now," he wrote to Chrissie. "I feel God nearer to me than ever. I will wait on Him and He will open the way."

Letting go was an expression of trust, but not the end of the struggle. Letters and diaries reveal his continuing distress:

> *How can I dabble in art, pleasing my own artistic sense when that burdening cry of the human is ever rising, 'What must we do to be saved?' 'Who will show us any good?' How can I think of artistic comfort and high self-culture when the Voice of Jesus, the Spirit of Jesus constrains me to go and preach the gospel? Oh it is not my worth, my ability, my talents, it is God that impels me.*
>
> *I hear a voice you cannot hear*
> *That says I must not stay*

I see a hand they cannot see
Which beckons me away.

But I do not know where to go, the blackness of darkness is before me and there is no way, but still the great passion grows within me to preach Christ and will soon be an agony and I must soon cry 'Woe is me if I preach not the gospel of Christ.'

Every prospect of work has now been withdrawn and I have not one thing to look to—but God. And is that not enough? If this is indeed the Spirit of Almighty God striving within me, He will speedily open the door, I will not fear.

By early December Chambers had talked to a local Baptist minister, a former student at Dunoon, who spoke enthusiastically of the college and described Principal MacGregor as "a man of great personality who infuses his enthusiasm into his students."

A letter from MacGregor to Chambers brought an invitation to join the student body of thirty at Dunoon. And, it offered the possibility of teaching fine art at the college or in the town. The long-hidden way was becoming clear.

"So this looks like the beginning of something," Chambers wrote to Chrissie. "This may after all be more conducive to gaining the ultimate end of being an ambassador for Christ in the art world than if I were merely a lecturer. God moves in mysterious ways."

Before going to Dunoon, Oswald hoped to organize a series of lectures in the Potteries near Stoke-on-Trent, then journey back to London. Neither materialized and he was keenly disappointed not to be home for Christmas.

All I can do now is to pour it all into God's heart. I feel only a child and such a child. I feel I need this time before entering College to be alone with God. This last step has taken me beyond my other friends, none of them follow, some of them think I have done wrong. Only you understand.

I tremble when I think of what I am going to train for. It will soon be Dunoon now. Pray for

> *me that the Spirit of God will fill me to the drowning of self and the exalting of Jesus.*

It would be easy to conclude from all this that Chambers' life in Edinburgh was one of constant soul searching and torment. There is no doubt that he struggled greatly, but it was, as it would ever be for him, a private matter. His outward appearance rarely revealed a troubled heart. A letter written to Chrissie on the day after Christmas, 1896, reveals the man that was much better known to his peers.

> *Christmas Day will long live in my mind as unique. John McDonald, a student of chemistry, and I determined to have a fine time. We were alone, and after much deliberation decided on a tin of salmon for our Christmas dinner, no potatoes; so I was cook, Jane, the butler and host all in one. Mark you, the salmon was just enough for two, and because of that who should step in but Cordiner, just off the London mail. Well, we did have a time, we laughed so much and so heartily, and so rich and luxuriant were the viands that I question very much whether there was a more truly bright and jolly trio anywhere.*

During the past eighteen months in Edinburgh, Oswald had enjoyed the cultured surroundings of artistic homes and stimulating contact with gracious personalities. In letters he had often told Chrissie his cherished dreams of someday having his own home where students would be influenced and uplifted as he had been. Now, he put all that behind him.

When he left for ministerial training a few weeks after Christmas, it was a bittersweet parting.

Diary, 15 February 1897: Tomorrow I start for Dunoon. Professor Baldwin Brown and other friends want me to go and see them; I do not lack many hearty, staunch and kind friends. On Sunday morning I heard a grand and soul-stirring discourse from Dr. Alexander Maclaren, the great Manchester preacher. What a fire his sermon made to blaze inside you! Great fervent passion. A splendid old man.

I have no doubt I am doing the right thing in going to Dunoon, and the next five years by the grace of God will silence the careful misgivings of my considerate friends and relatives.

I am sorry to leave Edinburgh, specially my 'grandfather' and 'grandmother' [Mr. and Mrs. Bell]. Old Mrs. Bell laid a parcel on my packed box this morning with 'Mrs. Bell to Mr. Chambers' written on the top. A brand new shaving brush and some special shaving soap! She hoped 'I would'na be offended!' Good old soul. Don't I long for the time when in some substantial way I can show some of my gratitude to them.

Oswald had no idea what lay ahead as he boarded a train bound for Glasgow, then farther west to Gourock, where he would catch a steamer across the Firth of Clyde. He knew only that his aim had once been art for God. Now it was only God. Months before, he had told Chrissie, "I feel I shall be buried for a time, hidden away in obscurity; then suddenly I shall flame out, do my work, and be gone."

Many years later his friend, George Oxer, reflected on this period of Chambers' life:

"I knew him through the crisis of some of the great renouncements which put so much of the tugs and triumphs into his early life. While it remains true that his soul alone held the secrets of experience, the fighting quality that was ever in him is the heritage of everyone he touched at all intimately. There was not much doubt or mysticism in the definite impact of courage and grace in his hand grips and soul grips.

"The friend I remember traveling to the Art School at Kensington, and later to the College at Dunoon, was the Oswald Chambers of early days—days of soul travail and delivery reflective of Paul's dualism of the 7th Romans.

"The posthumous published literature reproducing his specialized and Spirit-filled ministry, portrays the fisher of men, the man of God thoroughly furnished, the vessel unto honour, meet for the Master's use.

"My memory is keener concerning some of the boats of his natural ambitions God deliberately cut adrift, some of the ordained derelictions. In many a letter of those days his experience was reflected in one of his favourite quotations therein—

> That life is not as idle ore,
> But iron dug from central gloom,
>   And heated hot with burning fears,
>   And dipt in baths of hissing tears,

And batter'd with the shocks of doom
To shape and use.

"There is generally an unrecorded background to the pathway of full and glad surrender. The clinching 'Yea' may come in a moment, in the twinkling of an eye, and yet have travelled all unknown throughout the labyrinthine ways in which the mind has fled Him. Thus I believe was the 'fulness of the spirit' in Oswald Chambers linked to the 'distresses' of the days of our comradeship.

"I write this for the guidance and encouragement of any who may think that Oswald Chambers had an a easy passage to the heights God took him. The measure of the valley is the height of the mountain. My friend's soul was a lone rough rider passing through the wilderness to his Canaan, oft-times launching on his intimates at home and the social circle the unexpected and unexplained.

"Consistency was 'the hobgoblin of little minds' to him. The so-called practical side of life had little attraction. Art and Poetry gripped him deeply, in and through all this his great spirit marched on to a certain time of which he wrote—

There comes a mist and a blinding rain
And life is never the same again.

"In that 'mist' our ways somewhat parted. The aftermath of the clear shining is evident and will be recorded by other pens. But he was a great chum. He lives in God to-day, and in my life, made better by his presence.

"I pen this tribute as one who touched him in the De Profundis and for the enunciation of his soul's service in the hidden years."

6
DUNOON

(1897)

Oswald stood near the bow of the Caledonian steamer for the half-hour crossing from Gourock to Dunoon. With hat pulled low and topcoat buttoned against the wind, he breathed deeply of the winter air. In the distance, across the Firth of Clyde, he studied the Cowal Peninsula and the snow covered hills rising behind the town of Dunoon. In spite of the gray February sky, it was a breathtakingly beautiful sight.

In the summer, Dunoon attracted thousands of tourists who came by ferry to enjoy band concerts in the Castle Gardens and quiet walks along the four-mile waterfront promenade. Trips into the surrounding countryside offered the diversity of craggy uplands, wooded glens, and a fjord-like coastline with salt water lochs penetrating inland.

As the ferry neared the famous Dunoon Pier, Chambers strained to see the bronze statue of "Highland Mary," erected by admirers of the Scottish poet Robert Burns. He thought of Chrissie Brain in London and wondered what the future held for them. She would love this land of rugged beauty, just as he did. Eighty miles behind him lay Edinburgh and his dreams of being God's messenger to the world of art. To Oswald, the distance seemed more like eighty thousand miles. Now, with every turn of the steamer's paddlewheel, the gulf between his former goal and his present call grew wider and deeper.

Many of his friends and family thought he was throwing his future to the wind by leaving the University of Edinburgh. It made no sense to them and seemed a very ill-advised move. Chambers was stepping out of a cosmopolitan student body of 2,700 into a seemingly insignificant group of thirty young men, most of whom could not gain entrance into a university. He was abandoning world-renowned professors and placing himself under the tutelage of one man, the Rev. Duncan MacGregor. Oswald, to his critics, was leaving the ocean and entering a mud puddle. In all likelihood, that opinion was evenly divided between those who knew something of Mr. MacGregor and those who knew nothing of him at all.

MacGregor was Highland born and a graduate of the University of Glasgow and Theological College. After pastorates in Manchester, England, and Wales, he traveled to America and served Chicago's North Ashland Avenue Baptist Church for three years, from 1882 to 1885.

While in Chicago, MacGregor established the short-lived Scottish Land League of America, working for reform on behalf of the landless Scottish crofters (farmers). During Britain's 1885 Parliamentary election he campaigned actively on behalf of a Roman Catholic crofter candidate. Some Protestants had still not forgiven him for that. People would accuse Duncan MacGregor of many things, but never of being lethargic or bland.

In October 1885, MacGregor returned to Scotland and shortly thereafter became pastor of Dunoon Baptist Church. Under his powerful preaching and affable leadership, what had begun as a summer chapel in a tourist town became a thriving year-round congregation.

By 1893 MacGregor had grown impatient with the internal bickering and the floundering efforts of the Scottish Baptist denomination to educate and train its ministers. The Gospel Training College at Dunoon grew out of his dissatisfaction with the conventional academic approach to ministerial training. On his own, he assembled a few students, set up some chairs in his small church vestry, and began to teach them from his heart and life.

MacGregor believed that in most colleges and universities an intellectually antagonistic atmosphere retarded, rather than encouraged, spiritual growth. Even in seminaries he felt that the purely academic approach stifled men instead of igniting them for effective service. He saw a vast difference between teaching and training. The latter, he maintained, combined the discipline of the classroom with the crucible of practical experience, all under a wise guiding hand.

"In ministerial training, there should be less of the factory and more of the garden," MacGregor said.

While he was a staunch Baptist and deeply involved in denominational circles, MacGregor's college at Dunoon was interdenominational. Students were free to attend any church. The only entrance examination was an interview with MacGregor based on a single question, "When were you converted?" As long as a man was born again, his age and previous education were secondary.

From the outset MacGregor determined that Dunoon would not be a second-rate school. All students studied Hebrew, Greek, Theology, and Homiletics under him. Other subjects were added in time. But mere intellectual achievement was never his ultimate goal.

"My aim," he said, "is not sending forth ministers, but men with prophetic fire—men who cry, 'Give us souls, or we die!' If a student can be brought to believe that God walked this earth with naked feet, then he is a mighty man."

In spite of the twenty-five year age difference between Oswald Chambers and Duncan MacGregor, a deep friendship quickly developed between them. After two months in Dunoon, Chambers wrote to a friend: "Grand old 'Mac.' I wish you knew him—character, character, character!!! to the backbone, noble, unselfish, and holy. I look upon him as a re-incarnation of Jesus Christ by His Spirit, so like is he to his Master. I never loved a man as I love him."

Chambers entered the college as quietly as a gentle breeze from the hills but soon became a whirlwind of activity. When MacGregor entered the local school board election, Oswald became his campaign manager, preparing two large posters and offering to become a sandwich-board man to carry them through the town. The principal won the election without Oswald's marching through the streets of Dunoon.

When the college moved from the MacGregor home at Boston Villa to more spacious quarters, Chambers was an artistic and engineering dynamo. The magnificent estate called Dhalling

Mhor sprawled across a hillside in nearby Kirn. The front of the large house faced east toward a spacious lawn ringed with flowers, shrubs, and trees. Tall arched windows on all four sides of a large third-story room offered a breathtaking view of the Firth of Clyde. Dhalling Mhor provided ample living space for the students as well as the eight MacGregors. In addition, the large drawing room and dining room were well suited for lectures and larger gatherings.

Extracts from Chambers' letters to Chrissie during this time are enthusiastic and optimistic. From correspondence dated May 17, 1897, he wrote:

> *Great doings in connection with the College last week. The removal was grand with fun and work and comicality. Drains, chimneys and wall paintings have constituted a large part of my last week's work. The watercourse at Dhalling Mhor is most complicated and I went over the whole course with Mr. MacGregor and the plumbers and made a full and elaborate plan. That with my other work, and drawing a sketch of the College for printing, has caused time to dance past at a terrific rate. To-night after the class we are to have a prayer meeting in the new College at which we hope to have a good time.*

The MacGregor children were fascinated with Chambers. Easdale, a twelve-year-old son, noted that "he was amazingly thin and his hair was amazingly long—two things which made him a figure to be noticed wherever he went." Thirteen-year-old Mildred loved Oswald's impromptu drawing lessons during evenings in the home, along with his ability to inspire in them the love of music and literature.

Chambers' fellow students were equally taken by him. Thomas Houston first saw him across the dining room table at the principal's morning class and noted that Oswald's distinct facial features—"the eyes set under a broad cleft of brow, the mouth firm, with lips rather thin—might have created an impression of austerity." But just the opposite was true. "His countenance was unusually pleasing and inviting."

Everything about Chambers created the impression of a man who was impossible to categorize. Houston couldn't figure him out: "This decided cast of features gave him a look older than his years. You could not guess his age. One moment he looked a mere youth and the next a man of maturer years.

"When he rose to his feet he was surprisingly tall, and I have since thought that his physical aspect had its corresponding features in the structure of his mind. He naturally assumed the posture of sitting low at the feet of any teacher, but when he stood up to speak he would astonish with his utterance."

A lifelong animal lover, Oswald soon acquired a collie he named Tweed. Together they roamed the hills surrounding Dunoon and searched out the quiet waters of Loch Eck or the secluded beauty of Glen Masson. He loved to organize walks and take others with him. The impression he left during those times was unforgettable.

"When out walking together," Houston said, "Chambers had a great notion to keep in step. This we could never do for any distance, we always tried, but always failed. This played its part in our spiritual pilgrimage. We were in the main one and on the same journey, and Chambers would always be returning to get in step, and then anon would be carried away from me."

At Dunoon College, Chambers was busy, but not hurried, challenged, but not overwhelmed. MacGregor's goal was to nurture his students, not crush them.

On June 23, 1897, Chambers wrote to Chrissie:

> *My first session in Dunoon is over, and a splendid session it has been. Only the future can show the value of it. The quiet, the scenery, the few choice spirits I have met—the Principal and his wife, and Mrs. Muirhead, and all the unadulterated kindness of many, all this will have had a formative and restraining influence.*
>
> *A wonderful result financially was announced at the Conference—a balance of seventeen pounds on the right side. This is indeed a tribute to the faith of our grand old Principal. We all felt how really God does bless in temporal ways those who put implicit trust in Him.*

> *You will be glad to know that I have all Browning's works and Shelley's. They were a kind of payment for a portrait I did of a friend of one of the students; they are indeed a treasure to me.*

During this time, Chrissie's adherence to British Israelism became a point of mild contention in their letters. She believed that Britain was the lost tribe of Israel and would therefore fulfill the prophetic role given by God to His people, the Jews. Chambers saw things differently. They still maintained unity on the central tenets of faith, and agreed to disagree in the area of eschatology.

When the winter term of 1897 began, Oswald taught a drawing class in Dunoon Grammar school in addition to his college studies and active involvement in MacGregor's church. Immersed in a busy schedule, he still steadfastly pursued his ministerial training, never losing the vision of why he was there.

To Chrissie, on September 10, 1897, he wrote:

> *The College goes on well. I have great hopes for it, it is on the right lines. It is surely better for young men to be taught and personally influenced by godly men long in the work than to be crystallized to clear cold cultural concerns in a University curriculum.*
>
> *I have thought lately how fine the experience of a few years' ministry in a country place among country people would be, despite all the disadvantages. To be out of the competition, and to have but to think and study and preach, and pray and visit, and then come back into the swirl and competition of city life amongst the earnest, striving, worn-out multitudes of men.*

Soon, Oswald became a tutor in the College, teaching moral philosophy and using Schwegler's *History of Philosophy* as a text. When his students found that book and its concepts too obscure, Chambers wrote and published an introductory textbook of his own, *Outlines for the Study of Historical Philosophy.* The twenty-page booklet gave students a structure in which to examine the principal philosophers and the development of their ideas from ancient through modern times.

"[Chambers] positively adapted his lectures to our mental capacities," a Dunoon graduate recalled, "and helped us in private with what we could not understand in class. His enthusiasm knew no bounds, he could never do things by halves. He lived for his work and threw himself whole-heartedly into teaching us the different philosophies, expounding them with such clarity that he soon imparted a working knowledge of them."

Some of Duncan MacGregor's greatest gifts to his students were the great men of faith he invited to the college. Their lectures were inspiring, but their personal interaction with Chambers and the others was life changing. William Quarrier, founder of the nearby Orphan Homes of Scotland, was a great man of faith and prayer. His homes for children, like those of George Müller in Bristol, England, operated by faith, making no financial appeals.

Quarrier was a close friend of Duncan MacGregor and a frequent visitor to Dunoon College. His informal talks with students often concluded with everyone kneeling in prayer. Chambers was among those who listened as Quarrier simply and confidently approached his Heavenly Father for the needs of his "bairns."

In addition to faith, Quarrier was a man of action who never expected God to do for him what he could do for himself. While driving a visiting preacher to the railway station in Bridge of Weir, Quarrier and the clergyman spotted the train rapidly approaching. The preacher, fearing he would miss the train, shouted, "Don't you think we should pray about it, Mr. Quarrier?"

"No, not yet," Quarrier said as he cracked the reins. "Wait till we see what the horse can do."

When local authorities told Quarrier he would have to pay school taxes even though he provided a private education for all his children, he took to the streets. He marched a thousand of the children in his orphan homes two miles to the gates of the public school in Kilmacolm village and demanded that the school board make provision for their education. The board refused, and the court later decided that Quarrier must pay the taxes, but it wasn't because he sat on his hands.

Two distinguished preachers from Edinburgh often visited Dunoon—Dr. Alexander Whyte, pastor of Free St. George's Church, and the Rev. Dinsdale T. Young of Nicholson Street Church. And from London, the internationally known Baptist minister Dr. F. B. Meyer paid a visit to preach and then interact with MacGregor's ministers-in-training. It was Meyer who became the human catalyst in a spiritual reaction that brought Chambers to the absolute end of himself. The journey began with a spark of consecration and ended in the ashes of self-despair, a time Chambers himself described as "four years of hell on earth."

7
DARK NIGHT OF THE SOUL

(1897–1901)

In Oswald's preaching and teaching he seldom spoke of his personal spiritual experiences. The one rare exception is his account of what happened to him during his first four years at Dunoon. It is best described by Chambers himself:

> After I was born again as a lad I enjoyed the presence of Jesus Christ wonderfully, but years passed before I gave myself up thoroughly to His work. I was in Dunoon College as tutor of Philosophy when Dr. F. B. Meyer came and spoke about the Holy Spirit. I determined to have all that was going, and went to my room and asked God simply and definitely for the baptism of the Holy Spirit, whatever that meant.
>
> From that day on for four years, nothing but the overruling grace of God and the kindness of friends kept me out of an asylum. God used me during those years for the conversion of souls, but I had no conscious communion with Him. The Bible was the dullest, most uninteresting book in existence, and the sense of depravity, the vileness and bad-motivedness of my nature was terrific.

While others thought everything was fine in Oswald's life and spoke of him as a saint, he alone understood the plague of sin in his heart. It was a lonely, undeclared struggle, as much like Jesus' temptation in the desert as Chambers would ever know. A letter to Chrissie from Dunoon in May 1897 hinted at what was to come:

> *Everything goes with me in amazing prosperity. Perhaps the consciousness that I am thought of too highly makes me want to get away at times. They all place me so high that I am weary of it. Oh, that I might be away with Nature, and see and not be seen.*

The hills around Dunoon provided brief respites for Chambers, but he craved longer periods when he could walk with his collie, Tweed, and seek renewal in God's creation. During summer breaks, he often traveled a hundred miles north to the Highlands near Fort William, and the home of John Cameron, an old friend.

Cameron pastured sheep on the slopes of Ben Nevis, Britain's highest mountain. Chambers found emotional release in the hard labor of shepherding, and he loved to climb the towering mountain often called "the Ben." From the base, a footpath snaked its way for five miles toward the barren 4,400-foot summit. When hiking with others, Chambers would usually enjoy the walk at a leisurely pace. But when he was alone, he sometimes pushed himself with long strides until his lungs ached and his muscles cried for relief. Without stopping, he climbed through the swirling mists, perspiring even in the chilling wind.

If he reached the summit on a clear day, he could feast for hours on the panorama spread out below him. Even in summer, a thick crust of snow clung to the northeast rock face, with its sheer drop of 2,000 feet onto the crags below. To the west, the sleepy town of Fort William lay at the northern end of Loch Linnhe. Snow-capped peaks spread to the east and south as far as he could see.

Chambers loved Ben Nevis best in the early morning, before sightseers struggled up the mountain and hurried back down. He would walk the footpath in the dark of night in order to reach the summit in time to see the sunrise. Before most of the people awoke in the valleys below, he had watched the finger of God paint the morning sky.

In Chambers' estimation, John Cameron was a man who matched the mountain where he lived. The rugged old bachelor lived simply and gave the bulk of his income to the Lord's work. Cameron entertained hospitably and prayed as regularly and naturally as the sunrise. During one of Chambers' visits, he and Cameron were out shooting rabbits, accompanied by two dogs. When they reached a heather knoll, the old man suggested they stop for a while and pray.

"We knelt down and he led in prayer," Chambers wrote of the occasion. "Then I began to pray, but the young collie dog, who had been perfectly quiet during the old man's prayer, imagined I was meant for nothing but to play with him, and he started careering around, pawing me all over, licking my face and yelping with delight." Cameron rose from his knees, sternly took the dog by the neck and said, "Hoot, hoot, I will sit on the dog while you pray." And he did.

A few days later, Cameron took Chambers aside and said, "If you get permission to speak to my ploughman about his soul, do so." Oswald expressed surprise that Cameron had not spoken to the man himself, because he had watched the old farmer speak about Jesus to all sorts of people.

"My laddie," Cameron replied, "if you don't know what the permission of the Holy Ghost is in talking to a soul about salvation, you know nothing about the Holy Ghost."

Chambers pondered the remark on the train back to Glasgow. How much did he know of the Holy Spirit and His power? He had asked in faith to be filled, but it seemed that nothing had happened. Was he holding something back from God?

He wrote to Chrissie saying he felt compelled by God to go solitary, for the time being, and shut himself up alone to God and his studies. "I hear the imperative command of my own inner soul," he told her, " 'cut every tie and wait.' Shall I obey or disobey?" She knew his action was taken in sheer obedience to what he sensed as a definite call of God. That gave them courage, but didn't lessen the pain for either of them.

Oswald had renounced his ambitions in art and had now cut the cords of his relationship with Chrissie. If there was anything else he loved ahead of God, he was ready to place it on the altar as well. But the power and presence of God did not come after his renouncements. Instead, he became more aware of his own sinfulness than before. He could pluck out his offending eye and cut off his right hand, but he could not escape the plague of his own heart.

On May 4, 1898, Oswald and Mrs. MacGregor heard the sound at the same time—an awful shattering of glass and a sickening thud, followed by absolute silence. They rushed upstairs into the hall at Dhalling Mhor and found Duncan sprawled unconscious on the floor, his face ashen and his breathing irregular and shallow. In an attempt to make a minor repair to the roof, he had fallen through a skylight.

The doctor's report was grim—MacGregor was near death with one bone broken, several dislocated, a severe concussion, and internal injuries. If he survived, he would certainly never recover to his previous level of health and activity. No one thought the college could go on without him.

For the next three months Chambers personally attended Duncan MacGregor and nursed him back to health. Their relationship deepened beyond natural affinity into one of unshakable mutual admiration and respect.

Chambers shouldered the extra load of teaching, administration, and spiritual leadership in the college while the principal recovered. By the end of August, MacGregor surprised everyone by preaching again in church and declaring that he would resume his academic responsibilities in October.

During the years 1897–1901, Chambers appeared to be doing exceptionally well. Articles he wrote on music, nature, and Robert Browning's poetry appeared regularly in *The Dunoon Herald* newspaper. In addition, he often reported important events of the college and Dunoon Baptist Church. He was highly regarded by students and townspeople alike and known for his cheerful disposition.

In May of 1899, during the college's annual Day of Thanksgiving, Oswald was ordained to the ministry. Increasingly he was asked to speak at meetings outside the college and Dunoon. But his high visibility in Christian circles seemed to accentuate his growing sense of inner emptiness and longing.

Once again, Chambers' poetry written during this time reveals his inner struggle:

MOODS
(Kirn, March 4, 1899)

Rain on, dark skies, through the night,
The waters have burst their bound;
Destruction may rule till the light,
But day follows night, ever round.

Scowl on, dark moods of the mind,
Threaten, lower, and storm your way;
But the soul must bleed ere it find
The good you are seeking to slay.

Moods pass away like the rain-clouds,
Good is as day in the soul;
After the gloom of the earth-shrouds
Cometh complete heaven's whole.

Oswald continued his cheerful outward appearance while one by one his hopes and dreams were being put to death. Some he laid willingly on the altar while others seemed to be snatched from him by the hand of God. In either case, the pain of heart-break and loss felt the same. The most severe was the end of his long relationship with Chrissie. The absence of his letters to her after this time indicates that any hopes they may have had for marriage ended by the close of 1899. The decision came from Oswald as a cross-bearing sacrifice he felt compelled to make in order to follow Christ completely. The break-up represented a great loss for both Chrissie and him. For nearly eight years, a steady exchange of letters, along with holiday visits, had kept the flame alive. Some of their friends in London thought they might even be secretly engaged. Now it was over.

In the sorrow of those days, he wrote of the pain and peace which fought for supremacy in his heart:

AFTERWARD
(Kirn, January 22, 1900)

O my beloved Jesus! Not Thy cross
Nor any portion of Thine earthly life
Revealed Thy love to me.
But when my heart broke in its first true love,
And all my feelings like a lash of pain
Recoiled and stung me, till my tortured nerves
Refused to aid my spirit—

Then, in that pain, I saw Thee, O my Christ!
And that my first love, which so hopeless seemed,
Was after all for Thee disguised indeed.
But I mistook the form assumed by Thee,
And now I love Thee, Jesus, with the love
That lovers think they have for those they love.
O rapture! where there was such pain before.

If Oswald hoped that by relinquishing his fondest loves only his love for Christ would remain, he was deeply disappointed. He had won a costly victory, but the war was not over. He longed for peace in his soul, but found only turmoil inside and out. God's gifts of keen intellect and handsome appearance seemed to work against him. When a young woman in a local church accused Chambers of misconduct with her, it seemed to be more than he could bear. There was no truth to her story and a thorough investigation vindicated Oswald, but the damage had been done. Slander of all kinds followed the episode. He was misunderstood, shunned, avoided, and became the object of whispers throughout Dunoon.

More than causing damage to Oswald's reputation, the charge had heightened his own awareness of what lay within him.

"What any human being has done," he had heard a preacher say, "any other human being is capable of." He had not sinned sexually with the girl, but he knew he *could* have. The disturbing realization of what he was capable of thinking and doing began to oppress Oswald's mind.

He became aware of an abhorrent dualism in his personality. The sham and hypocrisy he detested in others had a foothold in his own heart. He could proclaim that God must be given glory for all his good works, but he enjoyed the praise of men. While many people in Dunoon thought he was a near-perfect saint, he knew the truth about himself. Within him lurked a frightening pride that was beyond his power to conquer.

His anguished poems reveal that behind his vindicated reputation lurked the reality of sin known only to him.

SIN IN PENITENCE
(Kirn, September 24, 1900)

Let me lay my life here
Where my sin is known,
Where the rapture and the fear,
Where the laughter and the tear
Isolate my heart, alone.

Jesus, here, my wandering heart
Turneth now to Thee,

Till in all its inmost part
Sweetly bitter is the smart
Of my sin in me.

Cowardly sorrow maketh plaint,
"This is hard to bear."
Makes a shape at being saint,
While the loathsome sin doth taint
All that others think so fair.

Jesus, Jesus, I can't pray,
For the horror of the thing
Haunts my waking thoughts alway,
And I have no word to say
For my wicked, wicked sin.

By the summer of 1901, this interior struggle intensified, building toward a crisis. Chambers' letters to the editor of the *Dunoon Herald* were caustic, cynical, and filled with frustration as Oswald mounted a one-man crusade to preserve the aesthetic beauty and spiritual health of Dunoon. In the April 11, 1901, edition he wrote:

> *Sir: "Improvements" and "alterations" attract attention. Some alterations are improvements, not all. The new bridge leading to the Bull Wood is a decided alteration, but one hesitates in calling it an improvement without necessarily qualifying the word. The bridge is an improvement, a great improvement for traffic.*
>
> *But the bridge is not an improvement from the artistic point of view. It is a straight, ugly erection, entirely out of keeping with its surroundings and the end and aim of Dunoon.*
>
> *I am, etc. Oswald Chambers, Dhalling Mhor, Kirn*

On June 19, 1901, he continued the attack:

> *Sir: The trees will surely be spared in the proposed widening of the roadway alongside the convalescent homes! All those trees in line marking the curb edge of a pavement would greatly add to the appearance of that approach*

> *to Dunoon. The few trees out of line might be sacrificed and new ones planted to fill up the gaps, but to take the trees away!!—surely our councillors will give this matter consideration before sacrificing the whole of those splendid trees.*

On June 28, 1901, Oswald wrote as follows on the Sunday steamer question:

> *The question of Sunday observance or non-observance is of vital interest to many people at the coast just now as the Sunday steamer, and its advocates, with a persistent insolence, determine to thrust themselves on us.*
>
> *However, not all who oppose our attitude at Dunoon are mere thoughtless Sabbath breakers. Many consider our attitude to be one of the narrowest of traditional and religious bigotries, and seem to feel it is in the interest of civilization and the onward march of the human race that the insolent determination to make Dunoon receive a Sunday steamer should be warmly encouraged.*
>
> *To all such broadminded—if shallow—people, we would like to urge that it is not a question of the highest of traditional religious bigotry, but a question of the highest moral, spiritual and civic importance.*
>
> *The Sunday steamer is a disgrace to the good manners of our British nation. It is an expression of shallow indifference to any of the higher concerns of the human race. God is not in all the thought of it. It is neither common human courtesy nor ordinary decency, the untoward impudence of these poor, infatuated Sunday steamer people.*

During this period few people beside Principal and Mrs. MacGregor knew of the battle raging inside Chambers. Waking in the night, Duncan could have walked to his bedroom window and seen a tall figure pacing the mist-shrouded grounds of Dhalling Mhor, head bowed, followed at a slight distance by a collie dog, trotting to keep up with the long strides of his master. If

MacGregor ached to see a resolution and release for Chambers, he knew he could help most by waiting, praying, and loving unconditionally.

Still, Oswald wrestled with himself. How could he speak to others of God when the deepest realities eluded him? What right did he have to represent Christ when his heart was so filled with the selfish impurity he said Christ came to cleanse?

"STRIVE TO ENTER IN AT THE STRAIT GATE"
(Kirn, June 7, 1901)

"Cut it off." My heart is bleeding,
And my spirit's wrung with pain,
Yet I hear my Jesus pleading,
"Cut if off or all is vain."

So I've stopped my ears in terror
Lest self-pity make me quail,
Lest at last I take the error
And God's purpose thwart and fail.

I am bowed to death in sadness,
For the pain is all too great,
But the dear Lord must find pleasure
In the way He maketh straight.

During the summer break, he traveled north again to visit John Cameron. As the train puffed along the shore of sparkling Loch Lomond, Oswald could feel the tightness in his shoulders begin to ease. He would climb Ben Nevis again and talk with old John. Perhaps he could find peace once and for all in the Highlands he loved.

Oswald loved to hear John Cameron pray. When they were alone, the old Highlander's words were simple and childlike. But when he gathered his workers around the table for prayer in his home, he prayed long, stately "architectural" prayers that would have seemed ponderous without his intense personal devotion and humility. From John's advice to others in difficult circumstances, Oswald gleaned a phrase to guide his return to Dunoon: "And you must be sure to ask Him why this came," Cameron said. "He knows."

Back at the college, Oswald's agitation became less concealed as summer merged into autumn. On September 6, 1901, he answered a letter from his father in which Clarence had apparently expressed his displeasure that Oswald was giving his teaching services free of charge at Dunoon College.

Dear Father:

I was glad to hear from you again, we are just nearing the new session and consequently very busy preparing for work. I am very well indeed after my trip north. Thank you very much for information re insuring my life. I had never thought of it before—I will think of it now.

About your attitude to me in my present circumstances, I know you would not hold them for one moment if you knew them. "Worthy of my hire?" my dear Father, I get more, far more than I deserve even of money. Here I have leisure to work at my will, here I have opportunity of doing a little to help men toward a realisation of their calling—The Ministry. Here I am clothed and fed and thought a great deal more highly of than I deserve. Here I have the inward conviction that I am doing God's will. You are not of some who can see nothing but the immediate present position and salary, as some have been who have talked to me. You can and do understand, they cannot and do not.

You say can I not earn money somewhere and someway else so that I can help my Mother and sisters to say nothing of you? I could at the expense of greater usefulness. What is money help to you and mother and my sisters compared to the eternal assistance I am certainly enabled to give here to souls. I dare to say, in Heaven, you will thank God for the life so few of you deem more than mere foolishness.

When my way opens to my own conviction to go from here I will, and no affection or friendship or leisure or ties will keep me. I see all along the run of life 'Many are called, few are chosen.'

I cannot alter my course today—God will in time as it suits Him. I am not good or worthy, but the ring of our Masters' passion is in my soul. How can I disobey His voice so clear to my own convictions even at the expense of being thought foolish, a dreamer, an idealist, at best; at worst, a fool and youth lacking common sense. Whatever happens cannot be outside the all things.

I understand your earnestness about me, I understand my former foolishness, my ignorant stubbornness, but God has been and is guiding me even when I do not see Him or understand. When you read and meditate near the heart of God you must know I am right; but when you remember me, your son, and the ways of the world, you think the way of life cannot be for me and my son. Believe me Father it can be and it is. Do not urge me because I cannot budge from my convictions. God will bring it all out clear.

This all seems a high tone, but it is necessary to take a high true tone.

I hear and know continually the cry and the irritation, for what purpose is this waste, could it not be sold and given to the poor? Let my life answer by its whole devotion for the sake of the wounded palms, and feet and side of the Saviour of the World.

I am neither great nor good nor noble, nor do I think I am, but I am impelled by the persistent mercy and love of God.

I know you shall know it someday, that I did well in sacrificing the present for His sake.

With much love to Mother and yourself.

Your loving son,
Oswald Chambers

His claim to be "very well indeed" may have been true of physical health and mental capacity, but his quiet moments alone brought him back into the presence of the enemy—himself. He realized as he had never believed possible what the disposition of sin in him could do.

A poem written in September concluded with this stanza:

O Lord Jesus, hear my crying
For a consecrated life,
For I bite the dust in trying
For release from this dark strife.

Oswald was living dangerously close to the edge of a complete breakdown. Deep in his soul, he echoed the words of Robert Browning,

I give the fight up: let there be an end,
A privacy, an obscure nook for me.
I want to be forgotten even by God.

Only three times during the past four years had Oswald been conscious of God speaking personally to him: Once, when sitting in his room late one night, his collie, Tweed, had come in through the window, put his head on Oswald's knee, looked into his eyes for a few minutes, then gone out again. Another time, his door opened and in came the baby boy of the house, barefoot and in his night-clothes. He came up to him and said, "Mr. Chambers, I loves you" and went back to his bed. Again, while conducting a Christian Endeavour meeting, a mentally retarded girl walked down the church aisle and laid a bunch of withered flowers on the table. A piece of paper tied to the flowers said, "With love from daft Meg." Each event seemed to be a tender touch from the Father conveying His presence and love.

Chambers' account of this period continued in his testimony:

I see now that God was taking me by the light of the Holy Spirit and His Word through every ramification of my being. The last three months of those years things reached a climax, I was getting very desperate. I knew no one who had what I wanted; in fact I did not know what I did want. But I knew that if what I had was all the Christianity there was, the thing was a fraud.

Then Luke 11:13 got hold of me—'If ye then, being evil, know how to give good gifts to your children, how much more shall your Heavenly Father give the Holy Spirit to them that ask Him?'

But how could I, bad motived as I was, possibly ask for the gift of the Holy Spirit? Then it was borne in upon me that I had to claim the gift from God on the authority of Jesus Christ and testify to having done so. But the thought came—if you claim the gift of the Holy Spirit on the word of Jesus Christ and testify to it, God will make it known to those who know you best how bad you are in heart. And I was not willing to be a fool for Christ's sake.

But those of you who know the experience, know very well how God brings one to the point of utter despair, and I got to the place where I did not care whether everyone knew how bad I was, I cared for nothing on earth, saving to get out of my present condition.

At a little meeting held during a League of Prayer mission in Dunoon, a well-known lady was asked to take the after meeting. She did not speak, but set us to prayer, and then sang, 'Touch me again, Lord.' I felt nothing, but I knew emphatically my time had come, and I rose to my feet.

I had no vision of God, only a sheer dogged determination to take God at His word and to prove this thing for myself, and I stood up and said so. That was bad enough but what followed was ten times worse. After I had sat down the lady worker, who knew me well, said: 'That is very good of our brother, he has spoken like that as an example to the rest of you.'

I got up again and said: 'I got up for no one's sake, I got up for my own sake; either Christianity is a downright fraud, or I have not got hold of the right end of the stick.' And then and there I claimed the gift of the Holy Spirit in dogged committal on Luke 11:13.

I had no vision of heaven or of angels, I had nothing, I was as dry and empty as ever, no power or realization of God, no witness of the Holy Spirit. Two days later I was asked to speak at a meeting, and forty souls came out to the front. Did I praise God? No, I was terrified and left them to the workers, and went to Mr. MacGregor and told him what had happened.

He said, 'Don't you remember claiming the Holy Spirit as a gift on the word of Jesus, and that He said: "Ye shall receive power . . ."? This is the power from on high.'

And like a flash something happened inside me, and I saw that I had been wanting power in my own hand, so to speak, that I might say—Look what I have by putting my all on the altar.

Glory be to God, the last aching abyss of the human heart is filled to overflowing with the love of God. Love is the beginning, love is the middle and love is the end. After He comes in, all you see is 'Jesus only, Jesus ever.' When you know what God has done for you, the power and the tyranny of sin is gone and the radiant, unspeakable emancipation of the indwelling Christ has come.

Chambers never looked back on this spiritual experience at Dunoon with the smug satisfaction of having "arrived." Instead, on the few occasions when he mentioned it in public meetings or private conversations, he spoke of it as a new beginning; a gateway instead of a goal. To most observers, he was the same as he had always been—a gifted, engaging, humorous, articulate, deep-thinking man of God. Only Chambers himself understood the extent to which his inner turmoil had given way to transforming peace.

Many years later, Chrissie Brain wrote about Oswald's struggle in Dunoon: "One can trace the mature years of service back to these formative and wonderful years of 'Genesis,' and watch the plan of God develop under His guiding hand. The master of 'Black and White' had his share of both in the landscape of his life at this time, and those who knew him most intimately in these days of sunshine and shadow can best interpret his later teaching. God's purpose is progressive, and his ultimate life work was as the fruit to the flower.

"He was no 'church window' saint, that is the last thing he would have desired to be—very real and human; not faultless, but blameless, a true knight of God, obedient to death, laying his 'Isaac' unquestioningly on the altar. To such is given the Crown of Life.

"After this the seal of God came in floods of blessing, irrigating countless lives. 'Because thou hast done this thing, . . . I will bless thee, . . . and in thy seed shall all the nations of the earth be blessed.' God does not lead many thus, but He does lead some, and they must obey."

Finally, the long night was over and peace had come. The citadel of his heart had fallen, not to a conquering Christ, but to the gentle knocking of a wounded hand. In a new and powerful way, at the age of twenty-seven, the story of Oswald Chamber's life had just begun.

8
THE WIDER SPHERE

(1902–1906)

Chambers' crisis of full surrender to God in 1901 profoundly altered his life. Some time after the experience, he spoke of it in a letter to a friend:

> *You ask a question about the baptism of the Holy Ghost—did I get there all at once, or easily? No, I did not. Pride and the possession of the high esteem of my many Christian friends kept me out for long enough. But immediately I was willing to sacrifice all and put myself on the Altar, which is Jesus Himself, all was begun and done.*
>
> *Holiness is not an attainment at all, it is the gift of God, and the pietistic tendency is the introspection which makes me worship my own earnestness and not take the Lord seriously at all. It is a pious fraud that suits the natural man immensely. He makes holy, He sanctifies, He does it all. All I have to do is to come as a spiritual pauper, not ashamed to beg, to let go of my right to myself and act on Romans 12:1–2. It is never 'Do, do and you'll be' with the Lord, but 'Be, be, and I will do through you.' It is a case of 'hands up' and letting go, and then entire reliance on Him.*

During the next five and a half years at Dunoon, Chambers developed into a powerful and much sought after preacher. To his gift of unique and forceful expression, he added tact and compassion, qualities evidently lacking in his earlier years.

Duncan MacGregor's son, Easdale, a close friend and keen observer of Chambers, notes that Oswald's earlier sermons "seemed to create a fear of God, in the sense of terror, in his hearers rather than of confidence and love." One request to the principal for a preacher from the college concluded with a prohibition against Oswald: "Dinna send us yon lang-haired swearin' parson!"

A friendship with the Rev. Dinsdale T. Young, then at Nicholson Square Church in Edinburgh, had a telling effect on Oswald's approach in the pulpit. During an address at Dunoon College in 1902, the Rev. Young explored the passion and genius of the late Charles Haddon Spurgeon. Chambers reported the address for the *Dunoon Herald*, noting Young's emphasis on "the grip and hold of the fundamentals" along with "the tender, passionate pleading of the preacher."

Easdale MacGregor believed that the Rev. Young convinced Chambers, "more by example than by argument, that there was work for him in preaching a simpler and friendlier gospel." But the softening was only in style and not content. Chambers maintained a lifelong stricture against "watering down the Word of God to the level of human experience."

Even with a demanding schedule of college and extracurricular responsibilities, Chambers took time to study and think. When a person or topic captured his interest, he plunged headlong into wholehearted intellectual pursuit until he had mastered the subject at hand. A casual conversation about Emmanuel Swedenborg, for example, so stimulated Chambers that he purchased all of Swedenborg's works and studied them in depth. This diligent inquiry led to a paper on the Swedish scientist, philosopher, and mystic, which Chambers presented in Glasgow in 1902.

"I am not a Swedenborgian," Chambers told the audience, "nor do I belong in the slightest way to the New Church." (The New Church was an organization founded by followers of Swedenborg's teaching.) Rather than hunting for heresy, Chambers appreciated the man's mind while carefully sifting and evaluating his conclusions.

When the Scottish New Church Evidence Society published the paper as a pamphlet, it brought a hail of criticism on Chambers from people who misinterpreted his intention. A vicious letter denouncing Oswald was published in the *Dunoon Herald*, but it brought no response from Chambers. At one time, he would have felt compelled to defend himself. Now, he had the power to keep silent.

Oswald read the novels of Balzac, the plays of Ibsen, and the stories of George MacDonald along with the latest theological writings of his day. The Revs. Alexander Whyte, James Denney, W. R. Inge, and J. H. Jowett were among his favorites.

Chambers and Duncan MacGregor shared a sparsely populated common ground in their attitude toward Christianity and the arts. In a day when many conservative Christians denounced the theater as the devil's workshop and avoided novels as an inherently sinful medium of expression, Chambers found that both presented useful, if painfully sharp, images of the human condition.

In 1901, MacGregor's own novel, *Lady Christ*, was published by Arthur H. Stockwell Company, a well-known London firm. The title alone was enough to send most evangelicals into a fit of objection. Chambers applauded the effort and contributed a drawing of a beautiful young woman sitting on a stretch of Highland seashore as a frontispiece for the book.

In the book MacGregor used his characters to tackle issues ranging from the landed nobility's oppression of the crofters to the church's insensitive stifling of common people who hunger for God. Infused throughout were tidbits of MacGregor's Highland humor: "It's a blessing Scotsmen are so few or they would conquer the world."

The novel underscored the uniqueness of the Rev. Duncan MacGregor and his vision expressed through Dunoon College. Chambers loved "Mac's" unconventionality and his uncompromising integrity.

Duncan MacGregor's most significant influence on Chambers during these years, however, was his daily life. "I never knew him in a controversy in my life," Chambers said. "He always let the other man have it all his way. I have known him to be defrauded over and over again; but I never knew him to be defrauded without knowing it."

Walking the streets of Dunoon and Glasgow with the principal, Oswald observed a man who lived what he preached. "One of the most touching sights to me," Chambers wrote, "was to see that man of God with the poor, the blind, the lame, the halt and the imbecile: they all seemed to feel that they had a strong refuge in him.

"Children were always very fond of the Rev. MacGregor and he never refused anything they offered him. I remember once a dirty little urchin, sprawling about in the puddles on the sidewalk, scrambled to her feet when she saw the Principal coming, and held up her grimy little hand with a mean [ordinary] piece of half-sucked candy in it, which the Principal took and put in his mouth with a most gracious, 'Thank you.' "

While still teaching at Dunoon College, Chambers first attended a meeting of the League of Prayer in Perth. He felt a special kinship with the "Leaguers" and their earnest love for God. Oswald's experience of the Holy Spirit's fullness and his study of the Bible convinced him that the organization's emphasis on scriptural holiness sounded a much-needed call for Christians in every denomination. He continued his involvement with the local chapter in Perth and began speaking on occasion at League gatherings in Scotland and the north of England.

When Reader Harris, founder of the League, first met Chambers, he took a special interest in the keen young tutor from Dunoon. They talked about Oswald's gifts and desires, and where God might be leading him. Harris helped raise Chambers' vision from Britain to the world. And the more Oswald learned about this tall man of dignified grace and decisive action, the more he liked him. Harris was a prominent London barrister and also a King's Counsel, a lifetime appointment recognizing his skill and success in the legal profession. His leadership in the League of Prayer was voluntary and unpaid. From the circles of royalty to the slums of London, Harris moved freely as a fearless but compassionate representative of Christ.

Richard Reader Harris was an unlikely person to establish a religious organization devoted to scriptural holiness and spiritual revival. As a teenager, Harris had sought God, but his conversations with a liberal clergyman left him so disillusioned that he later became a follower of Charles Bradlaugh, the well-known London atheist. Bradlaugh often lectured on Bible texts, ridiculing Christians for their weak response to its teachings while he called people to live moral lives and put into practice the ideas in the Sermon on the Mount.

Joining the Puritan Wing of Bradlaugh's Ethical Society, Harris pledged not to smoke or drink. If a man lived more uprightly than most Christians, he thought, why did he need their God?

"For ten years," Harris later said, "I remained an honest doubter because no one pointed me to Jesus Christ as the One Who saves 'to the uttermost.' I had wanted to know God, but the professing Christians I knew failed to introduce me to Him, because they did not know Him themselves."

His conversion to Christ came through Mary Griffin Bristow, a gifted and cultured young lady whom he married in 1880. Reader and Mary Harris could easily have remained well-respected, comfortable members of the upper strata of London society. But Reader could not forget the scathing accusations of Charles Bradlaugh from years past: "If Jesus had been divine," Bradlaugh thundered, "his followers would long ago have claimed the power He offered them, obeyed His command, and evangelised the world."

In 1884, a Moody-Sankey meeting in London fired the Harrises' concern for evangelism. Seven years later, they experienced a spiritual revolution identical to that of Chambers' complete surrender to God at Dunoon. The Pentecostal League of Prayer was founded in 1891 as "an interdenominational union of Christian people who, conscious of their own need, would join in prayer:

1. For the filling of the Holy Spirit for all believers;
2. For revival in the Churches;
3. For the spread of Scriptural holiness."

The organization celebrated its tenth anniversary in 1901, the year Chambers first attended a League meeting. By 1905, Oswald was speaking regularly at regional League functions and brought a message at the Annual Meeting in London. In a June editorial in *Tongues of Fire,* the League magazine, Reader Harris referred to Oswald as "a new speaker of exceptional power . . . whose address will long be remembered."

Along with Oswald's growing involvement in the League, his weekends and holidays were filled with speaking engagements in churches across the country. His reputation as a unique and powerful communicator of the gospel brought more requests than he could accept. He often filled his brother Arthur's pulpit, and in 1905 first preached for the Rev. Dinsdale T. Young in London's Great Queen Street Chapel, Kingsway.

During the Christmas holiday of 1905, Oswald held a week's mission at his brother Arthur's church, Eltham Park Baptist, ten miles east of central London. Among those listening to his impassioned call to yield fully to the Holy Spirit were two sisters, twenty-six-year-old Edith and twenty-two-year-old Gertrude Hobbs. Only two months before they had presented themselves for baptism and church membership.

It is likely that Mrs. Hobbs, their widowed mother, invited Chambers to their home for a midday meal or afternoon tea. Church hospitality called for members to take a turn in feeding each visiting preacher. At the table, Oswald showed none of the serious intensity that characterized him in the pulpit. With the family dog lying at his feet, he was quite content to discuss everything from politics to the plays of George Bernard Shaw. Of the two sisters, Edith, nicknamed Daisy or Dais, was closer to Oswald in age and education. Gertrude, known as Truda, was nine years younger than he, but struck him as very mature for her age. Mrs. Hobbs seemed gracious and proper while Dais impressed him as pleasant and kind. Truda's eyes, however, twinkled in a way that was hard to ignore. If a spark of interest was struck between Oswald and Gertrude at this meeting, it was two and a half years away from being kindled into flame.

A most intriguing topic occupied Oswald's time with his brother. Six months before, the church had sent Arthur to Wales for a first-hand look at the revival sweeping that land. He questioned Arthur about the spiritual fervor transcending denominational lines and bringing people of all social classes to faith in Christ and reconciliation with each other. What accounted for it? Had it resulted from dedicated prayer? Or was it simply a sovereign act of the Holy Spirit? Could it cross the borders into England, Scotland, and Ireland? Might it span the Atlantic to America?

Oswald returned to Dunoon with a verse burning in his heart for 1906: "Go ye into all the world and make disciples of all nations." He sensed that God was about to issue him a new set of marching orders, but he had no idea how they would come or where they would lead. He plunged back into his teaching, and a few months later, at a League meeting in Perth, he met Juji Nakada. The diminutive Japanese evangelist was in England, ostensibly to rest and be spiritually recharged. Even with that goal, he rarely slowed down.

Juji Nakada was a foot shorter than Oswald Chambers physically, but spiritually, they looked each other in the eye. From their first meeting they felt a unique kinship and calling to work together. In May 1906, they shared an evening platform at the League's annual convention in London, both testifying to the work of the Holy Spirit in their lives.

During long walks and talks together, Chambers was enthralled by Nakada's story of leaving Japan, going to Chicago, and entering Moody Bible Institute in 1897 in search of spiritual power. Although already recognized as a bold and effective evangelist in Japan, Nakada alone understood the dryness of his own soul. "If I don't find the power of the Holy Ghost," he told his wife before leaving Japan, "I'll come back, leave the ministry, and be a dentist."

Through the writings of John Wesley and the ministry of friends at Moody, Nakada found the filling of the Holy Spirit he sought. At a nearby church, he became acquainted with a Western Union executive named Charles Cowman, and his wife, Lettie. (Mrs. Cowman is remembered today for her book *Streams in the Desert.*) Through the Cowmans, Nakada was introduced to Martin Wells Knapp and his Cincinnati training college known as God's Bible School. Nakada returned to Japan and in 1901, the Cowmans sailed as missionaries and joined forces with him to open the Tokyo Bible College.

When Nakada launched into a humorous description of the providential twists and turns that had brought him to Britain in 1906, Oswald laughed until tears filled his eyes.

"You must come to Japan," Nakada told Chambers. "We need a man like you to teach at our Pastors' college." It was an intriguing but impossible invitation. Chambers had no money, no sponsoring organization, and no permission from Duncan MacGregor to leave his post at Dunoon. But the words lodged in his heart next to his Lord's command, "Go ye into all the world."

The two decided to begin where they were. After praying long and fervently, they made plans to visit Wales and preach the holiness message to the recent converts in the revival. Chambers returned to complete his work in Dunoon and became seriously ill. Nakada went on to Wales accompanied by others.

A few years earlier in Dunoon, the usually healthy Chambers had suffered from what his brother, Arthur, called "a severe illness that nearly cut short his career." Mrs. MacGregor was so concerned for him then that they brought him up from his room in the caretaker's cottage to care for him in the main house at Dhalling Mhor.

Because Chambers' writing usually grew out of his experience, an unusual poem introduces the strong possibility that he may have suffered from a form of recurring respiratory illness, perhaps tuberculosis:

THE CONSUMPTIVE
(Edinburgh, September 14, 1896)

"Waiting—wistful still?"
Yes, just for tonight,
Tomorrow, with the light,
I'm sure to be all right,
Don't you think I will?

"Waiting—wistful still?"
Yes, just for today,
Tomorrow, I'll away,
Just now I'm forced to stay,
For they say I'm ill.

"Waiting, wistful still?"
Yes, just for this year,
Because they say they fear
The cost will be too dear,
So I'm waiting—till!

"Waiting—wistful still?"
Yes! From the still white bed,
Came whispered from the dead,
"Till to God you're led,
Waiting, wistful still."

Chambers' greatest difficulty in leaving Dunoon was Principal MacGregor's hesitancy over his departure. His deep respect for MacGregor and personal attachment to him made it all the more difficult. Duncan would not stop Oswald from following what he saw as the clear leading of God, but he had no sense that it was time for this gifted tutor of philosophy to go. Oswald's personal record of his feeling at their parting was metaphoric. "It was night," he wrote.

He had spent nine and a half years with Duncan MacGregor and learned to love him, in some ways, more than his own father. Through the most tumultuous decade of Oswald's life, MacGregor had been a staying power for him. Knowing he could never repay that debt, Chambers determined to be the same influence in the lives of young men who might someday come to him as he had come to Duncan and Mrs. MacGregor.

During summer and early fall, Nakada and Chambers visited churches and League centers throughout England and Scotland. July found them at the famous Keswick Convention, soaking in the preaching of G. Campbell Morgan, F. B. Meyer, J. Stuart Holden, and W. H. Griffith Thomas. By the time the convention was over, they had made plans to go to America and then travel on to Japan. "This small Japanese is very good at stealing hearts and minds," Chambers said. "He stole mine, and then visited my home and stole the hearts of my father and brother, and he made them willing to send me to Japan."

On September 25, 1906, Oswald wrote to his mother:

> *My dear 'brick' of a Mother,*
>
> *I am proud of your letter, and more than proud of such a mother. I read a portion of your letter to Nakada, and he said—'Your mother is a noble woman.'*
>
> *God has undertaken mightily, the enervation caused by the fondness and attachment of home folks has so often been terrible in an out-*

going missionary's life. If it is possible, I love you more than ever for being so robust and strong in your mind. Thank God for you and upon every remembrance of you.

October found them in company with James Gardiner, League secretary for Scotland. They preached at Perth, Dundee, and Glasgow, then traveled up the Caledonian Canal, holding meetings in towns and villages all the way to Inverness. In Fort William, Chambers pointed to massive Ben Nevis, Britain's highest peak at 4,400 feet. Nakada was unimpressed. His tall friend's mountain would reach only a third of the way to the summit of Mt. Fuji.

With their characteristic good humor, rare camaraderie, and great difference in height, they presented a striking sight wherever they went. Glancing up at Chambers one day, Juji remarked, "You are long like a poker." Oswald countered with, "You are short like a shovel. And it takes both to make a fire." Their laughter endeared them to the townspeople who listened with interest to their message of salvation and sanctification in Christ.

By the time of their November 6 sailing, plans called for them to spend the winter in the U.S. and Canada. The arrangements were sketchy but Chambers was unconcerned.

Aboard the *SS Baltic*, bound for New York, he wrote in a letter:

Nov. 11, 1906

The passage in Exodus 33:20–25 which God gave me this morning has been a wonderful portion to my soul and heart and mind and body. 'Satisfied with Jesus every day.'

My own heart and life is at leisure from itself, and God's call is on me and in me, and in the heaving ridges of the deep and the ponderous distances rolling around, and the huge and thoughtful expanse above enfolding us, and we forging a way through it all—I never felt God's call so clear, or His meaning so certain.

Nakada has become a universal favorite on board. The grace of God has so endowed him with a sense of oneness with God that he really beams with the Spirit of God perpetually.

> *Probably the most persistent sentiment with me is the watch of the angel hosts in answer to the prayers of the numerous saints in the homeland. It seems to me as if a special watch surrounded this boat. How many go out into the world with so much unselfish love lavished on them as I have? Sometimes hands are too insistent, and human affection wickedly selfish, almost strong enough to break the ties to God. But all this I am free from, in much peace, in a perfect sense of God's call and leading, I go forth. The world is very wide and God is reigning. Thank God I feel strong to bear and do.*

Nakada watched in amazement every morning as Chambers lay on his heaving berth, slowly turning the pages of his prayer notebook, bringing scores of his friends before the throne of God. Juji tended toward seasickness while Oswald loved the open deck where he could watch the swelling, crashing waves of the North Atlantic. On this first voyage, Chambers marveled at the vastness and power of the sea, drawing strength and refreshment from it.

Oswald's letter of November 11 concluded on a confident note:

> *The goodness of God strikes me. People don't know Him, but it is not a wicked ignoring, it is ignorance. The full compassionate love of the Holy Ghost for the crowd is a precious, though intolerable, compassion. But to the ones who have tasted God, how nothing on earth again can satisfy. Once we think with God, all the rest is far and sinks to a relative place. Pray and keep my hands up while I do what our Father wants me to do.*

PART 3

"Unless the life of a missionary is hid with Christ in God before he begins his work, that life will become exclusive and narrow. It will never become the servant of all men, it will never wash the feet of others."
—So Send I You

9
THE WANDERING PROPHET IN AMERICA

(1906–1907)

The *SS Baltic* steamed into New York harbor on November 15, 1906. Chambers stood at the rail, enthralled with the Statue of Liberty and the towering skyline of Manhattan. So this was America. Was he really here? With the curiosity of a child, he scanned the bustling harbor and feasted on the reality of arriving in this new land.

Excited voices, shouts, and cheers from the decks below gave new meaning to Oswald's understanding of the words "freedom and opportunity." Of the *Baltic*'s 1,426 passengers, more than half were immigrants traveling in Third Class. Chambers had gone out of his way to talk to many of them during the voyage. He would especially remember the look of anticipation in their eyes and the ring of their names—Olson, Nyberg, Isaac, Johanson, Levy, Bajefsky, Barovitz, and Rabenda.

They came from Norway, Sweden, Latvia, and Russia; their surnames speaking the history of nations, the oppression of minorities, and the universal longing for peace and a new beginning. A few were identified by specific occupations—tailor, farmer, and weaver—but most appeared on the passenger list as "laborer." Chambers was coming to visit and would return to his homeland. But they had left home and were coming here to stay. Where and what was "home," after all? He tried to imagine their feelings as the tugboats guided the ship toward its berth.

Above, in First Class, the Honorable Earl of Suffolk and his wife, the Countess, prepared to disembark. Her maid and the Earl's manservant had already left their own First Class accommodations to prepare the mountain of luggage and steamer trunks for arrival.

Nakada and Chambers had shared a Second Class cabin during the ten-day journey. It was not luxurious, but much more comfortable than the crowded compartments below. Underneath the water line, shirtless men glistening with sweat labored in the engine room and the stokehold. Oswald's literary mind could easily have seen a simile in this voyage of the *Baltic.* The world was like an ocean liner, filled with an incredible variety of people from every station in life. Some understood their ultimate destination and others did not. Whether they wore fine silk or ragged wool, people were the same, and Oswald believed they all hungered to know His Lord and Savior, Jesus Christ.

In America, a great land of freedom, people in mansions as well as tenements suffered from spiritual oppression. The thin Scotsman and the stocky Japanese watched as the gangplank was maneuvered into place. As the passengers began to disembark, they shook hands with broad smiles. They had come to do battle and see how God might use them for His glory in "the land of the free and the home of the brave."

For a month Chambers and Nakada stayed with people on the East Coast, taking part in church services and preaching at special missions. Oswald's fascination with these new friends grew along with his appreciation for them:

From John Kimber's home in Newport, Rhode Island, he wrote on November 27:

> *I am staying now with a family of Quakers and it is all 'thee' and 'thou' and 'thy.' One of the lads did something wrong, and in the mildest way possible the mother said, 'Thee will be punished for that, dear'; the lad's countenance fell and he was punished. A most judicious method, almost bordering on the impossible.*
>
> *These saints have had experiences, as I have, of two distinct works of grace, and I find the bonds of the Spirit are closer than anything I have ever known before.*
>
> *Just now I hear Mr. Kimber calling 'Sophie,' she is a saved and sanctified Negress of about 60, simply shining with the beauty of the Lord.*

She came up to me the first day I was here and said, 'I love thee, thou'st brought heaven with thee.' These black people are gems . . . and so enthusiastic. They laugh and shout 'Glory' and interrupt the preacher to tell the audience an incident they think illustrates the point—gloriously unconventional.

Brother Nakada and I are being handed around through these States in a wonderful way. The saints are actually squabbling over us! All we do is to eat and sleep and talk and God witnesses. It is doing me endless good. I have only one desire growing more and more, that the Lord may be glorified.

On December 17, Oswald wrote from Brooklyn to his sister Florence:

We had a blessed time on Sunday here, many came out for sanctification and for salvation and for healing. You see, I believe that Jesus Christ our Lord has all power in heaven and on earth; do you? I find most people believe that He has all power in heaven, but are not sure about earth. I am finding out day by day more and more wonderful things about Jesus our Lord and what He can do. I am getting overwhelmed with calls for missions and services, and God is leading and using me blessedly.

I am now en route for Cincinnati, all the bottom berths are taken and the top ones are supposed to rock more; but, Hallelujah, I shall sleep like a babe and arrive in that city where as yet I do not know a living soul, but God knows and that is enough for me.

His letter to Florence continued the next day.

I slept like a top, really, every moment of the day reminds me of my Father's care, tender, watchful and grand. Truly I think I am one of the Lord's spoilt bairns.

For seven hundred miles, nearly twice the distance from Edinburgh to London, Oswald's train rolled across New Jersey and

Pennsylvania, then southward through Ohio toward the junction of three rivers and "The Queen City of the West"—Cincinnati.

He arrived on Friday, December 21, and was promptly whisked by streetcar to the top of a hill known as Mt. Auburn. There a warm welcome awaited him at God's Bible School and Missionary Training Home. Founded in 1900 by Martin Wells Knapp, the school functioned as the hub of a growing holiness movement in the United States.* In spite of Knapp's sudden death during a typhoid epidemic in 1901, the school continued to grow, and by 1906 it served nearly two hundred students.

Chambers and Nakada arrived just in time for the school's ten-day Christmas Convention. Juji was listed on the slate of expected speakers, but Oswald was a surprise. That mattered little to the convention organizers who were always ready for God's surprises. In holiness circles, most meetings were advertised as: LEADERS: God the Father, God the Son, and God the Holy Ghost; WORKERS: Names of those invited to preach and lead. Invariably, a final line was added: "And others whom the Lord may send."

Chambers was enthusiastically welcomed as one of their own, asked to speak at the gathering, and involved in ordaining nine candidates to the gospel ministry. In the January 10, 1907, issue of *God's Revivalist* magazine, Oswald described the evening meetings, held in the school's George Street Mission, as taking place "away down in the heart of that awful city of Cincinnati, in a street of unblushing sin and shame."

His assessment was more than Victorian prudery. Cincinnati, with four hundred thousand inhabitants, had its genteel, religious, and cultured side. But, like every metropolis, it was an "awful city" in many ways. In the slums bordering the Ohio River, crime, drunkenness, prostitution, and family disintegration left their scars on a poor, often transient, community. Children suffered most from the harsh existence in and around

*Holiness was widely accepted to mean "the Bible doctrine of regeneration and entire sanctification as taught by the original founders of Methodism, John and Charles Wesley." The "full-gospel" message of the early twentieth-century holiness movement included "regeneration, entire sanctification, healing, and the second coming of Jesus."

Shantytown, a collection of tarpaper shacks littering the banks of the Ohio down to the water's edge.

Cincinnati's tenements and back alleys became the arena in which God's Bible School students put their Christian principles into practice. They were in training as Christian workers, preachers, and missionaries, and that involved more than classes at their two-acre hilltop campus. Besides working one hour each day at the school, students passed out tracts, conducted street meetings, visited hospitals, and held gospel services in jails, infirmaries, missions, and churches. In the area around George Street, they were often greeted by jeers and physical threats.

Every Thanksgiving Day, God's Bible School held its annual dinner for the city's poor children. In 1905 seven hundred pounds of turkey with all the trimmings were served to eighteen hundred children. The neediest received better clothing and all were given a "goody bag" as they left the dining room. A service presenting the message of Christ completed the day. Students spent a week cooking and preparing for the Thanksgiving Day event, then worked into the night cleaning up. That evening they fed five hundred men at the George Street Mission

A primary school in Kentucky, an orphanage and farm, a publishing company, and a rescue home for girls were also operated by the school. It is not surprising that Chambers said of the whole enterprise, "This is truly Holiness socialism."

At the Christmas Convention Nakada remarked on the exuberance of people during the services. "I, having come from England lately, notice especially the liberty in the demonstration. May the Lord rub off the starch of every Holiness people in every country."

Chambers was keenly aware of the differences between a quiet, orderly Pentecostal League of Prayer service in Britain and the shouting, arm-waving, open emotion of an American holiness meeting. He had no problem with happy religious enthusiasm or weeping penitence, but he looked to criteria other than these for evidence of the work of the Holy Spirit.

He wrote in the January 10, 1907, *Revivalist*,

> There was nothing to hinder the blessed Lord having His way at this Convention. The hearts of all were eager and expectant and hungry. Many were the signs

of God's mighty presence—the full altars, the spontaneous freedom, and the prominent place the Bible received, but perhaps the most significant sign to some of us was the opening of God's truth to us and the ability granted us by the Holy Spirit to understand and grip the Lord's vital truth.

On January 1, 1907, he wrote in his diary:

The Bible School is situated on a hill overlooking Cincinnati, and the school is called The Mount of Blessing. The Bible School in Tokyo started from here and is largely supported by them. It is all run on faith lines, such as I have been used to.

For many months they have been praying for a teacher, and at their request I have agreed to stay until July and teach and write some books. My heart swells at the big thoughts and visions that come of founding Bible schools on these holiness lines in Britain and different parts of the world. Zech. 8:21–23 came to me with power today.

While Nakada traveled to renew old ties around the States, Chambers began teaching on January 4. Eight days into his Biblical Theology course, he greeted his students with an examination: 1. What do you understand by Biblical Theology? 2. Define science. 3. What do you mean by Bible facts being Revelation facts? 4. Show the difference between common sense and the common people. 5. Define Agnosticism, theory, and hypothesis. 6. Give Scriptural proof that God created both the material and Bible worlds. 7. What do you understand by insanity? 8. What is Biblical criticism? What is higher criticism?

If Chambers had a pet peeve it was, in his words, "intellectual slovenliness, disguised by a seemingly true regard for the spiritual interests." The solution? "Extermination by honest, hard-working, sanctified students of God's Word."

His course outline set forth bedrock convictions about the importance of diligent study and sound teaching. To his students he said: "More than half the side-tracks and *all* the hysterical phenomena that seize whole communities of people, like a pestiferous epidemic, from time to time, arise from spiritual laziness and intellectual sloth on the part of so-called religious teachers. There are a host of Holiness adventurers whose careers would suddenly end, if vigorous sanctified saints were abroad."

His warning to prospective teachers of Christian doctrine came in the words of Dean Alford's Golden Rule: "What thou has not by suffering bought, presume thou not to teach."

With all his emphasis on truth, Oswald was never content to affect the mind alone. His goal was to stir the will to act on sound principles of Scripture, so that people might demonstrate the love of Christ. He looked intently at his eager, earnest students, ready to go out and battle for the truth, then read from Dr. Alexander Whyte's exposition of Job: "Oh, the unmitigated curse of controversy! Oh the detestable passions that corrections and contradictions kindle up to fury in the proud heart of man! Eschew controversy, my brethren, as you would eschew the entrance to hell itself! Let them have it their own way. Let them talk, let them write, let them correct you, let them traduce you. Let them judge and condemn you, let them slay you. Rather let the truth of God itself suffer than that love suffer. You have not enough of the Divine nature in you to be a controversialist."

On February 4, he wrote to Franklin and his wife Ethel:

> *'Go with Him all the way.' The end and aim and meaning of all sanctification is personal, passionate devotion to Jesus Christ. Keep bold and clear and out in the bracing facts of His revelation world, the Bible. Never compromise with those who water down the word of God to human experience, instead of allowing God to lift up our experience to His Word.*
>
> *I go to Japan in July I expect; we shall most probably not stay there longer than four months. I know in my bones that it is 'Go ye into all the world and make disciples of all nations,' and glory to God I am going.*

A mid-February speaking engagement in Providence, Rhode Island, prompted a typical display of Chambers' playful yet practical spirit. Sensing the physical and spiritual tiredness of his hosts, Meredith and Bessie Standley, he convinced them to travel east with him for a few days of rest. They found inexpensive, off-season accommodations at a summer resort in Pennsylvania where Chambers promptly located a horse-drawn sleigh. Morning and afternoon Oswald took them skimming across the snow-covered roads and fields. Outfitted in fur hats purchased for $2.50 each, they looked like a threesome out of a Leo Tolstoy novel.

"That week was exactly what we needed," Standley said later. "We didn't know what was coming on, but God knew, so He got us ready by giving us that rest."

The Standleys were welcomed back to Cincinnati with a lawsuit and a complex legal tangle created, in large part, by Martin Wells Knapp's faulty will. When Knapp died in December 1901, he had bequeathed God's Revivalist Publishing and God's Bible School to God. Although he named three trustees to oversee things for the Almighty, controversy ensued and Knapp's family couldn't agree on who owned what. Early in 1906, a Cincinnati court decided that God could not hold property in Hamilton County. A judge put the school under a court-monitored trusteeship. When Meredith and Bessie Standley became particularly burdened by all the opposition, Chambers told them of the false accusations he had faced during his days of struggle in Dunoon. He urged them to keep on doing God's work through the school and let the Almighty defend their reputation.

Life in America was a tonic to Chambers. The people, the ministry, and the travel combined to fill each day with new adventures. In February of 1907, he wrote home from New York after viewing the magnificent Niagara Falls:

> *Niagara is an unspeakable marvel. The rapids are maniac waters and boil to great heights in erratic fury, and the sense of the sublime and awful they inspire, breaks through language and escapes, so I cannot give you any adequate idea. Niagara does not make you feel ecstatic, it overawes you; also, strange to say, it disappoints you. Its dimensions are so enormous, its fall of waters so colossal—the mountains of frozen mist, the icicles of a hundred feet long. It is so great, so awful, and after hours of watching, it gradually breaks into your conscious thinking that you are face to face with perhaps the most wonderful wonder in the natural world.*
>
> *If you have never read Victor Hugo's Toilers of the Sea, read it. It gives you something akin to the impressions you have when face to face with this power of nature. There is nothing freakish about this, it is a sublime and awful*

> *torrent that beggars description, it paralyses wit and inspires reverence. For long after when you wake perhaps in the quiet night, and hear again the ceaseless majesty of the thunder of those torrents, and see those clouds of white water mist rise and float, and catch the endless coloured sheen of winter light through icicles and snow cones and glacier fields—when the noise of the recent and the commercial has gone, you can easily picture it hundreds of years ago when the Red Indians ruled supreme.*
>
> *Tomorrow I am going to the Red Indian reservation to the Baptist church and an old Indian chief will interpret. This will be very interesting. What ceaseless and amazing interests pack my life! but best of all is the blessing of God. The letters, the people He is building up, the breaking hearts, the wrongs He is righting, the souls He is saving and sanctifying! Glory to His name.*

The months in America allowed Chambers to step out of his usual responsibilities in Britain and thus see his life and ministry from a different perspective.

In a letter dated February 16, 1907, he wrote:

> *I want to tell you a growing conviction with me, and that is that as we obey the leadings of the Spirit of God, we enable God to answer the prayers of other people. I mean that our lives, my life, is the answer to someone's prayer, prayed perhaps centuries ago.*
>
> *It is more and more impossible to me to have programmes and plans because God alone has the plan, and our plans are only apt to hinder Him, and make it necessary for Him to break them up. I have the unspeakable knowledge that my life is the answer to prayers, and that God is blessing me and making me a blessing entirely of His sovereign grace and nothing to do with my merits, saving as I am bold enough to trust His leading and not the dictates of my own wisdom and common sense.*

> *The sense of 'my Father' has been wonderful lately. The access in prayer is so ineffably sweet and natural, I am just flooded with a deep settled peace in my soul. That is the great message to my heart these months.*

On the morning of February 23, Chambers arose at 5:30, along with all the students and faculty, for a regularly scheduled day of fasting and prayer. "I tell you it is a blessed thing," he wrote his brother Arthur. "I never spent days like them for rejoicing."

God's Bible School was very different geographically and culturally from Dunoon College, yet Chambers found the emphasis on faith and prayer to be much the same. Principal MacGregor had often suspended classes and called a day of fasting and prayer at Dunoon, especially when food and finances had come to an end. Oswald smiled in recalling a day of prayer at Dunoon when the morning mail brought a letter with five pounds, more than enough for the current need.

The students were elated but MacGregor said, "We thank God for His provision, but we're still going to spend the whole day in fasting and prayer." The great result that day, and during many others at Dunoon, was a spiritual breakthrough in the lives of students who came to the principal or to Chambers to confess deliberately hidden sin and set things right.

The purpose of prayer, in Chambers' mind, was to get into step with God, not to manipulate or coerce Him into blessing personal plans. He told his theology students in Cincinnati, "Prayer is not a preparation for work, it *is* work. Prayer is not a preparation for the battle, it *is* the battle. Prayer is two-fold: definite asking and definite waiting to receive."

Part of Oswald's gift of teaching was his own insatiable hunger for knowledge. Always reaching, always curious, his voracious appetite for reading took him along a wide range of literary pathways. He rarely went anywhere without a book.

An April 7 letter to his sister Florence reveals his joy in learning and teaching:

> *I have been having a reveling few days. My box has at last arrived. My books! I cannot tell you what they are to me—silent, wealthy, loyal lovers. To look at them, to handle them, and to*

> *re-read them! I do thank God for my books with every fibre of my being. Friends that are ever true and ever your own.*
>
> *Why, I could have almost cried for excess of joy when I got hold of them again. I see them all just at my elbow now—Plato, Wordsworth, Myers, Bradley, Halyburton, St. Augustine, Browning, Tennyson, Amiel, etc. I know them, I wish you could see how they look at me, a quiet calm look of certain acquaintance.*
>
> *I find the people here very open-minded and teachable. There are no theological prejudices, no pre-conceived notions backed by hundreds of years of hereditary prejudice. In the homeland I continually heard—'Don't preach like that, people will not understand you.' Here I find them very teachable and mouldable, and my responsibility is increased for they take what I say as of lasting authority.*
>
> *It is blessed how God has opened my way to study theology hard and thoroughly as I studied psychology and philosophy. More and more I thank God for calling me to be a theological Ishmaelite for a dozen years, tramping the globe and insisting on the holy and sanctified life as Jesus gifts it to men immediately they are willing to close with His offer.*

Chambers was not given to reminiscing, but letters that reached him in March 1907 brought news of the deaths of three people he had loved and left in Scotland. He wrote to Franklin:

> *How easily I recall Donald McIntosh, a pure, rugged Highlander, the great old type, big build, with the close raven locks, and well I remember the many times I tramped the moors for fourteen miles on a Sunday with him to Kilfinan and back from Kames.*
>
> *Great thoughts were in that man and great utterances, and I recall him with a chastened grace and a profound gratitude for my friendship with him. I recall his family worship—the larger, the more liberal views were his, and he allowed hymns to be sung, and he had his own quiet humour. He was as tender as a lamb to*

his children, and how they loved him. My heart goes out to them now as the widowed mother enters a life that can never be the same again. Death does profoundly alter life. But Praise God how gloriously ready he was to go.

And Mrs. Livingstone. I remember very vividly the last night I saw her in Dunoon, the twilight was grey and gold, and the great warm heart of the old lady flooded out to me. I feel the strong almost painful hug of her old arms as she smothered me with kisses, 'Laddie, I'll never see ye here again—how can we live without ye!'

I recall the time two years ago as I watched her husband die, and in the early dawn heard her praying in that big house on the hill's top when nothing was stirring but the dawn birds. As the stern strong prayer carried, I remember how I bowed and waited in my own bedroom while a woman, whose sorrows were deeper than I have ever known, bowed while the billows of God went over her.

And then old John Cameron. But that hits hard! Few knew him, but I knew him. I remember him on his death-bed in his home on the slopes of Ben Nevis, he could not speak but held out his arms and I bent down and kissed him. The snows were deep not only around him, but on his own head. A stern mountain crag, but the heart of a moss rose was his.

If anyone has felt the tenderness of a rugged old Highlander's embrace and love, they'll know why I thank my God upon my remembrances of old John Cameron. How he knew God! How he talked with God! and how he taught me out on those hills—at midnight, at dawn-light, and at noonday have I knelt before that old veteran in prayer. Truly it was a great goodness of God to allow me to know such men. I learnt a bigger stride, the stride of the mountains of God, with these royal, elemental souls.

I am growingly more and more convinced that God makes our own our own for ever, and that He brings and removes friends and teach-

> *ers when He knows it best. The older I get in the things of God, the more I find of the good and the blessed and the noble in men. How few mean men I have met; and here it is the same, God is introducing me to the choice souls.*

Chambers enjoyed the bold, uninhibited personalities of men like Arthur Greene of Massachusetts. One day, while walking together on a main street in downtown Cincinnati, Greene shouted at the top of his voice, "I hate the devil!" Chambers yelled after him, "So do I!" Immediately after, "A man came up to us with tears in his eyes and asked us the way of salvation," Oswald wrote to his brother Ernest. "We pointed him to the Lord. Oh, these delightful unconventional ways suit me down to the ground. . . ."

Charles Stalker, the noted Quaker evangelist, and his wife, Catherine, hosted Chambers for an April weekend in Columbus, Ohio. During Chambers' illness the year before, Stalker had been summoned to England to accompany Nakada to Wales. A big man standing 6'3" tall, with a soft, kind face, he had already made two trips to Japan and held meetings with Cowman and Nakada at the Tokyo Bible School. Chambers plied him with questions in anticipation of his own visit to Japan in a few months.

Stalker, like so many other Americans Chambers met, was a man of great faith and decisive action. He once expressed the missionary imperative by saying, "People are going to the uttermost parts of the earth to take the beer that made Milwaukee famous. We must go and take the gospel that is the power of God unto salvation to them that believe." The story of Stalker's early missionary travels appeared in 1906 as a book titled, *Twice Around the World With the Holy Ghost*.

At the Quaker church, Oswald preached on "God's Hope, Eph. 1:18" and noted, "I was struck with a phrase in Bro. Stalker's prayer, 'Give us sermons and secrets and songs for the people.' "

Chambers deeply appreciated these men of God, but devoted more space in letters home to his relationship with a young lady named Dorothea Standley.

To his sister Bertha:

> *The other day when I was dealing with a minister I heard someone outside say: 'Dorothea, you mustn't,' but the handle turned and in she came. She said a word to neither of us, climbed upon my knee and went sound asleep resting on my shoulder while I talked with that poor backslidden soul; and she was not the slightest hindrance, in fact I felt she brought the blessing of the Lord with her. Dorothea is only three years old. I have two other friends, Lucy Knapp and Hazel Bell. 'We just love ye to death,' is their phrase.*

To his sister Edith:

> *Dorothea came to my room yesterday with a very serious expression—'I must write a letter to Jesus,' so up she scrambled into my chair, took a sheet of paper and proceeded to scrawl. She would scribble awhile, then look about her with deep abstracted concern, just as she had seen grown-up people do, then she read it to me with deep earnestness—as if she were reading her scribbling—'My dear, dear, God, I love you very very much. Mamma is crying. Amen.' Then I folded the paper and she trotted off with it.*

Again,

> *My irresistible companion Dorothea nearly made me split the other day. She lifted her baby brother round the waist and put him on his feet expecting him to stand, but of course he flopped on the floor and began yelling, and Dorothea said, 'Oh, he ain't sankified yet'!*

Oswald's great love for children gave him a strong bond with Lucius B. Compton, founder of Faith Cottage Rescue Home and Eliada Orphanage in Asheville, North Carolina. Compton, often known as "The Mountaineer Evangelist," was a rugged, pioneering man with a tender heart toward children. In a day when sexual abuse was hidden behind doors of silence, and prostitution flourished in rural as well as urban areas, Compton's work with "fallen girls" was bold and innovative.

Chambers shared the platform with Compton at several holiness meetings and joined him for a camp meeting in North Carolina, near Asheville. Chambers wrote of the site:

> *This place is a veritable Garden of Eden for beauty, right on the top of the mountains with an inimitable view, surrounded by grand and lofty oaks and pine trees, with the great rolling river at your feet in the valley and a vast space of heaven. The camp meeting had been in the midst of this lovely scenery and also of squalid human misery. The big tents pitched in a dingle [a small, deep, wooded valley] are crowded with people in the evening. I cannot picture to you the hunger of the people for the word of God, in the morning and at noon the workers from all around come for Bible readings. I go on talking to them out of the Bible for hours at a stretch. Bro. Compton and his wife are doing blessed work here.*

The crowning event of Chambers' six months at God's Bible School was the annual Camp Meeting in June. For ten days, God's Bible School became a tent city inhabited by hundreds of men, women, and children. Many out-of-town visitors slept in classrooms lined with beds. Specially constructed doors along one side of the seven-hundred-seat Tabernacle were raised so that overflow crowds could be seated in a large, adjoining tent. Nakada returned from his travels to take part in the meetings, along with holiness leaders from around the country and overseas.

Chambers had been scheduled to speak each morning only to pastors. But so many people thronged the first meetings that they were opened to the public. In language typical of the day, George B. Kulp wrote: "Thank God for the teaching every morning of that stalwart piece of sanctified Scotch granite, Oswald Chambers. Cultured, and all his culture captured by the Holy Ghost, he in turn captivated men and women by the fiery, scintillating, scorching truths he hurled forth from a hot heart, like a live, sanctified Scot from the land of Knox. God bless him and keep him on this old earth to preach, teach, and bless others till Jesus comes."

Enthusiasm and emotion were highly visible elements of the Camp Meeting, but in the minds of many who attended, they were by no means the most important. One observer noted the boys and girls from Compton's North Carolina orphanage enjoying the daily meetings conducted especially for children. Someone else mentioned an unnamed young man, a student at the Bible School, seated in a quiet corner of the dining room, feeding a wheelchair-bound man unable to care for himself.

However, at many meetings exuberance overflowed. An evening service, held downtown in the Cincinnati Opera House, was described in the *Revivalist* as a scene where "holy confusion reigned." Before the meeting began, people throughout the crowd were singing, dancing, and testifying. Two accounts reported that those on the platform were "prancing and shouting and jumping." Adherents of the holiness cause considered it a sign of divine blessing, but the boisterous meeting became the subject of a mocking cartoon in the evening *Cincinnati Post*.

What did Chambers think of it all? He wrote in the *Revivalist*, July 25, 1907:

> Christ's Camp is finished, as far as the gatherings are concerned. The one strong impression left on the heart is that God had His way.
>
> Another impression that is very strongly in the front is that the people gathered were hungry beyond words for the Bible, not so much for the shouting, uproarious, blessedly joyful testimony meetings, but souls were athirst for God.
>
> This city for ten days was marvelous; hundreds upon hundreds of the saints turned out nightly with banners and placards announcing the meetings, marching in three lines, two on the sides of the road and one in the center, with the band at the head, marching through the whole city praising God, singing and testifying and inviting to the meetings.
>
> The Opera House meetings were marked by great joy and deep conviction, and hundreds found their way to the altars. This impression regarding Cincinnati is one that has laid hold on some of us with very great power. Worldly men and worldly women respect character, when the same men and women ridicule testimony and uproar, *unless backed by character.* Of testimony and uproar there was no lack; of glorious manifestations and shouting and jesticulations there were an abundance; but these were not the things that won the respect of the city we are persuaded, but the lives of the people who have lived here year in and year out, and whom the Holy Ghost has maintained.

However words fail completely to give adequate expression to the time of blessing on the 'Mount of Blessings.' One thing that will remain with us as long as we live was not the preaching, not the meetings, nor the marches, nor testimonies (these were grand) but the splendid, supereffacing service of the students who waited at tables, washed the dishes, erected tents, pulled them down and did the drudgery. Their lives for ten days were one unbroken testimony to the blessing of God and to one at least, the impression grew strong, that if our Lord was here, He would still again be hidden and obscure as ONE WHO SERVED.

Oswald received a $500 honorarium for his six months of teaching and writing at God's Bible School—enough to send him on his way to Japan. He left Cincinnati with a great love for his new friends and an invitation to return the next year. His last letter home from America was written to his sister:

En route Seattle, July 6
My dear Florence:

This scenery is superb, imagine running 6,000 feet above sea level among the Rocky Mountains. It is truly grand. Just before you come to the Rockies there are hundreds and hundreds of miles of prairie, great plains, no hills, scarcely a mound or tree. They secured a sleeper for me and observation car, so as usual I live just like the King's son.

But the Rockies—I cannot hope to describe these to you. Massive, unspeakable heights, all snow-clad. The air raw, piercing and cold; mighty pine trees are clustered in thousands all round; sublime rivers and waterfalls, and daring ingenious railways. It all needs to be seen to be realized ever so faintly, and on this railway it is as comfortable as sitting in a room; I am as much at home at sea or on rail as on land.

I meet Nakada at Seattle and three other Japs and seven Yale graduates who are all going to Japan. What a glorious time it will be on the Pacific for sixteen days.

I wish I could convey to you the overpowering sense of God's love and protection as 'my Father.' I have met nothing strange, all treat me as friend and brother, Negro, Jap, Red Indian, American. I feel unspeakably at home among men now [that] I know God. Glory to His name.

I just looked up and saw the Rocky Mountains towering in the distance, pine trees and railway track, with rarely a hut or a human being. I can simply leave you to imagine the unspeakable bliss to me of these travelling days. I have a continual 103rd Psalm in my heart all the time. One of the blessed things about this life is that a man carries his kingdom on the inside, and that makes the outside lovely.

10
JAPAN

(1907)

Chambers' article titled "Missionary Ignorance" appeared in the June 13, 1907, issue of *God's Revivalist*. In it he spoke his mind on the tragedy of sending young missionaries into difficult foreign assignments without adequate preparation.

"Our training for both home and foreign work is all too slight," he wrote. "Three hours' training for thirty years' work is far more of the modern stamp than thirty years' preparation for three years' service."

Although Chambers had not technically been to "the foreign field," he had talked with veterans of overseas missionary service. Many had returned broken and discouraged simply because they had not been prepared mentally or spiritually to live in a radically different culture.

"To ignore the vast and competent literature relative to every country under Heaven today and to go to work for God, living more or less a hand-to-mouth spiritual life is to be utterly unfitted and unable to rightly divide the word of truth," he continued. "Missionary ignorance . . . has at its heart laziness or a mistaken notion that the Holy Ghost puts a premium on ignorance."

Chambers was anxious to reach Japan and test his conclusions in the reality of life in a "heathen" land. He knew that even if he stayed his intended four months, it would afford him little more than a visitor's perspective. Still, he was eager to learn and hoped he could make a contribution to the work of which he had heard so much from Nakada.

But first, it was time to relax and enjoy the voyage. His diary reveals the unflagging enthusiasm for life as it came each day:

Seattle—July 10, 1907: The Empress of Japan came to harbour shortly after we arrived and the sight of the Union Jack flying caused me to understand the deep 'make' of the love of one's country. I was surprised at the surge up from my deeps which the sight of the British flag brought.

I have three books with me for the voyage—The Lure of the Labrador Wilds; Plato and Platonism (Pater) and The Strenuous Life by Roosevelt.

There are seven Yale University graduates on board. We have the doctor presiding at our table. 'We' are—Nakada, Sakai, Higashi, and myself, a very bright company, although I for the most part am silent as they talk in Japanese. I must say I like the Japs more and more. Of course my attachment to Nakada has a great deal to do with it, he is a noble little man, with a great soul and a great mind.

12th: Very grey and rough; nevertheless I am out all day long reading in this magnificent air. No trace of sea sickness though the boat rolls right royally. Read most of Crocket's Kit Kennedy yesterday. It is inspiring to touch the Scotch pulse in a book again.

13th: A text came to me this morning with the irresistible grip of Bible words—'Glorify God in your body.' I know the Spirit will expound it to me as that other word of Paul's—'The Spirit maketh intercession for the saints according to the will of God.' To know that God knows the heart and is answering the prayer of the Holy Spirit is unspeakably blessed. Again, as on the Atlantic, the sense of answered prayer is in and around me. A perfect sense of safety and of being kept is blessedly mine, God bless all the saints who pray.

The morning is still cold and grey. Nakada is a delightful comrade, and he has great times with the students, they are obviously very fond of him.

14th: Sunday morn. What a blessed habit I have found my prayer list, morning by morning, it takes me via the Throne of all Grace straight to the intimate personal heart of each one mentioned here, and I know that He Who is not prescribed by time and geography answers immediately.

Today I have a rare treat in Westcott's Gospel of the Resurrection, a splendid book.

15th: Yesterday was a very happy day. We had a service in the little music room conducted by Nakada's son. He is a genuine favorite on board and no wonder, he is simply brimming over with interest and earnestness and wit. We sang some hymns together, several of the Yale students and Nakada and Sakai and myself; Sakai sang two solos, and Nakada talked on—'This perfect soundness in the presence of you all' with great power, God helped him, it was absorbingly interesting.

I have just finished Balzac's The Wild Ass's Skin, it is an enormous 'slice.' It gave me the sensation I had on first reading Les Miserables. Great unwieldy matters are handled shrewdly with more than ordinary penetration into human beings, yet there seems to me a strange lack of understanding of the supreme nobility of man, viz. that of a character produced by realizing one's responsibility to God. Self-realization or self-annihilation seems the utmost reach of these great novelists. The Bible note of the realization of another self in life, that other self being God, is completely undetected.

July 17: Today has been wild and stormy, I never saw such waves. I lay all morning on deck and watched the grandeur. The waves have been mountains high, grand but terrible seas; about 3 o'clock I caved in, Nakada and Sakai did the same, so that was a consolation.

18th or 19th: I am not sure whether this is Thursday or Friday because we drop one day and I will not know till I see the chart. Whatever day it is, it is just as calm as yesterday was stormy.

Had a delightful talk on art generally, and religion specifically, to several of the Yale boys after supper last night, they are an interesting, well-educated crowd. I am reading Pater's book with great profit.

20th Saturday—as to whether yesterday was Thursday or Friday I must leave the individual to imagine, anyway, this is tomorrow! Had another interesting talk with two Yale boys, they are open to spiritual conviction. I am more and more convinced that the personality of Jesus Christ is the Truth, and anything about Him that does not lead to Him is not the truth.

I am reading a very able scholarly book, Things Japanese. Tonight I am going to speak on 'Discipleship' to the students.

July 23rd: I was introduced to an admirable boys' book by one of the students, Mr. Taft (nephew of Taft who is in great prominence in America), it is entitled The Golden Age by Kenneth Grahame, and illustrated superbly. I am very struck by these Yale boys, they are delightful young men of the world, yet they study their Bible constantly and we have some delightful chats. I am sure we cannot understand any 'set' but our own, hence the need for the servant of God to be like Paul and have humanity as his 'set.'

'I am become all things to all men—not that I might be nothing in particular to any man, but 'that I may by all means save some.'

I came across a powerful portion on which I am going to chew the cud. 1 Cor. 4:20—'The kingdom of God is not in word, but in power.' Its chief power is to me the perpetual vision of Jesus Christ, the perpetual indwelling of the Holy Spirit, Who loves Him to utter self-effacement, perpetual intercession that God's will may be perfectly done, and the perpetual carrying of the cross. Nakada is enamoured of Jowett's little book The Passion for Souls, and says he is going to translate it into Japanese.

July 24th: My birthday morning. This year I spend it on the Pacific, last year I was at Keswick. 33 today, praise God. The text for the morning on the League calendar is 'The Lord rewarded me . . . for I have kept the ways of the Lord.' These weeks on the Pacific have been an unspeakable spiritual boon for they have physically refreshed and recreated me, and I am more and more convinced that this is essential to true full-orbed spirituality.

This evening marks a red-letter birthday for me. Without any warning at the close of dinner the head waiter and all the others in a string lined up to my table with trays, with presents on each, the head waiter was carrying a splendid birthday cake with a candle burning on it. They presented the presents to me, and then burst out with cries of 'speech,' which I duly gave, and I then cut the cake and handed it all round. It was a great occasion, and on reflecting I do not know how I got through it as well as I did, but it was the suddenness of it. Then they took me to the deck and serenaded me with Scotch songs and Jubilee singer pieces. Of course Nakada had put them up to it all. Well, God bless them, it greatly affected me I can assure you.

25th: Every recalling of last night fills me with pleasure. It was a very beautiful thing of those students to do, and exhibited their inherent, generous natures, for I neither smoke nor drink nor play cards and simply have met and chatted with them.

Yesterday we had a display of ju-jitsu, very fascinating and robust, and the elegance of the posturing and the courtesy they showed was wonderful.

July 26th: Yesterday we sighted Japan, and this morning early we saw the outline of the hills. The morning is dull, but the people are not. Poor Nakada, I have never seen him so restless. He says he feels more longing for home now he is near than he did all the time away.

July 27th: Oriental Mission Society Bible School, Tokio. Japan at last. We arrived in Yokohama midday. Nakada's boy and nephew were aboard one of the launches and the little fellow spied his father out first of all. On the pier were Bros. Cowman and Kilbourne, Mrs. Nakada and the two girls and about ten students. After much palaver re the luggage (not one thing of mine did the Customs demand to be unlocked, I had no trouble, praise the Lord), Cowman and Kilbourne and I took jinrickshaws to the depot; how these fellows can run! Then we took a train and what a reception we had at the station on arrival. All the Bible School students were there, and they escorted us to the premises and we had a welcome meeting to Nakada, chiefly in Japanese. He is really a deservedly great man among all here. Cowman and Kilbourne agree to this and certainly the students adore him. I am charmed with the premises, they exceed all I had dreamt of. Well-laid-out grounds and plenty of well-appointed houses. Mrs. Cowman is a royal soul and truly a saint, they have taken me into their home in splendid style. But I cannot hope yet to convey my fascination for Japanese homes, they are inimitable—but more hereafter. The meeting was a blessed one this morning and God was mightily present. I spoke through an interpreter, it was splendid, but restraining.

The Oriental Mission Society, founded by Cowman and Ernest Kilbourne, was only six and a half years old at this time. The Cowmans had arrived in Tokyo in February 1901 and joined forces with Juji Nakada, whom they had met at Moody Bible Institute. Eighteen months later, Ernest and Julia Kilbourne and their three children joined the Cowmans in Japan.

Charles Cowman led Ernest Kilbourne to faith in Christ when the two were telegraphers with Western Union in Chicago. Together they introduced seventy-five of their fellow workers to Christ in the next year, and the Christian fellowship in their office grew into a "Telegrapher's Band" with a missionary heart and a worldwide outreach.

The Cowman and Kilbourne Mission, as it was first called, soon became known as the Oriental Missionary Society. Through close ties with holiness friends in the United States, Canada, and England, the work was undergirded with prayer and financial support. *Electric Messages*, their monthly publication, sent news and pictures of the ministry in Japan into homes around the world.

Charles Cowman was the visionary organizer and articulate spokesman in the homelands for the work. His passion for bringing the gospel to Japan drove him beyond the point of physical and spiritual exhaustion. Lettie, equally if not more effective as a speaker, carried the burden for their expanding work with him on many fund raising trips around the world. Because of Charles' poor health and the need to raise money for the fledgling mission, the Cowmans were away from Japan as much as they were there.

It was E. A. Kilbourne's faithful presence on the foreign field that moved the mission forward. From 1902 to 1908, he served without a furlough, and when he finally came home for a few months, his wife and youngest child stayed in Japan. Yet, Cowman and Kilbourne were a team, committing their different gifts to a common goal.

Chambers found every day in Japan full of wonder.

July 28–31: Three days in Japan! It is exceedingly difficult to realize that it is all real. You feel continually as if you must soon wake up to the stern realities of daily life. But no, the 'Earl's Court Exhibition' goes on, not only all round you but to your very mouth in tea, food, etc. but I cannot hope to state the impressions and sensations of the place. It is unbearably pathetic to see the temples with their god of healing, the idol is worn quite smooth with the hands of the people. As I stood watching today, a man with a baby on his back came up to the idol, rubbed his hand over the legs of the idol and then rubbed it on the legs of the child, his face was the picture of anxious solicitude.

Tomorrow we begin the three days of welcome at the Y.M.C.A. Every moment is surprisingly and endlessly interesting. You return tired at night, and with not too much time before you have to get up in the morning. The eagerness of the people to hear at all the meetings is simply wonderful, one sees nothing like it in the homeland.

From August 1 to 3 Chambers and Nakada preached each morning at a meeting for Christians, then in the evening at evangelistic services. Of these gatherings, Chambers wrote: "The meetings at the mission, the open-air meetings under the vast shadow of a huge pagoda within the precincts of the temple grounds, the Bible School, the delightful courtesy, the eager hunger after salvation and the Bible, the expositions, are all elements of the wonderful and perplexing mystery of human nature. Truly the noblest work in this world is making disciples in His Name."

Throughout his visit in Japan, his amazement grew at the response of the people, who, he said, swallowed salvation wholesale. "I never imagined or saw anything quite like it," he wrote. "Nakada is a mighty preacher here. To see the altar service is wonderful, they come out fifty to a hundred, without any persuasion, and then the work begins. Every worker gets on his knees with his Bible and instruction goes on for hours, for they know nothing of the Christian revelation; they will stay all night, and when they do get through it is wonderful. God puts His seal on these people as He rarely seems to do in the homeland or America. Their faith is marvellous and God answers it. But it is simply too baffling to try and speak of it all."

On August 6 Oswald accompanied Kilbourne and Nakada to a missionary convention at Karuizawa. "This place is a summer resort for missionaries," Chambers recorded, "and the convention is held in the little wooden Episcopal Church." One diary entry continues with a candid account of his reactions:

> Today I met a group of people I am not at all drawn to. There is the stamp of the effeminate and sanctimonious about them which is languid. They carry large Bibles and speak in extravagant terms of 'such a lovely man, a sweet man of God, dearly beloved brother so and so.' To put it in rugged language it is enough to make a fellow 'puke.'
>
> One man gave a Bible reading on 'The Lord for the body,' mildly apologetic and very diffident—'Really, don't you know, it would be such a savour to the Lord Jesus if you were to be sanctified,' this said with clasped hands and a sweet inoffensive smile and then you have a faint impression of this ambassador of the King of Heaven to men and women entirely in danger of becoming children of the Devil.

Mantle [another missionary] followed after, splendid, strong and grand on the same subject. I felt enlarged and uplifted, God certainly spoke through him.

Some of these missionaries are afraid of the Oriental Bible School and its strong advocacy of holiness, uncompromising and manly. It is amazingly interesting to see all this from a spectator's point of view, and am sure God must enjoy and pity it. Oh, He'll forgive them, for there's nothing much to punish. Had a very good talk with Mantle. What must he think? It is strange if he does not pity these unsexed namby pambyists.

The page on which these words appear reveals inner thoughts Chambers would never have spoken in public or private.* He was not a Pollyanna, nor was he a spiritual ostrich with his head buried in the sand of ignorance or fear. Yet his diary at this time was a personal journal of thoughts, observations, and reactions, not intended for the eyes of others.

Clearly, Oswald had no use for religious phraseology used merely out of habit, or for any Christian message delivered in an uncertain or whiny tone. He would rather hear a fiery heretic than what he considered a weak-kneed presentation of the gospel. He preferred the "dynamite" of God.

Likening himself to the amazed Queen of Sheba during her visit to Solomon's empire, Oswald called Japan "the most entrancing country" he could imagine. Of Cowman and Kilbourne's Mission, he said, "I never expected such an elaborate, splendidly organized work as it is."

Chambers had been in Japan for less than a month when the Cowmans asked him to accompany them to Britain. Charles Cowman's already poor health had suffered during the extreme summer heat and he needed to recuperate. In addition, the Cowmans felt a pressing need to raise support for the mission activities. Interest in the work was increasing in Britain, and the Cowmans felt Chambers would be more valuable as a spokesman in his homeland than as a teacher at the Bible College in Tokyo.

On August 9, Oswald wrote to Franklin:

So I am likely, more than likely, certain God willing, to be in Britain at the end of the year. The proposition has come so naturally and is

---

*Chambers' diary mentioned specific missionaries by name.

evidently of God. Brother and Sister Cowman have asked me to accompany them to Britain and give my impressions of this work in the homeland.

We leave on August 21st, and the route is as follows—Shanghai, Hong Kong, Singapore, Colombo, Aden, Red Sea, Suez Canal, Port Said, Mediterranean Sea, then we go to Rome and I hope to meet Rev. Pullen of Spezia, and may go to Switzerland, Marseilles, and Paris. This will be a magnificent round-the-world trip. I will have much to tell you, much that will make you laugh and cry, but it is a wonderful opportunity and He reigns and leads.

The *SS Bingo Maru* carried only twelve first-class passengers, plus Peter Bingo, whom Chambers identified as "a great big tom cat as dignified as the reincarnation of all the divine cats of Egypt."

During a Sunday layover in Kobe on August 25, Charles Cowman stayed in bed suffering from neuralgia while Lettie delivered tracts and portions of Scripture to the coolies and crew. "They came on board selling things," Chambers noted, "but when we told them we did not buy on Sunday, they bowed and did not molest us any more. Peter Bingo grows more condescending."

The Chambers diary continues to chronicle the daily delight of new discoveries:

August 26: Yesterday was a lovely day, we went through the Japan Inland Sea, without doubt the most lovely place I was ever in—indescribable, a placid sea, brilliant sun and rare clouds. We sailed through the southern passage last night, a dangerous narrow passage with a swift and raging current running, this was to gain time, having lost so much at Kobe. Every berth is full now; my mate is a fine young Canadian. God is unspeakably blessed to me. Hallelujah!

August 28: We had a fine little time down in the chief officer's cabin, he is a Christian and wants us to hold meetings there for the Japanese crew which, God willing, we will do.

29th: A beautiful morning. Cowman called me at quarter to five, the chief officer had awakened him to see a comet, we saw it but it was dim, although the star above it was intensely bright. Had some very interesting conversation with Mr. and Mrs. Anderson, the Chinese missionaries, and Mrs. Anderson lent me David Smith's The Days of His Flesh, very fine indeed it is.

Sept. 2: Just one day from Hong Kong. Yesterday evening we held a service arranged by the chief officer and Mrs. Anderson, I was asked to speak. Very few came down. I spoke on Discipleship and its sterner meaning.

4th: Bro. Munroe of Yammatsi came for us early yesterday and we went with him to his own mission station. He and his wife live in a Chinese township where the devil is worshipped. Their home is in a very quaint building, yet they thank God with evident joy for such a palatial residence. I am more and more convinced that one needs a Divine call unmistakable in its effect before coming to such fields.

5th: My state-room is now mine exclusively and I am glad for in the morning hours it is unspeakably blessed to spend the hours in prayer and meditation.

7th: I am reading Geo. MacDonald's There and Back, of course MacDonald appeals to my bias, I love that writer.

At times a strong compassion alternates in my mind with a strong scorn of the low aims and satisfactions of many one meets. Bless God, the sense of His will is more and more graciously real. Doing His will—what an aim!

Sept. 10th: Just entering Singapore. Last night I saw the Southern Cross in the heavens quite distinctly. Cowman referring to the phenomenon, and also to the one in the Rocky Mountains [Colorado's Mount of the Holy Cross], said it always struck him as significant that in these places where people go for holiday making, God has placed the sign of the Cross.

For the rest of September, the ship trekked westward for three thousand miles across the Indian Ocean with only a brief stop in Colombo, Ceylon, to break the journey. As October neared, they traversed the Gulf of Aden, slipped through the narrow strait between Africa and Arabia, and entered the Red Sea.

Oswald's diary continued on October 1:

A glorious and boisterous morning. At sunset the sea becomes the most wonderful purple, a purple so startling that you are obliged to notice it. A passage came to me with peculiar force this morning and awakened the thought that possibly I will remain in the homeland and do steady Church-building work. We shall see. The passage is 1 Chron. 28:9–10, particularly verse 10: 'Take heed now, for the Lord hath chosen thee to build an house for the sanctuary: be strong, and do it.'

On October 3, he wrote to his brother Arthur from the Gulf of Suez:

> *What a sunrise! We are surrounded by visible land now and it is most interesting, we are told to expect to see Mt. Sinai. The beauty is too absorbing to write more.*

> *It is night now, a great pall has settled on all that wild, majestic desolation, and the wall of cliffs and desert mountains facing the afterglow from the African side looks like the pillar of fire. Nothing but the tongue of an inspired writer could avail to convey the day's impressions on me. I encamped with the children of Israel 'before Pi-hahiroth between Migdol and the sea,' and crossed the Red Sea with them in the breathless awe inspired by that miraculous east wind that clove the deep into a highway for the people of God.*
>
> *I danced a veritable Highland fling as Moses sang his imperial Glory Song, and shouted as Miriam and her women added their tribute. For three long weary days I wandered with them to Marah and heard their wild and fierce murmurings. I ate the manna and reveled myself at Elim's Palms. I trudged with eerie caution in the wilderness of Sin and skirted round Sinai. I spent the forty days and nights on that uncouth awesome height with Moses . . . But it is of no avail, the thoughts and emotions will be with me for ever.*
>
> *Imagine it, at 12 o'clock today we were abeam of Mt. Sinai! It is a lonely, fierce, paralysing desert, full of the great ache of speechless loneliness and arid heat, brooding with unspoken and unfathomable mystery—nothing familiar, nothing usual, nothing homely; for thousands of centuries the scarred, serried range of sand-blighted mountains has held the mystery of modern civilization making its boast of* progress *sound like 'the crackle of thorns under a pot.' But tonight the memory of our Lord Jesus Christ comes with ineffable peace. Truly the human race as displayed on this planet of earth is a great and mighty experiment.*

The *Bingo Maru* entered the Suez Canal, passed through the Bitter Lakes, and paused for a time in Lake Timash, near the city of Ismailia. When the final canal segment was clear of southbound steamers, they entered it and pressed north past Al Qantarah, toward Port Said and the Mediterranean.

The ship steamed out of Port Said at midnight on October 5. Chambers' thoughts were focused on "the most beautiful ultramarine blue" of the Mediterranean as they followed the course of the apostle Paul westward across the sea. The anticipated stop in Rome did not materialize, and on October 10 they were in Marseilles. A day later the wandering prophet was reunited with his family in London. He had been gone almost a year.

The Egyptian names and places that seemed so strange to him in October 1907 would become the scene of Oswald's final years on this earth. In less than a decade the Great War would burst upon an unsuspecting world, calling thousands of men from the British Commonwealth to their final destiny in the deserts, rocks, and hills of the Middle East.

Chambers concluded in his diary: "Here ends this most profitable voyage, as an education very difficult to estimate. I hope to reap benefits therefrom all my after life, however long or short."

PART 4

"The great word of Jesus to His disciples is Abandon. When God has brought us into the relationship of disciples, we have to venture on His word; trust entirely to Him and watch that when He brings us to the venture, we take it."

— ***Studies in the Sermon on the Mount***

11
THE LEAGUE OF PRAYER

(1907–1908)

Chambers reached London in late October 1907 and arrived home to a warm family welcome. He had a fortnight to catch his breath before the League of Prayer's big Autumnal Meetings at Speke Hall. In his address there on "Holiness and Brotherhood," he warmed the audience with his humorous analysis of current trends: "Some years ago, amongst the young fellows that I used to know, there were those who used to call themselves agnostics, because it was fashionable. These fellows were agnostics for the same reason that my dog was; they had never paid the remotest attention to the subject: therefore they did not know. When I come back to this country this year what do I find? That the fashionable word is not *agnosticism* but *socialism.* One can sum up all the definitions of socialism in the words of the Irishman who said, 'Sure one man's as good as another, only better.' "

While the audience was still laughing, Chambers shifted the focus from the follies of the world outside Speke Hall, to the frailties of the people within. "The snare of an audience like this is not the snare of a shallow socialism," he said. "It is the snare of a selfish holiness with no God in it. Holiness is an individual protest that God may lift the life of the Church to the standard He made for it, not an individual pet based on my little convictions. What does holiness magnify? 'Jesus ever, Jesus only, Jesus all in all.' "

Reader Harris was especially glad to have Chambers back. During the past year, he had faced an unusual amount of misunderstanding and opposition. There were ongoing claims that the League of Prayer was a sect, a church, or even a denomination that taught the false doctrine of sinless perfection. Others assailed it as a stern and spiritually elitist group. The most serious accusation, however, was that it encouraged Christians to leave their churches and form separate fellowships. Harris had always been able to refute that charge until recently.

David Thomas, a long-time associate of Harris, had broken away from the League and formed an organization of his own, calling for Spirit-filled believers to leave the churches. Their parting of the ways, which was painful for Harris, became even more difficult when Thomas established his "Holiness Mission" in Battersea, not far from the League's headquarters at Speke Hall.

This widening rift greeted Chambers and the Cowmans when they arrived in London. Apparently Charles and Lettie's friendship with David Thomas placed them in the difficult situation of divided loyalties. They had no quarrel with Reader Harris and the League, but they spent a month staying in Thomas's home and knew they couldn't have it both ways. Their planned tour of Britain with Chambers endorsing their work was evidently scaled back to a few scattered meetings. On their previous trip to England in December 1905, the Cowmans held a week-long mission at Speke Hall. During their 1907 visit, their presence in Britain is not mentioned in *Tongues of Fire*. Without any outward animosity, everyone seemed to accept the necessity to travel down separate roads that were only slightly less than parallel. Oswald deeply loved the Cowmans and maintained a lifelong respect and appreciation for them.

In mid-November Chambers held a nine-day Special Mission in Speke Hall. Rested by his voyage and enlivened by his past months of learning, Oswald was in rare form. Even Reader Harris found it challenging to describe his unique presentations.

In a December 1907 editorial, Harris wrote: "The Scriptural truths of full salvation have been preached in fresh language which was both definite and drastic. Indeed, sometimes, as the missioner warmed to his subject, his language took on a lightning intensity that was almost lurid in its illuminating effect. Next to his remarkable vividness of diction, Mr. Chambers' special characteristics are his knowledge of the Scriptures and his faith in God."

Mrs. Donaldson, a long-time League worker, wrote: "The Holy Ghost spoke through the missioner [Chambers] with great power, although sometimes he put his facts into a few such drastic words as to be startling, and while we thought them out, we missed the explanation that followed."

After the November mission, Harris was pleased to announce to his readers that "after fulfilling one or two old engagements Mr. Oswald Chambers hopes to devote his time, energy, and rare gifts to the work of God in connection with the Pentecostal League."

Chambers' task involved visiting League centers around Britain, speaking for their monthly meetings, and helping them stay on target spiritually and organizationally. He traveled constantly, stayed as a guest in scores of homes, and made new friends throughout Britain.

On November 24, 1907, he began a ten-day mission in Hanley and a much anticipated reunion with his brother Ernest's family in nearby Stoke-on-Trent. Ernest's daughter, Irene, was typical of children everywhere who welcomed Oswald with open arms. Knowing that Uncle Oswald was expected in the afternoon, ten-year-old Irene and her two younger brothers sat glued to the window watching for a tall lanky figure dressed in clerical gray. Finally they saw him coming toward the house, now close enough to see his thin, gaunt face and piercing gray-blue eyes. Irene threw open the door and the house erupted into a volcano of laughter and fun. Before Oswald had time to remove his frock coat, he was down on all fours with two small boys clambering over him. He was on their level, at their disposal, and happy to be part of their world.

The next morning and on many mornings to come, Irene crept down the stairs at six o'clock, knowing she would find her beloved uncle in the kitchen. There he sat, wrapped in his plaid, with the inevitable teapot close at hand. Whether she found him reading, writing, or on his knees, he greeted his niece with a smile and a welcome word. He gave her a book and a chair nearby where she sat feeling important and happy, content just to be with him.

When one of the children balked at doing a family chore, Oswald would make up new words on the spot and sing them to a familiar tune:

It's better to shine than to whine,
It's better now than before,
It's better to wash the tea things up
Than sulk by the kitchen door!

At family prayers in the evenings, Oswald talked to His Heavenly Father so naturally that Irene longed for the same trusting relationship with God. When he preached in their chapel, he spoke in the same natural way—clear, ordinary, forceful words delivered in a penetrating voice that had a Scottish tang. There was no emotional appeal and no manipulation.

Looking back on those days, Irene said: "He came into our quiet home life with its parochial outlook like a west wind, waking us up and bringing an exciting sense of limitless possibilities. He was always ready at any moment for anything anywhere. One never knew what lovely, exciting thing might happen where he was, and maybe catch us up in its train. He had a great scorn for small petty outlooks and actions, 'small potatoes, rather frosted' was his expression for all that."

One night after a meeting, Irene and Oswald were about to leave the church when a woman came rushing up: "Oh, Mr. Chambers," she said, "I feel I must tell you about myself."

Oswald sat with the woman in a quiet corner and Irene resigned herself to a long wait. To her surprise, he was back again in a few minutes.

"That was quick," said Irene as they walked home.

Oswald chuckled. "I asked her if she had ever told God all about herself, and she said she hadn't. So I told her to go home and tell God as honestly as she could, and then see if she still needed or wanted to tell me. If only folk would go to Headquarters!"

Oswald's wisdom and gentleness in dispatching that case of simple vanity endeared him to Irene all the more. Yet she knew how many times he had talked with people far into the night, being patient and understanding with those in genuine perplexity and distress.

Children gave Oswald a welcome respite from the tangled webs he faced with adults. League members were not always tactful or patient with their fellow church members whose spiritual flame appeared to burn lower than their own. No one could be faulted for praying for revival, but human urgings and efforts to bring it about often created misunderstanding and fear of the League.

The Pentecostal League of Prayer whose magazine was named *Tongues of Fire* was immediately associated with the emerging "tongues movement." When Harris founded the League in 1891, the terms *pentecostal* and *tongues of fire* had no connotations beyond the familiar passage in the second chapter of Acts. Within a few years, however, the growth of Pentecostalism as a movement in Britain and the attendant emphasis on speaking in tongues caused confusion about the League's orientation.*

Reader Harris distinguished between the gift of speaking in an unlearned foreign language (Acts 2:6–12) and the ecstatic utterance or *glossolalia* mentioned in the letters of Paul. Harris had no quarrel with either "gift" but strenuously opposed those who made "tongues" the litmus test of being filled with the Holy Spirit. In a January 1908 editorial he wrote: "There is nothing wrong with speaking in tongues; it was the privilege of the early Church, and it may be the privilege of any believer today. What we condemn in that movement is this; that by their literature they teach that people are not baptized with the Holy Ghost until they speak with tongues. The Bible never says so."

An article titled "Tongues and Testing" by Oswald Chambers appeared in the same issue. "Let a teacher once get the set of the people off our Lord Jesus Christ to any sign or manifestations or power and he is deserving in this day of as severe and drastic rebuke as Peter gave Simon Magus (Acts 8:23). Character, not anything less, is the result and immediate stamp of the Baptism with the Holy Spirit and Fire."

This was the spiritual climate in which Chambers began his work as a full-time missioner (evangelist/preacher) for the League of Prayer. If his goal had been simply to respond to the League's critics or to denounce its detractors, he would have

---

*The mistaken association of the Pentecostal League of Prayer with the tongues movement eventually prompted the League to drop the word *Pentecostal* from its title. In 1916, they changed their magazine name from *Tongues of Fire* to *Spiritual Life*.

been little more than a debater. But that was not Chambers' way. His objective was to present Jesus Christ and the fullness of life in Him. He spoke of the League's goals and tenets, but they were secondary, not primary, in his mind.

From November 1907 to May 1908, Chambers criss-crossed Britain by train many times, holding meetings from Plymouth in the south of England to Aberdeen on the northeast coast of Scotland. Sometimes he would stay in a city for a week or two, speaking each afternoon and evening and three times on Sunday. For one-day engagements, he arrived by train, delivered an evening message, stayed with a host family, and departed early the next day by rail for his next destination.

An entry in his prayer journal reveals his struggle against physical weariness and spiritual stagnation: "O Lord, this day I have to speak in Thy name three times, and I am un-moved and uninspired till now. If Thou canst convey Thy mind to me in my spiritual dullness, Oh, for Jesus Christ's sake, do it."

By the end of May 1908, he was nearly exhausted. During the previous four weeks, he had spoken more than twenty times in eight different locations. On May 28, he was due to sail for the United States and two months of Camp Meetings, beginning at God's Bible School in Cincinnati on June 19.

He pushed himself through the final League meetings in Wallington on May 26 and Wimbledon the next day, knowing that he could sleep on the train to Liverpool, then completely relax for ten days across the Atlantic. How he cherished the prospect of that time to read, think, pray, and prepare for the rigors of his coming ministry in the U.S.

This time, however, he wouldn't be alone as he usually was. Mrs. Amelia Hobbs had written saying that her daughter Gertrude whom he knew from his brother Arthur's church in Eltham, would be traveling to America on the same ship as he. She hoped it wouldn't be imposing to ask if he'd look out for her, and give her a hand, especially when they arrived in New York.

Life was always interesting in the providence of God.

12
THE YOUNG LADY ON THE BOAT

(1908)

Gertrude Hobbs was twenty-four years old when she watched the docks of Liverpool slip away behind the churning foam of the *SS Baltic*'s propellers. In the early twentieth century it was not unheard of for a young woman to make a trans-Atlantic voyage unescorted, but neither was it common. The fact that Oswald Chambers happened to be traveling on the same boat added an element of certainty and security, more for her mother than for herself. Gertrude was on her way to New York City to visit her good friend, Marian, who said secretarial jobs were plentiful. It was a grand adventure and she was quite unconcerned that she had only $16 in her purse.

As the ship steamed up to full speed, Oswald's thoughts ranged back to his voyage with Nakada on this same ship, eighteen months before. That journey had been pure comradeship and adventure, but this was different. Not a foot away from him stood a lovely, intelligent young woman whom he had known casually for some two and a half years. With her head turned toward the receding coastline of England, he had a chance to study her face for the first time. He had to look down because the top of her head just reached the level of his chin. He saw that her brown hair was parted just to one side of the middle and swept back into a bun. Almond shaped blue eyes twinkled under arched brows, and her mouth rested in a straight line that resembled a kind of perpetual smile. How would he describe her face in a word? Pretty? Soft? Kind?

It was a view of Gertrude he had never seen from the pulpit or even across the table at tea. Why was he seeing it now? Strange thoughts and feelings rose within him, and he wasn't sure if he liked them or not. No matter, for the next ten days courtesy required that he at least accompany her to meals and help her get acclimated to the ship. Once in New York, she would begin her new job, and for the next two months, he would be so occupied in preaching and counseling that thoughts of her would be the farthest thing from his mind.

For now though, he had to decide how to address her. Gertrude was too formal and besides, he had a sister with that name. Her family called her Gertie or Truda, but he needed a nickname of his own. For reasons unknown, he decided on Biddy, a friendly name with none of its current negative connotations.

During walks on deck each day, he learned more about this intriguing young lady. When she was a child, winter bouts with bronchitis kept her out of school every year for two months at a time. She eventually left school to help her mother at home and allow the family resources to be used for educating her older sister, Dais, and her brother, Herbert.

While other children might have languished in self-pity, young Gertrude was not deterred by her winter confinement and lack of formal education. She had a single ambition—to become secretary to the Prime Minister of England. So she set herself to studying Pitman's Shorthand at home and learning to type.

Knowing that many young men and women could take shorthand, she therefore decided to outdistance the field in speed and accuracy. Mrs. Hobbs and Dais took turns reading articles and book selections as Gertrude transcribed them into shorthand. Not content to function like a machine, Gertrude listened for the sense and context of what was read. Along with speed and accuracy, she sought understanding as well.

Two weeks before Gertrude's fifteenth birthday, her father died at the age of fifty, leaving the family in financial difficulty. Dais finished school and secured a good position with the civil service. She continued to live at home, generously contributing to the family income.

By the time Gertrude was old enough to work full time, she could take shorthand dictation at the phenomenal rate of two hundred and fifty words per minute—faster than anyone was likely to talk. This skill won her a position as secretary to a high ranking officer at the Woolwich Arsenal, Britain's sprawling munitions factory some ten miles east of London. She didn't seem to mind working in close proximity to thousands of tons of highly explosive cordite, gunpowder, and filled artillery shells. She did, however, object to men who saved their dictation until the end of the day and expected her to type and post the letters before she went home. She was happy to leave the arsenal for a job with a firm of solicitors in the prestigious Lincoln's Inn Fields in the heart of London's legal district. Now Biddy was off to a new adventure in America.

Every day aboard the *SS Baltic,* she and Oswald walked together, ate together, and discovered new things about each other. She admired his keen mind, his bright humor, and the deep love he held for Jesus Christ. Oswald was impressed with everything about Biddy, from her determination and ability, to her love for animals and her genuine interest in people. How could they have shared so much in common without his realizing it before?

When the voyage ended they parted company, but a steady correspondence quickly developed between the two. He wrote to her from Cincinnati on June 20, a day before he plunged into the camp meeting at God's Bible School:

> *Be very patient and very confident in Him. Do not be a little bit perturbed that you cannot answer Mr. Moore's questions regarding God. God is not a fact of common sense but of revelation. Tell him God lives—evidenced to your heart when you abandoned your right to yourself and let Him take the rule.*

On July 3, after two draining weeks of preaching and counseling, Oswald's tone was more personal:

> *It is a great refreshment to think of you for I have had such a drenching with the sad and sordid sorrows of so many blighted lives, but glory be to our God how blessedly He saves and delivers and heals.*

During July Oswald's travels took him from Cincinnati to camp meetings in North Attleboro, Massachusetts, and Old Orchard, Maine. New York City and Biddy were right on the way. Undoubtedly, he called on her as he traveled north, and again before he left for England. An August 19 letter, written as he sailed back to England, indicates a rapid progression of their feelings for each other: "All in His good time we have the love, thank God, and the discipline of our characters alone or blended, it is all in his hands."

Biddy remained in New York to finish her job commitment while Oswald returned to a demanding schedule of League meetings in Britain. For the first time in many years, however, he had someone to whom he could pour out his deepest thoughts and feelings.

On August 20 he wrote:

> *The great hunger is on me more than ever for Him and His work. O how few love Him and how feeble is my most passionate love. I scarcely know anyone who is consumed for Him. It is all for creeds and phrases and belief, but for Him how few! To know Him—that is it. How I fear and hate the pattern and print of the age.*

August 23—London:

> *It is Sunday night and I have finished my second Sunday at Wesleys Chapel. God, as usual, undertook. He looms large again tonight. Oh that I had more of heart and brain and body for Him. My mood tonight is one of sorrow that I cannot serve and be spent for Him better.*

September 16—Eltham:

> *How does your spirit develop in intimacy with Him? Nothing else is right if that goes not well.*
>
> *He has all the circumstances in His hand—in His hand my whole life and yours with me must be for Him and not for domestic bliss.*

October 4:

> *I have a blessed and beautiful text for you—'For I know the plans that I am planning for you,' saith the Lord, 'plans of welfare and not of calamity, to give you an end and expectation.' A new translation but it is exquisite.*

October 5:

> *I do not think anyone realises more keenly than I do the struggles and difficulties of people, and yet all my messages broke them on the wheel.*

On October 18, he wrote to Biddy's mother from Plymouth:

> *Dear Mrs. Hobbs:*
>
> *Do you object to my corresponding with your youngest daughter, Gertrude? I love her, and naturally would like to write her and see her occasionally as my missions allow.*
>
> *But we should like to know that this is with your sanction and certain knowledge of the kind of friendship forming.*
>
> *I return to London on Friday, Oct. 23rd. I shall esteem your reply as early as convenient—highly.*
>
> *Yours heartily, Oswald Chambers.*

As he awaited a reply from Mrs. Hobbs, his letters to Biddy continued.

October 19—Plymouth:

> *God should make our faces radiant and patient for all the sordid cares of others. Our love but makes a more sure haven of rest for multitudes of strained and stressed lives. From our love should spring great patience and gentleness and service for others, for love is of God.*

October 21:

> *High over us shadows His Cross —This have I done for thee—what hast thou done for me?*

The world is our parish and He will open the way.

Mrs. Hobbs replied immediately but indicated that instead of clearing the air, Oswald had merely muddied the water. He wrote to her again on October 21:

Dear Mrs. Hobbs:

Thank you very much for your letter, and I am deeply concerned that my letter gave you more trouble than it otherwise would if I had only thought to have told you the sort of friendship I mean.

I certainly do not mean 'Platonic' (which to me is apt to mean the meanest [most ordinary] of all friendships) but I do mean a friendship with view to an engagement and ultimate marriage.

Regarding a mere ordinary friendship I should never have thought it necessary to ask your sanction—but I could not hold correspondence with your daughter having in my mind and heart what I have without your certain knowledge.

Please forgive my causing you unnecessary anxiety over and above the inevitable anxiety such a letter as mine must certainly cause a mother.

My present position as a 'missioner' is just temporary and quite a Godsend, it has been a good break to me from my College tutorial work and already permanent work is inviting me and as soon as that is settled I should like to become engaged.

Again thanking you for your letter and hoping you will be able to reply to me before I leave here Friday morning. I am yours heartily,
Oswald Chambers.

After posting the letter, he walked along the waterfront and gazed out at Plymouth's famous harbor known as The Sound. Far out on Penlee Point, the lighthouse cast its beam of welcome and warning. "You're almost home," it seemed to say to ships off the rugged coast of Devon. "Beware of the rocks as you near your goal." Oswald thought how quickly God had broken into his life of solitary service and given him a love for Biddy. He was astonished by the longing he had for her, and staggered that she loved him too.

His letters to Biddy continued:

October 23—Plymouth:

> *I have nothing to offer you but my love and steady lavish service for Him. I can hear you say: Foxes have holes . . . but the Son of man hath not where to lay His head.*
>
> *I have His Word, let us both take it, subsequent days will prove His meaning in it—Let us go forth unto Him, without the camp, bearing His reproach. Mark it in your Bible and I will do the same, with the date.*

Following the mission in Plymouth, Oswald traveled north to the little Yorkshire village of Denby Dale. It had been two years since he and Nakada stepped off the train and "put their feet down in Denby Dale for Jesus Christ." The results of their first meetings were still being felt upon his return.

On October 28, he wrote to Biddy:

> *He takes what we present Him (Romans 12:1) and from the basis of a heart at leisure from itself He can pour out His blessing to others.*
>
> *Pour out lavishly all you have on others. You have surely far more reason for making dull sordid places bright and beautiful because of the love of your heart. No good thing will He withhold from us.*

With pen still in hand, he contemplated the next letter he needed to write. Until it was sealed and posted, he could not move on to anything else. He had already put it off too many times and expended far too much time and energy thinking about it. He must write it now and put the matter behind him. He scribbled out the heading, then gripping the pen tightly in his long, slender fingers, he stared out the window, paralyzed. For a thirty-four-year-old man known in England and America for his unique vocabulary and powerful clarity of expression, this was an agonizing impasse. After several false starts and crumpled pages, he took a deep breath and began to write:

> *'Hortulan'*
> *Denby Dale*
> *October 28, 1908*
>
> *My dear Mother and Father:*
>
> *I want to tell you that I am in love and it is quite such a new experience that it opens up so many unknown things that I do not know quite how to put it.*
>
> *I love plenty men and women and am loved in return, not slightly but grandly and truly; yet this is quite different. It did not come passionately or suddenly but all permeatingly and now I have abruptly told you the fact.*
>
> *I have been more usually absorbed in Him and work for Him than even you would suppose, that this 'thing' has been a trial foreign to me, and now has come a sense I never had before, a sense of my own loneliness came to me. Of course I do not know what the future holds out and I do not intend to anxiety. My call is still as strong as ever. 'Go ye into all the world and make disciples of all nations' and I will go and ultimately I expect Miss. Gertrude A. Hobbs will go with me. I cannot yet conceive what good I can be to any woman, but I never feared until now, yet I am sure His hand leads.*
>
> *Of course I quite understand the avalanche of common sense and wisdom that my many kind friends will see fit to subject me to and I'll try my best not to [be] overwhelmed or frozen.*
>
> *But I want you to know from me and I find it awkward and difficult to write about myself.*
>
> *My thoughts for seven years past have never pictured me further on than 35 years of age and if you remember I sometime used to say I should like to go to more commodious premises then—and now this comes and in amazement I took the cup more or less dazed and stupid and am very and unspeakably thankful.*

Please tell Gertrude. I have ever lacked tenderness much to my distress and prayer and perhaps this new relationship will develop it.

Now my dear Mother excuse this letter writing so incoherent and abrupt because I cannot write this sort of thing well. I would like to bring her to tea before I go away next time, may I?

Your loving son, Oswald

There, it was done. He could almost predict the reactions when the letter arrived in London. His mother would read it with a smile and say, "Of course he can bring her to tea." She would think it was wonderful that her youngest son was in love. His father would frown and say, "Does Oswald have a position, a salary, a home, or any set plans for the future? No. His itinerant preaching with the League of Prayer is a hand-to-mouth existence providing nothing more than meals, lodging, and train fare to the next engagement. Does Oswald have any concept of what is needed to support a wife, and eventually children? Not likely. Yet it is time for him to bring his head out of the clouds and face the realities of life. Perhaps marriage will force him to do it."

Oswald was used to the criticism of his family and friends, particularly in the area of money. He believed that Jesus' words, "Give to everyone who asks," meant exactly that. One evening, walking back to his lodgings after conducting a League meeting, he was accosted by a drunken man asking for money. Chambers listened intently to the man's story, then told him, "Man, I believe your story is all lies, but my Master tells me to give to everyone that asks, so there is my last shilling." After putting the coin into the man's hand, Chambers noticed that it was not a shilling but half a crown worth two and a half times more. It didn't matter. "There you are," he told the man, "the Lord bless you."

When Oswald's hostess heard this story, she chided him for being foolish. "I believe beggars are sent to test our faith," Chambers replied, nonplused. "My duty is plain—to obey the command of God and give to everyone that asks. What the recipient may do with it is not my concern." As the woman shook her head in disbelief, Oswald added with a twinkle, "Besides, the

Lord always gives double for all I give away." The next morning Chambers received a letter enclosing a gift from a person who was bedridden and could not come to hear him preach. The gift was three times what he had given the drunken man the night before.

Humorous or barbed comments about his living on "nothing a year" had little effect on Chambers' dedication to his chosen path. When his way caused others pain, he deeply regretted it but was not swayed from his course. But now he was about to ask a fine young woman to join him in this life many people considered one of a spiritual vagabond. Was it fair to her?

He read again the letter he had just written to his parents and shook his head at the woodenness of his expression. How could a relationship that filled him with such anticipation and joy appear so cold and lifeless on paper? Laying the letter aside, he opened his Bible and thought ahead to the evening meeting. It was the same sometimes with his preaching. Many nights he fell into bed wishing that more of his love for Christ would have come through in what he said. "If I could only tell Him as I know Him."

Biddy returned to England in time for Oswald's special mission at Speke Hall. On November 13, he took her to St. Paul's Cathedral, a favorite place for both of them. For a time they wandered through the vast nave, unable to resist the pull of their eyes skyward toward the magnificent dome. Then, standing in front of Holman Hunt's famous painting, "The Light of the World," they pledged their love to each other and became engaged. A small ring set with three tiny diamonds sealed their promise.

It was more than a romantic gesture that brought Chambers to this place for this most important moment of promise. Hunt's painting shows a door, locked, barred, and overgrown with ivy. Christ holds a lantern in his left hand as he knocks gently with His right. Beneath the painting are the words of Revelation 3:20: "Behold, I stand at the door and knock; if any man hears my voice and opens the door, I will come in and sup with him and he with me."

Oswald would have been quick to notice that Christ came at night carrying light and a gentle request for entrance to a door that could be opened only from the inside. The meaning was clearly and skillfully portrayed on the canvas. He and Biddy were pledging their love, first and foremost, to Jesus Christ, and to His work in this dark world. Their commitment went far beyond a hope for personal happiness to embrace a calling to belong first to God, and then to each other.

At the same time, their engagement was a love-match of the highest order. No one who knew either of them would ever view their pledge as a utilitarian arrangement for more efficiently furthering the kingdom of God. Efficiency, in the usual sense of the greatest benefit for the lowest cost, was not in Chambers' vocabulary. His approach was "spend and be spent," with nothing held back.

Biddy loved him dearly and shared his vision. They left St. Paul's ablaze with hope, unmindful of the cold or the night.

13
LEADERSHIP IN THE LEAGUE

(1908–1909)

Oswald and Biddy had only three days to share the good news of their engagement with family and friends before he left on an extended mission for the League. His meetings in Speke Hall ended on November 16, and the next day he was due in Scarborough. From there he would spend all of December in Ireland and the month of January in Scotland. It would be nearly three months before he saw Biddy again.

At the close of the meetings in Speke Hall, Reader Harris sent Chambers off with a prayer: "Lord, take him to Scarborough, and Ireland, and Scotland, and bring him back to us laden with souls."

Oswald knew Reader and Mary Harris as few others did, and he considered them "the Lord's choicest saints." Some looked at Harris and saw only the prominent barrister. Others focused solely on his leadership in the League of Prayer. Chambers saw the man of God whose winsome, yet fearless testimony for Christ extended from the circles of British aristocracy to the poor in the slums of Battersea.

On November 13, 1908, the day of his engagement and imminent departure for Ireland, Chambers wrote: "What I owe to the League of Prayer only our heavenly Father knows. How it exalts me and humbles me when I remember so many hundreds are praying for me all over the country."

Perhaps Oswald might have looked longer at the bearded face of the organization's founder or gripped his hand more tightly if he had known it would be the last time he would see Reader Harris alive.

Oswald's first Irish mission took him to Donegal Square Church, Belfast, the Mother Church of Methodism in the capital of Northern Ireland. The Rev. James Alley, Superintendent Minister of the Methodist Circuit and of the church itself, had invited Oswald, praying that the congregation would be lifted into "newness of life" and empowered for service. In characteristic fashion, Oswald assured the Rev. Alley that if they allowed the Lord to help Himself to them, a good time was in store.

From Belfast, he wrote to Biddy on November 22:

> *This boarding-house I am in is conducted by the widow of one of my fellow students at the Royal College of Art, South Kensington. So I am in the awakening of the old days.*

The boarding-house held three permanent residents, two of whom were dead-set against a "missioner" staying as a guest in the house. A recent visit by a man "who made preaching his trade" had left them weary of hollow-sounding religious talk and shallow thinking.

They voiced their dismay before Oswald arrived. James Anderson, a rising barrister decided to ignore the preacher, certain they could have nothing in common. What knowledge would a missioner of some prayer group have of anything legal or parliamentary?

The other strenuous objector, forty-three-year-old Katherine Ashe, was more vocal. She was horrified at the prospect of another preacher coming. Rising from the breakfast table to her full five feet, ten inches, she said with an upturned nose: "Fancy having an ignorant evangelist in the house for ten days! We won't have any conversation at meals and nothing to talk about. He'll be absolutely appalling."

Miss Ashe, as she was always known, came from an old aristocratic Irish family on her mother's side. Although her father, Weldon Ashe, was a clergyman in the Church of England, Katherine was an entrenched agnostic—cultured, learned, musical, and extremely strong-willed, with no use for a God whose representatives seemed so uneducated and ill-bred.

Oswald accepted his house-mates' aloofness and focused table conversation on them and their interests. They found it difficult to avoid talking about themselves and what they believed. Then, after expressing themselves at length, common courtesy moved them to ask his views.

Oswald later wrote to Biddy of their exchange:

> *There are aching lives here and He is working. Last night we had a glorious 'clash.' They did not know Him and I did. I told them that I knew nothing of God apart from Jesus Christ, He was God to me; apart from Him, God was a mere mental abstraction.*
>
> *The hearts of these people are hungry, but their intellects seem satisfied with the worship of abstractions which is so modern, and to me so absurdly insufficient.*

As the week progressed, Miss Ashe was surprised to find that her "ignorant evangelist" played Mendelssohn and knew the plays of Henrik Ibsen. James Anderson wanted to know more about Reader Harris, a man at the top of the legal profession, and his commitment to Christ. The third member of the household, whose name is not known, was drawn by Oswald's genuine interest and the unmistakable reality of what he said. All three were deeply touched by his love for the beauty of Ireland and his understanding of its subtle expressions, seldom noticed by a visitor.

Within a few days, Oswald won their hearts simply by being himself and caring for them. Their conversations became, in the words of Miss Ashe, "delightful excursions of talk upon every subject under the sun."

Before the mission ended, Katherine felt she should at least show Oswald the courtesy of attending one meeting. She came expecting nothing and was arrested by his message on abundant life in Christ. At the close of the meeting, in an unusual departure from his normal ways, Oswald gave an altar call, inviting those who wished to give themselves to Jesus Christ to come to the front of the church. Katherine stood up and began to walk forward, her pride and self-sufficiency melted by the love of Christ for her. She described the event as "a wholly supernatural conversion, a very agonizing birth from above," followed by "an intensely painful period of readjustment of every point of view . . . to honourably accept the New Testament standard." Tall, imposing, aristocratic Katherine Ashe had turned around in mid-stream and would never be the same.

Oswald praised God for the visible results, but confided his deeper longings to Biddy. On November 23, 1908, he wrote from Belfast:

> *I speak and people get blessed. But I long to hear them say, 'He made me love Him better. It was through his sermon that my Lord Jesus became all in all to me.'*

November 24:

> *He looms large tonight. Nothing is worth living for but just Himself. I see churches and schemes and missionary enterprises and holiness movements all tagged with His name but how little of Himself! I wish every breath I drew, all speech I made could make Him come and seem more real to men.*
>
> *God grant you may never need to be disciplined as He has disciplined me. He has taken me through Sheol and a broken heart. In those days of agony beyond words (if you knew you would understand that pain must ever be the price of power), I wrote a few lines. I have never thought of them since but they come back again to me now just freshly, they are fragments torn from deep down:*
>
> *Hush! there comes the sound of weeping*
> *Of my spirit vainly seeking*
> *Through the passions that are sweeping*
> *Another sphere.*
> *And its great tears ever falling*
> *And its pained voice ever calling*
> *Rack my life with fear*
> *Never can I live in gladness*
> *Never can I turn from sadness*
> *But must dwell in tears.*
>
> *After that, I found my Lord Who sanctified me.*

His remembered poem, "De Profundis," had actually come from his London days. It was written in January 1895. His recollection of it indicates the length and breadth of his previous spiritual struggle, which commenced long before his days in Dunoon. His crisis of surrender was now seven years past, but never far from conscious thought.

December 1—Dublin:

> *I sound so stern and definite but He knows too the compassion for men and women, compassion for His sake.*
>
> *If I could only tell Him as I know him! I see heartbreaks all around and I know He can put it all right, but how to get them there, how to tell them, how to persuade them.*

From Portrush, on the far north coast of Northern Ireland, he wrote on December 6:

> *I feel as if I must go out and see the sea once more. This great power and groan of the mighty sea seems to awaken that longing loneliness of the prophet about me for God. I am filled with joy always but a tremendous sorrow seems to be interwoven with it all.*
>
> *The wind is out mightily tonight and I feel so sure the gales of the Spirit are blowing over me and conveying something to me—what, I do not distinguish yet. It holds me strangely alert. I wish I could catch its meaning but I cannot, yet I think I must be not spiritual enough to detect it.*

On December 15 Oswald began his final Irish mission in Antrim. He wrote:

> *My Lord Jesus Christ grows grander and more and more central to my mind and heart and being daily. How much, how intolerably much, we owe to Him, none of us begin to realize it. Such an indignation gets hold of me, such a passion of penitency, when I think of the days I have given over to thoughts and concerns other than Himself. How the prince of this world presses and throngs with clamours, more or less noble and good, but all in order to keep us away from devoting all to Him.*

With his Irish mission concluded, Oswald traveled by ferry across the North Channel to the English mainland, then by rail to Scotland. He spent the Christmas holiday in Perth with Franklin's family, and each day, a letter sped by train to Biddy in Eltham:

Christmas Day—Perth:

> *I am more and more certain God is leading to great and solemn things in the future for you and me together for Him. Never fear. He is training you.*

December 26:

> *I realize more and more that if we are not to forego the interests of His cross we must forego a great many other interests and how you will go, counting Him worthy of the cost.*

Oswald's letters during this week speak of his refusal to view God's call in terms of "usefulness," as others defined it.

December 27:

> *I am not appealed to on the line that I am of more use in certain places. It is with me where He wills. Bless the Lord He guides. Pay attention to the source and He will look after the outflow.*

It appears that his "temporary" work as a missioner with the League had been indefinitely extended, and nothing permanent was in sight. Undoubtedly, as he had anticipated, an avalanche of practical advice was being offered the couple from concerned family and friends.

December 31—Perth:

> *This is the last day of a momentous year to you and me. The best year of our lives. Yet He is preparing us for what He is preparing for us. The word that grows on me for the new year is His word: 'As the Father sent me, so send I you.' His first obedience was to the will of God not the needs of mankind. The voice of the age that says 'Here you will be most*

> *good' is to my mind the voice of the tempter. It is where He places us, and how few see it!*

Other than ten days on the ship to America, Oswald and Biddy had spent little time together. Telephone calls were expensive and reserved for unusual circumstances. The mail became their lifeline of love. From every letter, Biddy gleaned a line of encouragement.

> *I believe God's spirit is winning and wooing you with some great new thing. Let Him have his way, over all the light you have got.*
>
> *Be patient and so utterly confident in God that you never question His ways or your waiting time.*
>
> *One individual life may be of priceless value to God and yours may be that life.*
>
> *I am so amazed that God has altered me that I can never despair of anybody.*
>
> *Let mistakes correct themselves as Jesus ever did with the disciples.*
>
> *Be reckless for Jesus Christ!*
>
> *Criticism of others kills spirituality every time.*
>
> *Keep a sense of humour in divine things as well as in human things.*

Their engagement provided a context of confidence and trust in which they could open up to each other. Since only quoted fragments survive of Oswald's letters to Biddy, we are left to guess at what she wrote to him. Reading these fragments of his letters to her is like listening to one end of a telephone conversation, but the bits and pieces reveal the love that was deepening between them. Throughout January 1909, he poured out his soul and described what he saw for their life together.

> *With what power those words of His come back to me about you—a help answering to Him. Let me tell you what I see in outline. All comforts and comrades and countries are held*

> *lightly, all at His command. Can you, out of your love to Him and me forego every other interest saving the interest of His Cross?*
>
> *Do you know how it costs to write this—by grace mine eyes have looked on Jesus. I dare not think of that. Oh I know you will rise to any height of self-sacrifice—but you understand how many misgivings I have in calling you to come with me.*
>
> *I cannot give you any other warned couple as a specimen of what it will mean. We will be the two sent out by Him. I need you to keep me strong in the way He calls.*
>
> *I have no home to offer you. I have no money to give you. I have the great wild world and His commission — Go and make disciples.*
>
> *I am solemn with the awakening to the grandeur of His call — follow me.*
>
> *I see loyalty to Him and nothing else and you will help me to be loyal to Him.*

Major John Skidmore, the League's secretary in Manchester, shared a "no-holds-barred" relationship with Oswald Chambers. There was nothing they couldn't tell each other—a rare gift for two men in the sometimes repressive atmosphere of the day and the holiness movement itself.

When Skidmore found himself in a mental cul de sac, emptied by his role of continually giving the truth out to others, he shared his dilemma with Chambers.

"What do you read?" Oswald asked.

"Only the Bible and books directly associated with it," Skidmore told him.

"That's the trouble," Chambers replied. "You have allowed part of your brain to stagnate for want of use."

Within a few minutes, Oswald had scribbled out a list of more than fifty books—philosophical, psychological, and theological, dealing with every phase of current thought. In a follow-up letter to Skidmore, Oswald said: "My strong advice to you is to *soak, soak, soak* in philosophy and psychology, until you know more of these subjects than ever you need consciously to think. It is ignorance of these subjects on the part of ministers and workers that has brought our evangelical theology to such a sorry plight.

"When people refer to a man as 'a man of one book,' meaning the Bible, he is generally found to be a man of multitudinous books, which simply isolates the one Book to its proper grandeur. The man who reads only the Bible does not, as a rule, know it or human life."

In late February 1909, Chambers and John Skidmore met in Yorkshire for League meetings in the villages of Askrigg and Hawes. They stayed with John's brother, Jim, at his home above the family antique shop on the main street in Askrigg. Every afternoon in the shop, a contingent of local men gathered to talk with the Skidmores' father, the last of the famous Askrigg clockmakers. Through a haze of tobacco smoke, they gestured with their pipes and bantered with "Old Skiddy," now almost eighty, about the price of wool and the chance for snow. As the sun dropped toward the snow-covered fells, fifty clocks ticked and chimed the afternoon away.

Oswald enjoyed these people and their little village of old stone houses. He loved the valley of Wensleydale surrounded by rolling hills and the wild expanse of moorland. No visit to the Yorkshire Dales was complete without a tramp across the moors in the pure, bracing air. During a walk in the hills above Askrigg, a sudden storm sent Chambers and Skidmore scurrying for shelter. While they waited for the blowing rain to run its course, their conversation turned to "the ignorance of religious workers generally and their apparent inability to think and keep abreast mentally with spiritual growth."

It was a problem, in the League and in churches everywhere. Chambers had seen it in America and Japan, too. "Mental woolgathering" he called it; an unwillingness or lack of training in how to engage the mind in earnest study for God, with eyes wide open to the real world and the hurting people in it.

"If the man in the pew was trained to think for himself," Skidmore asserted, "very soon the man in the pulpit would have to give him something better to think about." A trained laity could encourage more diligence in the pastor's study.

They returned from their walk determined to address the issue. The difficulty was how. The work of God's Bible School and Cowman's college in Tokyo had convinced Chambers of the value of practical training carried out over a period of time. In heart and method, he had always been more of a teacher than a preacher. He and Skidmore decided to experiment with a different approach during Oswald's upcoming seven-day mission in Manchester. Instead of lecturing on his usual themes, Chambers tackled "Christianity vs. Socialism," presenting his material in colorful blackboard outlines while encouraging open discussion. A student from those early classes said: "Although Chambers regarded carelessness and stupidity in spiritual matters as a crime, he was able, by his rare gifts to obtain the best from his students. For many of us it was stimulating to be told that we all had 'intelligence' and we must use it for God. We began straightway to think."

Skidmore immediately made plans for Chambers to hold similar Bible training classes in Sheffield and other cities. The Manchester meetings gave both of them a powerful sense of being right on target. When the mission was over, Oswald wrote to Biddy:

> *What a blessed and a busy time I have had! The Lord literally poured the word. This mission has without question been the most wonderful and blessed of my life. What impressed me most was the way God opened up His word and poured out His Spirit. Years of study along the lines of philosophy and psychology and ethics suddenly seem to have come to fruition.*

He approached his March 22–April 3 mission in Lowestoft with special anticipation—Biddy would be there. He wrote her from Sunderland on March 19: "At Lowestoft we will have the chance of communion with our Lord and Master at the meetings, and of praying and working and watching together for Him."

For a few days, the letters could give way to life. They could speak face to face, walk the shore together, and talk of things to come. But just before the meetings, Biddy came down with influ-

George Oxer, Oswald's closest teenage friend. Pencil sketch by Chambers, August 9, 1895, just before leaving London for the University of Edinburgh. **Left:** Student, University of Edinburgh, 1895–1896.

Rye Lane, Peckham, in 1900. Chambers lived in this London suburb during his teenage years.

Courtesy: Southwark Local History library

Courtesy: Leonard Chambers

The Chambers brothers in 1886. Standing: Arthur–25. Seated, from left: Ernest–19, Oswald–12, Franklin–16. Arthur became a Baptist minister, Ernest a commercial artist, and Franklin a chemist in a dye works.

Above: Duncan and Gertrude MacGregor (seated center) with daughter Mildred pose with students at The Training College, Dunoon, circa 1912. **Left:** Tutor of Philosophy, Dunoon College, 1904. Age 30.

Left: Reader Harris in wig and court gown. **Below:** Seascape by OC, 1901, a spiritually turbulent time. *I would rather the flood went o'er me/ The flood of the great wild sea/ With its acres of secret waters/ Than mourn o'er the never-to-be*—Poem by OC, September 30, 1901

Interior, Speke Hall, London. Headquarters of the League of Prayer.

Courtesy: Christine Reynolds

Beethoven, a portrait in charcoal, by Chambers at age 19. Oswald loved to play Beethoven's "Moonlight Sonata."

Highland Mary's statue, erected in honor of poet Robert Burns, looks beyond Dunoon Pier, across the Firth of Clyde.

Tranquil seascape, another charcoal by OC, reflects the inner change brought by the resolution of his spiritual crisis at Dunoon in November 1901.

Top Left: Bound for America and Japan, November 1906. **Right:** Juji Nakada and Chambers traveled together in 1906–1907, preaching in Britain, America, and Japan. **Left Center:** Oswald taught at God's Bible School in Cincinnati, Ohio, for six months in 1907. Brother Chambers, as he was called, pictured with faculty members (left to right) Sister Lovett, Sister Nettie Peabody, and Sister Elizabeth West. **Right Center:** Oswald on a brief holiday with Meredith and Bessie Standley of God's Bible School, February 1907. **Bottom:** Annual ten-day camp meeting in June at God's Bible School. Chambers was a featured speaker during four summers, 1907–1910.

Courtesy: God's Bible School and College, Cincinnati

Wedding Day, May 25, 1910. Standing, Left to Right: Percy Lockhart, best man; Biddy's sister Edith (Daisy); Oswald's sister Gertrude; Biddy's brother, Herbert Hobbs; Oswald and Biddy, seated with his niece, Doris, in front.

Hannah and Clarence Chambers. Fiftieth Wedding Anniversary, July 16, 1910. **Center Right:** Returning from America to England on board the *SS Adriatic*, September 1910.

July 1910: Oswald and Biddy spent their first four months of marriage in America. Oswald spoke at many camp meetings like this one at Old Orchard, Maine. Standing, Left to Right: Capt. Charles T. Potter, Rev. Arthur Greene, Rev. Oswald Chambers, Mr. William Richardson, Rev. H. J. Olsen. Seated Right: Biddy Chambers, Mrs. William Richardson.

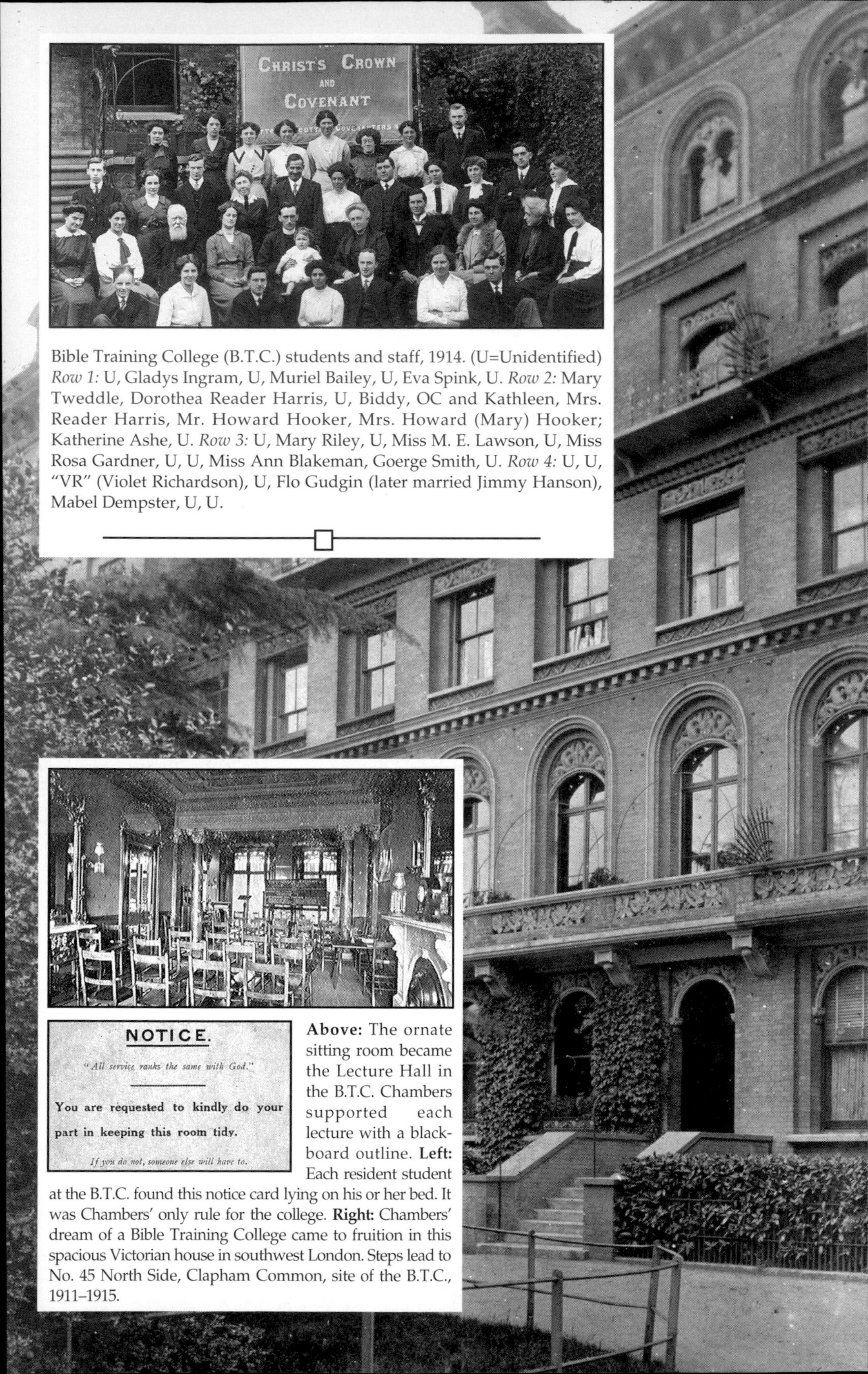

Bible Training College (B.T.C.) students and staff, 1914. (U=Unidentified) *Row 1:* U, Gladys Ingram, U, Muriel Bailey, U, Eva Spink, U. *Row 2:* Mary Tweddle, Dorothea Reader Harris, U, Biddy, OC and Kathleen, Mrs. Reader Harris, Mr. Howard Hooker, Mrs. Howard (Mary) Hooker; Katherine Ashe, U. *Row 3:* U, Mary Riley, U, Miss M. E. Lawson, U, Miss Rosa Gardner, U, U, Miss Ann Blakeman, Goerge Smith, U. *Row 4:* U, U, "VR" (Violet Richardson), U, Flo Gudgin (later married Jimmy Hanson), Mabel Dempster, U, U.

NOTICE.

"All service ranks the same with God."

You are requested to kindly do your part in keeping this room tidy.

If you do not, someone else will have to.

Above: The ornate sitting room became the Lecture Hall in the B.T.C. Chambers supported each lecture with a blackboard outline. **Left:** Each resident student at the B.T.C. found this notice card lying on his or her bed. It was Chambers' only rule for the college. **Right:** Chambers' dream of a Bible Training College came to fruition in this spacious Victorian house in southwest London. Steps lead to No. 45 North Side, Clapham Common, site of the B.T.C., 1911–1915.

A photographer captures a candid moment in the garden of the B.T.C., early 1914.

Left: A picnic near Askrigg in, as Oswald called it, "my heavenly Father's dining room." **Bottom Left:** Oswald loved children and found unending delight in Kathleen. He was almost 39 when she was born in May 1913.

Oswald in frock coat and Biddy in League of Prayer bonnet, ready for a mission together, 1914.

Chambers loved to fish the clear streams in the Yorkshire Dales.

Holiday in Askrigg, August 1915. Standing, Left to Right: Arthur Chambers, Biddy, Oswald, Eva Spink, Jim Skidmore, Jimmy Hanson. Middle Row: Gertrude Chambers, Bertha Chambers, Kathleen, Mary Riley. Front: Gladys Ingram, Flo Gudgin (later Mrs. Jimmy Hanson), Unidentified.

Just before Oswald sailed for Egypt in October 1915.

Left: "God be praised for our little daughter, and cause her to be a sister of the Lord Jesus Christ." **Above:** Instead of sending children away while he talked with their parents, Oswald often entertained them with simple sketches (Courtesy: Christine Reynolds).

Chambers and Stanley Barling, Y.M.C.A. Cairo, 1915. **Below:** Oswald surveys the latest improvements at Zeitoun. Diary, May 3, 1917: *The tendency is to argue—'It is only for so short a time, why trouble?' If it is only for five minutes, let it be well done.*

Evening study classes often spilled out the door of the Devotional Hut as men stood beneath the stars and listened.

Y.M.C.A. Hut, Zeitoun. Diary, October 27, 1915: *This is absolutely desert, in the very heart of the troops and a glorious opportunity for men. I am watching with interest the new things God will do and engineer.* **Right:** New Zealand troops in camp under the pyramids, early 1915. The area around Cairo was the scene of massive troop movements throughout World War I.

Above: Constant improvement and change were Chambers' way of life. **Below:** Zeitoun, 1916: Tablecloths and flowers revealed Biddy's touch at every Sunday "free tea." Over 400 soldiers came for sandwiches, cakes, and gallons of tea. Biddy, center, in wide brim hat. Oswald, top right, with arms folded.

During Chambers' two years in Egypt, thousands of men heard his searching presentation of the gospel, directed at their immediate needs.

Left: Peter Kay, (standing next to OC) a rough-and-tumble Aussie soldier, came to faith in Christ through Chambers. Ted Strack, kneeling beside Kathleen. **Center:** Troops often made a point of walking past the notice board to read Oswald's motto for each day. **Right:** Chambers would speak for an hour, using only an outline like this one written in his own hand.

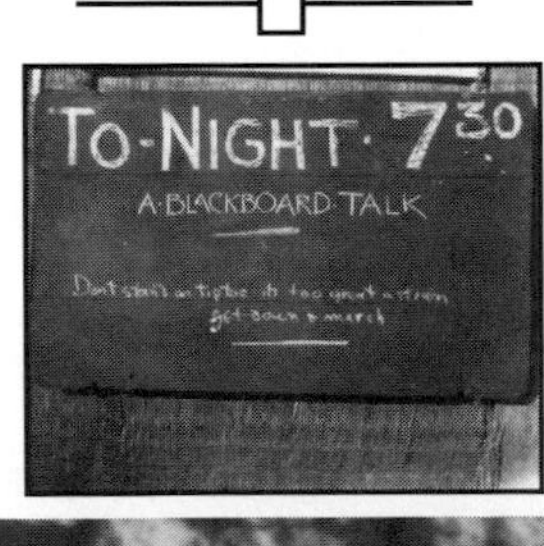

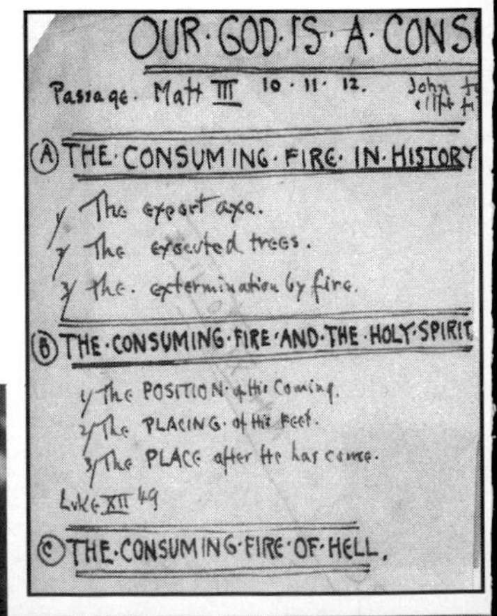

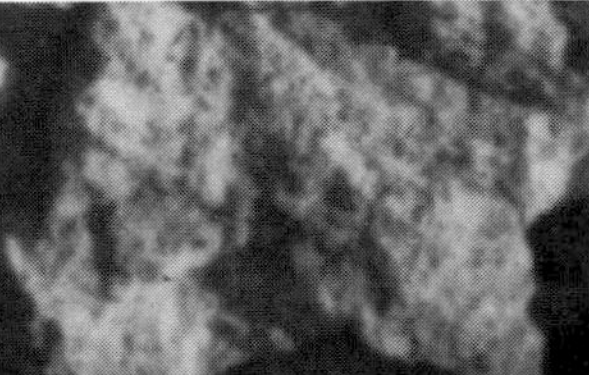

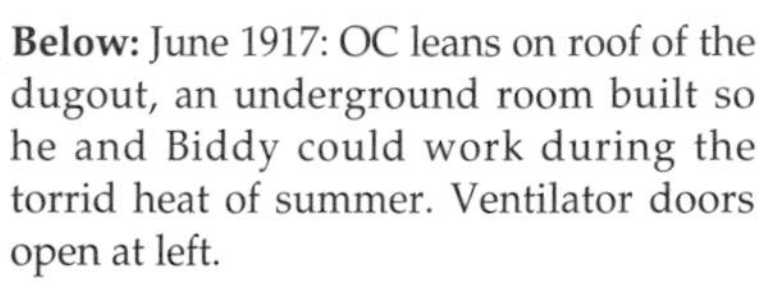

Below: June 1917: OC leans on roof of the dugout, an underground room built so he and Biddy could work during the torrid heat of summer. Ventilator doors open at left.

Flowers and stone-lined walkways among Oswald's huts. One Y.M.C.A. secretary called Zeitoun "The Mental Oasis."

Biddy never knew how many people would appear for tea or supper outside the bungalow at Zeitoun. **Right:** Chambers prized the broad-brimmed hat given to him by appreciative Australian and New Zealand troops. He holds the ever-present fly whisk in his right hand. **Below:** Ready for a jaunt into Cairo for lunch at Groppi's Greek Restaurant or tea at Shepheard's Hotel, June 1917.

Above: Zeitoun, 1916: Taken from second floor of Egypt General Mission home. Left to right: Study Hut, Devotional Hut, The Bungalow, with bell tent in front. Diary, October 7, 1916: *I have a great adjunct now in my double fly bell tent, it makes an admirable open air study.*

Above: From her perch in the post-card hut, Kathleen reigned as queen of the Y.M.C.A. camp at Zeitoun. **Left:** Diary, January 8, 1917: *Peter Kay, one of the Australian Remounts, has brought a little donkey for Kathleen and she is ecstatic over it.* **Below:** Chambers did everything he could to help soldiers find the Y.M.C.A. huts at Zeitoun.

September 1917: Sunken cheeks reveal the toll of demanding work on Chamber's declining health. **Below:** The B.T.C. Camel Corps at the Sphinx and the pyramids of Gizeh: Left to right: Biddy, OC and Kathleen, Jimmy Hanson, Miss Ashe, Mary Riley, and unidentified soldier.

Photos found among Eva (Spink) Pulford's mementos. Believed to be of Oswald Chambers' funeral, November 16, 1917.

Above: Chambers' grave in the British Military Cemetery at Old Cairo, 1918. Buried among the men he loved and served. **Below Left:** The British Military cemetery at Old Cairo, 1992. **Below Right:** Military authorities later replaced the wooden crosses with headstones. *Rev. Oswald Chambers, Superintendent Y.M.C.A. 15th November 1917 Age 43.*

Biddy and Kathleen, England, 1923.

enza and could not come. Far from being a mild illness, influenza could be life-threatening, especially for someone with Biddy's history of respiratory problems. Oswald wrote to her mother: "The influenza is a thing one cannot take liberties with and B.D. must realize it. God bless her and keep her still, the thing she ever complains to me that her mother will not be."

Chambers was five days into his mission at Lowestoft when the shocking news came on March 26 that Reader Harris had suffered a stroke and lay in a coma at his London home. Four days later, without regaining consciousness, Harris died at the age of sixty-one.

Chambers ended the mission early and left for London. During the past four months he had often looked forward to a long talk with Reader Harris when his marathon schedule of missions came to an end. Now his valued counselor, mentor, and friend had received the greatest call from God. As the train sped through the night, Oswald jotted a single verse in his diary:

I war alone, I shall not see his face
But I shall strive more gladly in the sun,
More bravely in the shadow for this grace,
He fought his fight and won.

On Tuesday afternoon, April 6, two thousand people overflowed Speke Hall for the funeral. Hundreds of others stood outside, lining the streets. Chambers gave a brief tribute at the service. Then, along with hundreds of others, he boarded a special train carrying the funeral party to Norwood and interment in the cemetery there high on a hill.

That evening in Queen's Hall, Langham Place, a memorial service paid further honor to Harris. Franklin Chambers came from Perth to preside at the organ, and Oswald joined a large party on the platform. His remarks reveal not only his personal relationship to Harris, but his awareness of people's questions regarding the future of the League:

"He was a King's Counsellor to me in the very highest sense," Oswald said. "By one of those strange turns of God's providence, Mr. Reader Harris came across me. How, I do not know; God knows, and he began to counsel me, and from that moment the counsel and the prayers and the guidance of Mr. Reader Harris have been to me as those of a commander.

"Others of you may have known of his winsomeness, of his beauty and humour. I have known of these also, but to me he had a clarion voice spiritually and he was indeed a man by whom God witnessed to my own heart with these words the first day he shook hands with me, 'I have chosen him to be a witness, and a leader and a commander,' and God knows he has been that to thousands.

"There is no second Reader Harris, and never will be. There never was a second Moses. God does not repeat His servants. But I have got one word for the Joshua. And Joshua in this case is every member of the League. I would like to remind every Leaguer here that, although we have lost the clarion voice and personality of the leader sent forth by God, we have still got a leader amongst us in his wife, and may the Lord bless her!"

He closed his remarks with a call for renewed prayer and dedication to the three-fold vision of his mentor and friend: "The filling of the Holy Spirit for all believers; the revival of the Churches; and the spread of scriptural holiness."

The next day the regular monthly meeting in Caxton Hall went on as scheduled. During an afternoon gathering Chambers and the League secretaries from around Britain pledged their continuing support to Mrs. Harris as the new leader of the League. Her daughter, Mary (Mrs. Howard Hooker), agreed to assume greater official responsibilities as well.

It was clear that Chambers never regarded himself as Reader Harris's successor, nor was he ever considered the figurehead of the League of Prayer. The death of Reader Harris placed a heavier burden of preaching and teaching on Chambers' shoulders, but also gave him a new perspective of ministry as a partnership between husband and wife. He wrote to Biddy:

April 13, 1909—London:

> *I can see how mightily God will use us as one. I am finding out how much Mrs. Reader Harris was behind her husband. The public saw him, but she was the power behind the throne. I remember also Catherine Booth what a woman of God she was. Blessed be the name*

of God. He is preparing us both for the same power and service.

April 25, 1909—Birmingham:

I love Him more and more. This service for Him is getting more of a consuming passion. I wish you were out in it with me, but it is coming glory to His name.

May 6, 1909—London:

We will have a spiritual surgery and dispensary and convalescent home and be spiritual reality to the aching wounded lives around—God give you the true inwardness and Divine life being health.

After an exhausting April and May, Chambers left for two months in America, reveling in the prospect of ten days to rest and study at sea:

June 3, 1909—On board the *Lusitania*:

How I have ached for this solid silent time of communion with Him whom my soul adoreth. The deep above, underneath, around and within. God bless you and help Himself right and royally out of us both.

14
TOGETHER FOR HIM

(1909–1910)

Each day aboard the *Lusitania,* Chambers grew stronger in body and spirit. He loved the sea and the way it spoke to him of God. Sitting in a deck chair, wrapped in a blanket against the chill of the North Atlantic, he watched the changing face of the ocean from day to day. Morning calm gave way to afternoon swells, whose whitecaps were lifted and scattered by the wind. In it all, he saw a picture of life. No matter how strong the winds or how high the waves on the surface, far below lay the great mysterious deeps with their strong currents and untouched calm. A man who would live for Christ in a turbulent world must draw his life from the depths of God Himself, not from the froth and foam of surface experience.

He arrived in New York, refreshed and renewed by his days at sea. A year before, he and Biddy had stepped ashore together, just beginning to recognize the stirrings of love for each other. Now they had been engaged for seven months and still could not make definite plans for marriage.

He wrote from Brooklyn to encourage her:

June 6, 1909:

> *It is unspeakably beautiful to be here and remember all the ways that God has led and how gracious and yet how unfathomably profound His ways have been. Keep strong in faith in God.*

En route to Cincinnati he wondered what this year's Camp Meeting at God's Bible School would bring. Last summer God had impressed him with messages for pastors. This year he would address the entire camp each morning at eleven as well as speak several evenings. In between, the days and nights would be filled with people wanting to talk, pray, and pour out their souls to him. He was never shocked by what they told him, but he was always deeply moved by the pain and heartache of their lives. The only hope for their spiritual healing and his spiritual health was the power of God.

"I am so amazed that God has altered me," he often said, "that I can never despair of anybody."

During the days of joyful friendships and exacting ministry, his thoughts were never far from Biddy and what lay ahead for them:

June 17—Cincinnati:

> *The love of this people is great, mighty. I have a greatly increased prayer list. I believe more and more that this is His way—intercessory prayer, this is the way He makes us broken bread and poured out wine for other people.*

June 30—Cincinnati:

> *These past days the tragedies of broken lives have been full. I should like ultimately to have a home where those in 'the blues' could come, not so much to be talked to as to be and to wander around until healing comes to them.*

In view of Chambers' artistic, romantic nature, it may seem strange that his letters to Biddy did not contain more expressions of tenderness and love. In all likelihood they did, but only selected fragments of the originals survived. A man like Oswald Chambers, who wrote poetry, played classical music, and exulted in the beauty of nature, was not likely to restrict his written communications to spiritual and practical matters alone. His written words of personal affection to his fiancée remain hidden. Two themes that clearly emerge from his letters to Biddy during this period are his vision for a Bible school and his excitement about the challenge of "forsaking all" to serve God together.

July 7—Cincinnati:

> *My mind and heart are full over the prospective Bible school. God unite us into that*

mighty purpose of His, whatever it is that I feel singing in my heart.

Oh what a grand strenuous life there lies out in front of us. The unbribed soul for His enterprises, that is my charge. Bless God He reigns and He will open all the way. Isa. 45:13

July 11—Brooklyn:

How little can I give you, a life of steady arduous undertaking for Him.

Let yourself go to all the forces around you for I am persuaded that they are some from our Father's hands and He knows just what to bring to bear on us. He is fitting us for a great and blessed life of usefulness to Him in the days that are coming. My utmost for the Highest is ever the motto.

July 12:

Again the loneliness of our Lord comes to me more and more. How few of us are concerned about satisfying His heart. How I hear Him saying, I thirst, Give me to drink. May my Lord never let me grow cold in my longing to be a cup in His hand for the quenching of His own royal thirst.

July 23—Old Orchard, Maine:

My whole soul is full of thoughts and prayers and of waiting and working for what God is preparing for us in the near future. My idea of a Bible Training School for about 10 years will yet come about. 4 years—the country. 4 in a city and 2 in a foreign field. Keep these schemes in your mind and heart.

By early August, he was back in Britain, scheduled to visit League centers in Scotland for the next six weeks. Following that there came a full slate of meetings and missions through the end of the year. His letters during the autumn of 1909 express a longing to go beyond the traditional structure of ministry and pioneer new concepts and methods.

Aug 25—Aberdeen:

> *God is answering prayer mightily and grandly, praise His name. I am more and more absorbed in the Great Word, our Lord Jesus Christ; and I am certain that the rush and hurry of civilised churches loses the sound of that Great Word. How I long to be absorbed more and more in hearing Him and loving Him.*

Aug 27—Dundee:

> *Let us pray much and see how He will open the way. Visionary? Yes, but who is to carry it out? Who better fitted than we are for this scheme of Bible teaching?*
>
> *How ideas and conceptions rise and stir and float and move in my mind and heart. I have a great vision of a Protestant movement where people of ability who could obviously make their living fair and flourishing in other domains, deliberately refuse to do it and live for Him alone going the world over for Him.*
>
> *How much will He allow us to reach these ideals and how much will he say it is well 'that it was in thine heart'?*
>
> *Then another great tract of ideas is literary work. Oh how much there is to overtake and I leap when I think of you and then sink back and wonder how ever is it to be accomplished!*

Writing had long been an avenue of communication that interested Oswald. From his teenage poetry in London to his newspaper articles in Dunoon, he expressed his thoughts with a unique and stirring vocabulary. With his love for books and their impact on his thinking, he saw the printed page as a powerful means of influencing others.

In the late nineteenth and early twentieth centuries, decades before magnetic recording, Sunday sermons and messages at Christian gatherings like the Keswick Convention were routinely taken down in shorthand by appointed stenographers and later transcribed for publication. The Sunday evening sermons of Alexander Whyte, Charles Haddon Spurgeon, and other notable preachers appeared regularly in major newspapers and were often published later in book form.

By July 1906, transcribed versions of Chambers' messages at League meetings were appearing as articles in nearly every monthly issue of *Tongues of Fire*. Similar "articles" began appearing in January 1907 in *The Revivalist*, published by God's Bible School.

His first visit to Cincinnati in 1906-07 had opened new possibilities with the publication of his sermon "The Discipline of Suffering" in pamphlet form.

Among the dreams of ministry dancing through Oswald's mind in 1909 was a partnership in which he and Biddy would combine their gifts to produce written material.

"It will be such a meagre home we will have," he wrote to her, "you and myself going heart and soul into literary and itinerating work for Him. It will be hard and glorious and arduous.

"I want *us* to write and preach; if I could talk to you and you shorthand it down and then type it, what ground we could get over! I wonder if it kindles you as it does me!"

By the end of December, two things had apparently been settled. First, the possibility of beginning a residential Bible school in London under the auspices of the League of Prayer had been delayed by lack of a suitable house and adequate finances. Instead of a residential college, the League would offer a six-month correspondence course under Chambers' direction. Second, Oswald and Biddy planned to be married near the end of May, 1910, and spend the summer in America, as he had done the previous two years. With the prospects of a Bible school in Britain coming closer to reality, Oswald's commitment to the League of Prayer held renewed possibilities. By faith, it was time for them to move ahead.

The year 1909 ended with the most definite plans since they pledged their love to each other in St. Paul's a year before. "I do want you to know the peculiar set of people you will be amongst by coming with me," Oswald wrote to Biddy. "They are all out and out for the Lord and nothing else. Keep praying and believing that the Lord will help Himself liberally to me and to these people.

"Just now my whole soul surges with the certainty that the line I am on in religious matters is right—the pushing to the most painful point of resistance the experience of giving up the right to ones self to our Lord and Saviour Jesus Christ.

"Hourly almost my sense of His call grows. It will have to be a rover life I am afraid, all over the world. There are grand days coming for you and me."

The January 1910 *Tongues of Fire* mentioned a "most gratifying" response to the correspondence classes and set forth the plan for eight lessons covering the next six months. A printed sheet of hints and a demonstration lesson would accompany the first assignment. "No one need fear to join," Chambers said, "as the utmost consideration will be given to each paper. The idea of these classes is an intensely practical one without the least element of competition."

The schedule allowed students two weeks to complete each lesson and post their papers to London. While they enjoyed a free week, Oswald would correct the papers and return them with the next lesson. For the first term, three hundred people were enrolled!

Even with this added responsibility, Oswald's speaking schedule for the League was heavier than ever. In February, he began a six-part Lenten series at St. James Hall, spoke every Tuesday and Wednesday at League meetings in greater London, and held a meeting focusing on personal holiness every Thursday night in Speke Hall. In addition he traveled to Bristol, Plymouth, Dover, and Gravesend for missions of one to five days. On February 12, he tackled a pile of three hundred papers from the Bible School Correspondence Course, marking and returning them all within a week.

How did he do it? The answer from those who knew him best seems to be, "Very gracefully and unhurriedly." For the six months before his marriage, from December 1909 to May 1910, Oswald headquartered in the spacious home of Mr. and Mrs. Howard Hooker on the north side of Clapham Common, just a mile from Speke Hall. Mary Hooker, Reader Harris's oldest daughter, was an accomplished musician and a frequent speaker at League meetings. Her younger sister, Dorothea, played and sang as well. After Reader Harris died, the leadership of the organization fell on his widow and the Hookers. At

Speke Hall meetings, members of the Harris family played a prominent role. Before every main speaker rose to preach, Mrs. Reader Harris called on Dorothea for a solo with the words, "And now my daughter will sing."

Mary Hooker described Chambers during those strenuous days as "a man who always carried with him, and therefore gave to others, a sense of the Presence of God. We noticed this in his merriest moments as well as in his ordinary life, or in the most serious part of his ministry. We loved having him in our home. He taught us so much. He played with our children, and was never happier than when crawling round the nursery playing at being a lion or a tiger, led triumphantly by a small boy or girl whom he allowed to tease him unmercifully."

Oswald's relationship with children is one of the most revealing aspects of his character. In a day when society believed they were to be "seen and not heard," he listened to them, loved them, and gave them a place of honor. Had he wished to be alone and undisturbed to prepare his messages, his host families would have made sure the children never bothered him. Instead, he sought them out.

During League missions in Blackpool, he often stayed with the William Docking family. The first time he met eight-year-old Dorothy Docking, she was seated in the drawing room alone. After introducing himself, he asked what she was doing.

"I'm writing a poem," she said.

"Really," Oswald replied. "What's it about?"

"It's about Queen Victoria and Buckingham Palace," the girl told him.

"May I see it?" he asked.

Chambers read the poem quietly and returned it with a smile.

"You must like to read," he said. When Dorothy answered with an enthusiastic "yes" they talked about books for a while before Chambers thanked her for her time and asked to be excused. He went immediately to the kitchen.

Dorothy's mother, Anne, was preparing the evening meal when Chambers appeared in the doorway. He mentioned the conversation with her daughter, then said, "Mrs. Docking, you must see that Dorothy goes to a university and not a teacher's training college. She must attend a university where she can do an honors course in English literature, because she is going to make her life in literature."

Anne Docking was taken back but knew Chambers to be a keen observer of people and a wise man. "Help her all you can with English now," he said. "Encourage her to write and guide her to the finest books for her reading."

Chambers planted the seed and left it to grow. With Dorothy he was content to be a playmate and a friend, chatting casually along her line of interest about anything and everything in the world.

Occasionally, Oswald's way with children left some parents scratching their heads in wonder. During a visit with London friends, the Reynolds, he stayed home with two little ones so the parents could attend a Sunday evening service. Upon their return they tucked the children into bed and asked if the Rev. Chambers had taught them a nice song or Bible verse.

"Oh, yes," the children said. "We'll say it."

> Little Willie in best of sashes
> Fell in the fire and was burnt to ashes,
> Later on the room grew chilly,
> But no one cared to poke poor Willie.

Oswald's ringing laughter could be heard from his room down the hall.

Chambers also impressed people with his use of time. During a jam-packed weekend in Dover, with four messages to preach on Sunday, he excused himself after lunch, saying he would sleep for ten minutes before the afternoon meeting. When his hostess asked if he would need to be awakened, he said, "No. I am going to ask my Heavenly Father for ten minutes' sleep and He will rouse me on the tick of the clock." To her amazement, it happened just as he had said.

He was a man of the mornings, rising early each day for Bible study and intercessory prayer. His personal approach to overcoming fatigue was: "Get out of bed first and think about it later."

Before each meeting he found time to slip away for a brief time alone with his Lord. Whether it was the privacy of his room in a home or the quiet of an unnoticed corner in Speke Hall, he always spoke to God before speaking to men. "Not to prepare the message," he said, "but the messenger."

He never complained about his heavy schedule and the demands on his time, but he struggled with what it would mean for Biddy. A month before their wedding, he wrote to her on April 29, 1910, from Birmingham:

> *The Lord has been slowly rebuking me for wanting to shelter you. And He is bringing me to understand that this union is His and that He will look after you and me. All we have to do is to obey and work and love.*

A week before they were married, he conducted a seven-day mission in Guisbrough, and wrote from there on May 17:

> *We have had no sun here—an almost unbroken fog and drizzle since I arrived, however I carry a wonderful kingdom inside, the Lord's mighty work and your love.*

Three days later, Britain draped itself in black for the funeral of King Edward VII. The eldest son of Queen Victoria had reigned for only a decade in contrast to his mother's sixty-three years on the throne. On May 24, the sense of national sorrow along with a gray drizzle lingered over the usually festive observance of Victoria Day, the late Queen's birthday.

On Wednesday, May 25, the skies cleared and Oswald awoke earlier than usual. After an eighteen month engagement, he and Biddy would pledge their love to each other and become husband and wife that afternoon. Magnificent roses and colorful spring flowers bloomed everywhere throughout the London suburb of Eltham. In front of every red brick row house, a bright profusion of blossoms basked in the sunlight and warmth from a cloudless sky.

Had the Eltham Park Baptist Church been registered with local government authorities as a place to conduct marriages, the wedding would undoubtedly have taken place there. In the absence of the required registration, the couple would exchange vows in the nearby Walford Green Memorial Wesleyan Methodist Church. Oswald's brother Arthur had come from his new pastorate in St. Leonard's to conduct the ceremony.

At the appointed hour, family and friends, many from the League of Prayer, filled the church. Percy Lockhart, Oswald's long-time friend from the town of Dunstable, stood as best man while Bert Hobbs, Biddy's brother, flanked Percy as a groomsman.

Biddy walked slowly down the aisle in a long white dress with a high collar, a bouquet of spring flowers cradled carefully in her hands. Each step brought her closer to the man she loved, the man with whom she was sure life would never be dull. At the altar, she handed her bouquet to her sister, Daisy, her maid of honor, and smiled at Oswald's sister Gertrude Chambers her other bridesmaid. Every aspect of the ceremony reflected Oswald and Biddy's unqualified desire to commit themselves first to God and then to each other.

Hannah Chambers beamed, thrilled to see her youngest son and his bride so radiant on this momentous day. She glanced at Clarence sitting arrow-straight beside her and recalled the day they exchanged vows in London fifty years before. In only two months, they would celebrate their golden wedding anniversary.

Following the ceremony, everyone gathered at the nearby Baptist parsonage for an outdoor reception. Laughter, speeches, and hearty congratulations accompanied the cake and delicacies of the tea prepared by friends. Oswald and Biddy were both nearing their July birthdays on which he would be thirty-six and she twenty-seven. Their age at marriage and the years between them were common for the time. And though they were mature, committed Christians, neither of them could fully understand the uncommon nature of their love for each other or what their lives would mean to the church of Jesus Christ and the eternal kingdom of God.

A week later the newlyweds sailed for New York aboard the *SS Coronia.* Ahead was a four-month whirlwind of activity promising little respite from Oswald's previous schedule. In his suitcase he carried three hundred papers from the Bible School Correspondence Course. Three weeks later he was to receive a box from England containing the same number for correction and return.

Along with his camp meeting commitments in the U.S., he had agreed to conduct an American version of the Bible correspondence course. From June through September, he would have to read and evaluate a total of four thousand papers—eight each from five hundred students. It is little wonder, then, that during most of June, Biddy remained in Brooklyn with a long-time friend. Even if she had been in Cincinnati, the chances of seeing Oswald were slim. From the camp meeting at God's Bible School, he wrote:

> *Every now and again I get fearful of being prosperous and settling down. There has been so much blessing and prosperity on my life lately that it has made us afraid—but it is for Him. Pray much for me that it may ever be Jesus only and all in all in my ministry and life more and more.*

During a week together in the Catskill Mountains of southern New York State, Oswald and Biddy devoted part of each day to a new experiment in ministry together. Sitting on a high rock, he dictated an article called "The Place of Help," based on Psalm 121. After she transcribed her notes, Oswald edited them for publication.

A series of articles on the Christian disciplines also had its birth in the Catskills. A year earlier he had told Biddy about his dream of collaborating with her in literary work. This was the testing ground, and it appeared to have almost limitless potential.

The only problem was time. After their few days in the Catskills, the weeks were taken up with a succession of camp meetings in Ohio, Massachusetts, Maryland, and Maine. The typical week in camp left little time for anything but the program and the people at each location. He tried to prepare his bride with a note of encouragement regarding the people she was about to encounter at the camps. "They are not the clever, the glittering or the worldly, but just the common folk who have gone through much uncommon sacrifice to belong to God. I am sure you will find some royal, heroic souls."

On July 21, they traveled by train from Boston to Harrington, Delaware. From there, a fifteen-mile journey by horse and carriage took them across the rich farmland of Maryland's eastern shore to Denton. The camp meeting site lay in a grove of tall red oak trees just outside town. Charles and Lettie Cowman were there along with several speakers with whom Oswald had shared the platform a few weeks before in Cincinnati.

Every American camp meeting had its own character, but all shared common elements that made them a mixture of community social gathering, family vacation, Bible conference, and spiritual renewal. Some people traveled for days and spent the entire week in a tent or cottage on the grounds. Others living nearby came to evening meetings or Sunday services as they could.

The daily schedule at the Denton Camp was certainly not organized for leisure. From the first morning prayer meeting at six through the altar service and personal counseling that lasted far into the night, almost every minute was filled.

Above all, a spirit of expectancy could be felt among all who came. When Chambers stepped up to the pulpit in the evening, he looked out on a thousand people sitting under the open-sided wooden tabernacle. Half-circle palm leaf fans given away by funeral parlors stirred the humid air as he spoke to them of discipleship, surrender, and joy.

From Denton, Oswald and Biddy traveled by train to Ohio, then to Maine, on the Atlantic coast. On August 1, he wrote to his parents, sending belated congratulations on their fiftieth wedding anniversary. "God bless you and fulfill to you both in your measure Psalm 87:7, 'All my springs are in Thee.' "

At the age of thirty-six, Oswald had gained a new appreciation for his parents. "The memory of mother's doings and managings are to me a growing stimulus and an amazement, while her detestation of can't and humbug also seems to have left in me no little measure of that same spirit. I thank God for you, and praise Him that neither of you ever offered any obstacle to my following out what appeared to me God's calls, for the ways and turns must have perplexed you much, but, thank God, He has allowed you to live to see that when He leads all is well."

By September 21, Oswald and Biddy were aboard the *SS Adriatic* plowing across the Atlantic toward England. She had enjoyed their time in America but was anxious to be home, even with all its uncertainties. They had no house, no furniture, and no money. And beyond the month of October, they had no firm plans. Instead of anxiously pacing the deck, Biddy opened a book while Oswald reclined in a wooden chaise lounge and gazed at the rolling sea. God was in charge and tomorrow was in His hands.

Oswald's approach to the future was simple, "Trust God and do the next thing." What duty lay nearest at hand? Take a nap. Wrapping a blanket around himself, he closed his eyes and went to sleep.

Biddy looked at him and smiled. "Mein geliebt," she whispered. He was such a gloriously unconventional man.

15
THE BIBLE TRAINING COLLEGE

(1911–1915)

While Oswald dozed on the Atlantic, John Skidmore was writing the initials "OC" on nearly every day in his October calendar. Their pilot Bible training class in Manchester a few months before had gone so well that Skidmore arranged a more ambitious undertaking for Chambers' first month back in England.

John placed a hand on top of his completely bald head and reviewed Oswald's teaching schedule. Every Tuesday night he would be in Stoke-on-Trent, where twenty students had already registered for the course in Biblical Psychology. Every Thursday afternoon and evening he would teach the same material to another twenty people in Blackpool. Two sessions would be held each Saturday in Manchester, where Skidmore knew the class would be larger. And, of course, he could count on Chambers to preach in local churches on Sundays and take the odd League meeting here and there when he wasn't marking papers.

No one else Skidmore knew could accept this kind of demanding schedule and fulfill it so gracefully, and he looked forward to hosting Oswald and Biddy for an entire month. Their visit was sure to be a tonic.

The *Adriatic* steamed through The Solent past the Isle of Wight and docked in Southampton on September 29, 1910. Biddy took Oswald's arm as they walked down the gangway and once again set foot on British soil. America had been wonderful, but it felt good to be home. Biddy couldn't wait to sit down to a real cup of tea with her mother and Dais, and talk face to face after four months away. The three shared a strong bond of love and faith that had sustained them through the death of Biddy's father and the continuing spiritual waywardness of her brother.

After a joyful but brief reunion with the families and two League meetings in London, the two were off to Manchester. It appeared that Oswald's dream of a Bible Training College was going to be limited to regional classes and correspondence courses. If that was the only door God opened, he and Biddy would gladly step through it. For now, Oswald determined to give his best to the people in and around Manchester.

"All of you have intelligence," he told each class at the first meeting. "You have a marvellous, God-given capacity to reason and think." Some looked eagerly at him, drinking in his encouragement while others glanced down at their note pads, wanting to believe it about themselves but not sure they could.

"All of you have intelligence," Oswald repeated, "and you must use it for God."

Biddy was there and took shorthand notes of Oswald's lectures. If they used Biblical Psychology as a topic for the correspondence course, she could type explanatory pages and lesson outlines from this material. Apart from that, it kept her stenographic skill sharp and helped focus her attention on what he said. Shorthand was her way of listening. Her pencil flew to keep up with Oswald's rapid fire delivery, and at times she couldn't keep from smiling as he ranged over the spiritual landscape in long strides.

"The reason why the average Christian worker is only the average Christian worker is that he or she will remain grossly ignorant about what he does not see any need for. The majority of us have been brought up on 'spooned meat.' " He continued, "We will only take the truths we see immediate practical use for, consequently the average Christian worker knows nothing about Bible Theology or Bible Psychology, and cannot therefore push the battle for God on any of those domains."

Chambers stressed that an active mind was essential to vital spiritual experience. In many of his lectures, he sounded a constant warning to people who said, "Thank God I'm saved and sanctified, now it's all right." The result of resting on experience, according to Oswald, was "fixed ideas, moral deterioration and utter ignorance of God's book. Always beware of the danger of finality."

Oswald led his students one step at a time into the Bible and its application to daily living. Life, not intellect, was his final objective, but the road to this goal required strenuous mental effort. When assignments seemed overwhelming, he assured students that the pains they felt were signs that their brains were working. "With a little practice," he laughed, "the pain will pass away."

His study principles were simple and direct:

"Always have a dictionary and a concordance by you."

"Never intend to look up a word, *do it now.*"

"A quarter of an hour a day on any subject will make you the master of that subject. Consistency is the key."

Oswald enjoyed the classes in the Manchester district but still longed for a place where students could live as well as study. In Dunoon he had learned more by living with Duncan MacGregor than from anything he said in the classroom. Listening to MacGregor preach had been inspiring. Observing him at home had been life-changing.

Oswald's months at God's Bible School had brought home the value of day-by-day interaction in an atmosphere of commitment to God. In community living, more was "caught" than "taught." During every Cincinnati camp meeting he had been most impressed by the unselfish work of the students who cooked and cleaned. In a class he could teach people to study and preach. In a home he could help them learn to serve.

Providing an adequate house in London was no problem for God. In His time and way, the Lord would give what was needed. Very suddenly, the Lord did exactly that and everyone was startled by His generosity.

In early December, 1910, a large house became available close to the home of Mrs. Reader Harris and only a mile from Speke Hall. The League rented it and immediately announced that the Bible Training College would open in January for resident and day students. In spite of the short notice, Chambers and others in the League felt it was time to move ahead even though they had no furnishings, no money, and no students.

On a gray winter day, Oswald took Biddy for her first look at their new home. The huge Victorian building known as the Cedars contained five spacious houses. Theirs was in the middle. They were like two children as they entered the front door of Number 45 North Side, Clapham Common, and started up a long staircase with wrought iron banister and rails. On the first landing a stained glass window displayed the family crests of a previous owner. As they climbed they noticed that many doors were emblazoned with coats-of-arms. The house was embarrassingly elegant.

A beautiful drawing room occupied nearly all of the second floor, from the front to the back of the house. Large mirrors in ornately carved wooden frames faced each other on two walls. "Incredible," Oswald muttered as he glanced at the imitation marble pillars and the ceiling murals painted fifty years before by an Italian artist. The back windows looked down into a private garden, while the front windows offered a magnificent view of the well-groomed, spacious parkway. There was little feeling of being in the city at all.

They continued through the house, astounded by its size and suitability for a college. There were nineteen rooms on six floors, including a basement. Properly arranged, it could accommodate twenty-five resident students and seat fifty people for meals. Seventy "institute chairs," with arms for writing, would easily fit in the drawing room. Electric trams from the nearest railway and tube stations stopped two doors from the house. It was hard to imagine anything more perfect.

Standing together in a room on the top floor, Oswald prayed that within those four walls, the Spirit of God would create and maintain the atmosphere of His own presence and abiding. Then, hand in hand, they began descending the ninety-six steps from attic to basement, pausing in each room to offer the same prayer. At the bottom of the stairs, they knelt a final time as Oswald summed it all up: "Lord, we pray that in this college, Thou wouldst charge the atmosphere from the top room to the basement with Thy Spirit. We thank Thee for Thy marvelous provision of this place."

These two devoted servants of God, without a shilling, were about to become residents of one of the finest houses in southwest London. "We're spoilt bairns of the Almighty," Oswald said as they locked the door behind them.

Within a few weeks gifts of generous League members provided the initial complement of beds, linens, chairs, and tables for the house, plus an all-important blackboard for the lecture hall. A married couple was hired to cook and keep house, and the college announced its opening ceremonies for January 12, 1911.

Two days before Oswald and Biddy moved in, the first resident student arrived. After dinner at Mr. and Mrs. Hooker's home, the young man accompanied Chambers and Howard Hooker to a meeting at Speke Hall. Mary Hooker walked across to the college and made the student's bed, feeling this was a historic moment in the history of the Bible Training College. Perhaps it was too much attention or the thought of being a one-man student body in a new college with no track record and no stated curriculum that changed his mind. The young man departed sometime during the night, leaving a note saying he had decided the college was not the place for him after all. No one could accuse the B.T.C. of getting off to a roaring start.

A few days later, Violet Richardson arrived to become a full-time student. Unlike the young man who preceded her, she stayed, and for several weeks she remained the only resident enrollee. Meals shared with Oswald and Biddy at a tiny square table set in the middle of the huge dining room might have been awkward, but instead the Chambers' warmth chased the uncertainty and chill from the huge, empty house.

Undeterred by this sputtering start, Chambers plunged energetically into his duties as principal. His goal was to make the training classes available to a broad spectrum of people, from full-time resident students to those who could attend only one lecture each week. The curriculum for the first term was built around two core classes: Biblical Psychology: The Bible description and explanation of ourselves, as we are, and as we ought to be, and can be; and Biblical Ethics: The Moral Life—the rightness or wrongness of human nature in every practical relationship judged by the moral standards of the Bible.

Chambers' schedule for the first six months was staggering. From January to June, he taught the Biblical Psychology course in three different London locations outside the college. The correspondence course continued, and he had agreed to take as many as six hundred students—twice the number of the previous term. His articles appeared regularly in *Tongues of Fire* and in *God's Revivalist* in America. Mercifully, his speaking commitments for the League in Britain had been somewhat curtailed.

In June he sent a letter of greeting through the pages of *God's Revivalist*, expressing regret that he and Biddy couldn't attend the camp meeting at God's Bible School: "This year God's will keeps my wife and myself from America, and with a glad alacrity we 'hold on with a steady pace' in the dear Homeland.

"Will you praise God for His marvellous undertaking for this Bible Training College, in the mightiest metropolis of the world, and pray that it may become world wide in its usefulness to God and His saints. Next year, God willing, I hope to see you face to face and talk with you again from His marvellous Book of books."

His request for their prayers augmented his own daily petition: "Send us more students, O Lord, until this place is filled with men and women through whom Thou canst glorify Thyself throughout the world."

Each term, as the number of students grew, Chambers expanded the curriculum, adding classes in The Gospels, Biblical Theology, Exegesis, and Exposition. Biddy taught Bible Memorization, Mrs. Hooker offered Bible Survey, and local ministers addressed a class for Sunday School teachers. As favorable word of the school spread, attendance grew steadily. A year after it opened, the college reached its capacity of twenty-five resident students. Day students and visitors were always welcome as well.

One of Oswald's basic life-principles—"Give to everyone who asks"—spawned a unique practice at the College. No one was ever turned away from the door and whatever the person asked for, whether money, a winter overcoat, or a meal, was given. Savvy London residents were appalled by Chambers' seeming lack of discernment in a city known for its network of beggars who quickly told each other the location of "easy marks." People were amazed that the College was not besieged by hoards of vagrants seeking handouts. "My responsibility is to give," Oswald explained. "God will look after who asks."

Most people who sought help weren't looking for money. One winter night, a student answered the front bell to find a young black man shivering against the cold. "Is this the house of Brother Chambers?" the stranger asked. "Reverend Standley at God's Bible School in Cincinnati gave me this address."

Brother Petros was traveling from America back to his homeland in Africa. Chambers and the students eagerly welcomed him and during his brief stay they listened raptly to stories of his Zulu childhood, his capture by Arab slave traders, and eventual escape. A missionary befriended him, led him to faith in Christ, and fueled his desire to take the gospel to his own people. Labor in the diamond mines gave Petros enough money for passage to America where he worked his way through God's Bible School. As the African man talked, Oswald's eyes could not avoid his branded flesh and the marks of the slavers' hooks, still inflamed after eight years.

On another occasion, Oswald and Biddy received two hours' notice that a missionary couple and their five children had just arrived from the Gold Coast of Africa and needed a place to stay for a week. Biddy immediately went into action to prepare for their arrival. She asked four students to vacate their room while some of the men brought in additional beds and furniture to accommodate the family of seven.

"They're on their way home to America for their first furlough," she told them. "Four of their children have never been out of the bush." Almost instinctively, Biddy asked one of the women to contact Mrs. Hooker about getting some clothing for the family. "Not missionary barrel castoffs," she told her quietly. "Something new they can keep wearing when they get to America."

And of course she knew that the children would be pleased to find something special. From her own purse she drew enough money to send two more students out to buy some small dolls and toy airplanes. Biddy passed through the kitchen to tell the cook of the new arrivals, pausing to taste the soup and pronounce it, "Wonderful!"

When the weary family arrived at the college, they found comfortable accommodations and a joyful welcome. The awed children frolicked through the house and shouted over their toys. Biddy, with the appearance of nothing else to do, served tea and listened to the missionaries' story of their voyage to England.

Late that night, when the visiting family and the students were asleep, Biddy brought the daily ledger book up to date and typed three letters of response to prospective students. This day, so full and at times frantic, had been typical of her work as Lady Superintendent of the College. She regarded this house as a loving gift from God, the students as her family, and every guest as a messenger of the Almighty.

The B.T.C. was a haven for anyone in need. One student observed, "The College kept open house for the broken, the bruised, the unfortunate, for the old, the forlorn, and the weary."

Student fees paid only a portion of the College costs and the difference was met from private donors through the League of Prayer. There was never an endowment, and never more money on hand to meet the needs beyond a week ahead. In spite of that, Chambers maintained a carefree attitude of faith and often paid for needed supplies from his own pocket. The house existed in a spirit of freedom and informality where every one came and went with perfect liberty.

At the first anniversary celebration, the noted London pastor, Dr. G. Campbell Morgan, delivered the keynote address and made special reference to the uniqueness of Chambers' courses in Biblical Psychology and Biblical Ethics. Morgan's presence was a great boost in morale to League members and a strong endorsement for the B.T.C.

Chambers saw the College in two ways. To make the school known and interest new students, the doors were flung wide to anyone. League members and friends were encouraged to take a class or simply attend lectures when they could and bring a guest. This was the broad outreach and equipping ministry of the school.

His second vision was the long-term training and personal investment in resident students who could take six months, a year, or even two years for intensive study and preparation. Some were candidates with missionary societies, while others were seeking God's will concerning their life-work. Resident students constituted a unique group, and Chambers prayed for them and worked toward building them into a community.

He had only one "rule" of conduct, which each student received on a printed card:

NOTICE
"All service ranks the same with God."
You are requested to kindly do your
part in keeping this room tidy.
If you do not, someone else will have to.

Visitors were welcome in all his classes except two. One of these was on sermon preparation and delivery. On the dreaded days when each man or woman stood to preach, Chambers made sure everyone was on an equal footing. Because every student's turn was coming, all were sympathetic listeners. It was Oswald's responsibility to be an honest but kind critic.

The other "student only" meeting was the weekly devotional hour. During these gatherings Oswald spoke from his heart about God's purpose and work in their lives. Why were they here? What was God doing? How should they react to difficult circumstances and heartache? So many times his keen insight and spiritual perception prompted a message that left students wondering, "How did he know exactly what I needed to hear today?"

Oswald unceasingly pressed the issue of personal fellowship with Christ:

"The great enemy to the Lord Jesus Christ in the present day is the conception of practical work that has not come from the New Testament, but from the systems of the world in which endless energy and activities are insisted upon, but no private life with God.

"It is not its practical activities that are the strength of this Bible Training College, its whole strength lies in the fact that here you are put into soak before God. You have no idea of where God is going to engineer your circumstances, no knowledge of what strain is going to be put on you either at home or abroad, and if you waste your time in overactive energies instead of getting into soak on the great fundamental truths of God's Redemption, you will snap when the strain comes; but if this time of soaking before God is being spent in getting rooted and grounded in God on the unpractical line, you will remain true to Him whatever happens."

Every observant student could see the truth of those words in Chambers' life. In the closely-knit community of the college where classes, meals, and conversation were shared each day, a person might pretend for a while, but not for long. There was no discrepancy between Oswald's walk with God and his talk, and in the final analysis, that was the power of his influence.

However, not everyone agreed with him. Often his drastic statements about some aspect of the Christian life brought forth a chorus of objections. During meals, students would bombard Chambers with questions about a point of his that had snipped the ribbons of their neatly tied theological ideas. Oswald never argued and never tried to force his viewpoint on the questioners. "Just leave it for now," he would say. "Brood on it and it will come to you later."

Chambers' study door was never closed to a student who wanted to talk about personal concerns. One student summed up his relationship to the principal by saying, "There was no such thing as compromise with him, yet he was never bitter. Nothing small or petty had any place in his make-up. He was a big man in every way, mentally and spiritually, and he never wore 'blinkers' [blinders]. Sham and make-believe could not live with him, but to those in need he was a tower of strength. Nothing was ever a trouble, and I do not know of anyone ever calling on him for help in vain."

Chambers possessed a rare capacity to trust matters to God in prayer and wait for Him to move. When one student informed Chambers that the couple hired to cook and clean were stealing supplies, he decided not to confront them, but to ask God to convict them.

The loss of food and linens continued for several weeks until one day the man came to Chambers, deeply guilty and sorrowful, to confess his thefts. "I've known about it all along," Oswald told him, "but we wanted to wait until God's Spirit spoke to you." The man was astounded, and both he and his wife came to a personal faith in Jesus Christ.

In another case, Chambers might have acted differently. He often said, "You cannot tie God down to a particular line. Get to know how God deals with you and how he deals with others through you in the most practical way."

The steady growth of the Bible Training College from 1911 to 1914 created a "family" of students, many of whom became closely tied to Oswald and Biddy.

Eva Spink, daughter of a prosperous jeweler, came to the college in 1913 with a desire to serve God, but with little idea of what to do or where to go. Her father had recently stopped funding her education in music, and now she faced an uncertain future. "Sphinx" as Chambers nicknamed her, was twenty-two years old, spirited, fiercely loyal to people she loved, and a bit of a flirt.

Gladys Ingram, with dark hair and attractive features, came to prepare for missionary service. During her first meal she glanced around the long dining room table and thought, *This must be the quaintest collection of people in any training school—men and women of all ages, classes, and occupations*. Chambers soon christened her "Gladiolus," and through his teaching she came to know Christ personally, where she had only known *about* Him before.

Jimmy Hanson met Chambers in 1906 when he and Juji Nakada held League meetings in the village of Denby Dale. Oswald figured prominently in Hanson's early spiritual development before Hanson came to the B.T.C. in 1913. Short and stocky, with a distinctive Yorkshire accent, Hanson was a dynamo. Jimmy and fellow student Philip Hancock both sensed God's call to foreign missions.

Hancock's mission board sent him to the college, but he came with great reluctance. He knew nothing of the League of Prayer, and the word *Pentecostal* in the name made him wonder what he might find in the way of theology and behavior. His first meeting with Chambers dispelled all his fears.

Gertrude Ballinger, or "Bill" as Chambers called her, came to the B.T.C. for a few weeks of "spiritual refreshment" and stayed on to prepare for Christian service. Like many of the women students, she found a true friend in Biddy Chambers and a wise counselor in Oswald. Philip Hancock had set aside hopes of marriage until after his first term overseas, but he couldn't keep Gertrude Ballinger out of his mind or his prayers. While his head told him to forget about her and pursue his call to the mission field, his heart still beat faster whenever she sat nearby in the lecture hall or at a meal. He found great encouragement and solace in Oswald's oft-repeated phrase: "Let God engineer."

Mary Riley first encountered Chambers at Speke Hall. She entered the college with the dual role of student and cook. Soon she also assumed responsibility for the "domestic students" who earned their way by helping with the kitchen and household duties.

Katherine Ashe, the outspoken Irish lady, renewed her acquaintance with Chambers during his September 1911 mission in Belfast. Still as aristocratic and imposing as the first time they met three years before, she was intrigued by the idea of the B.T.C. A few months later she arrived in London as a student and stayed on to teach Christian Sociology.

For a time, Oswald and Biddy took League meetings together around the country between school terms. He loved to hear her speak, especially from the Psalms, and when his turn came, she took out her notebook and faithfully recorded all he said.

On May 24, 1913, the most beloved member of the B.T.C. staff arrived. Kathleen Chambers was born at the college and immediately began her reign as queen over all. The women were excited, the men were intrigued, and Oswald was ecstatic. His previous love for children offered no preparation for the feelings he had for this small person who was a miraculous combination of himself and the woman he loved. A difficult delivery left Biddy exhausted, but joyful in this new life.

Kathleen became a fixture at meals, lectures, and informal social gatherings. Every smile or burp brought a chorus of approval from the doting students. When she cried at the top of her lungs Oswald borrowed a line from Mrs. Reader Harris, saying, "And now *my* daughter will sing."

Oswald and Biddy talked of returning to America, but Kathleen's birth and the growing demands of the college and the League left these hopes unrealized. His summer camp meetings now consisted only of speaking at the League of Prayer's annual week in Perth every August. On the spacious South Inch where he had played as a boy, Oswald now mounted a platform in a huge tent to urge his countrymen to give up their right to themselves to God and find satisfaction in His will.

Circumstantially, Oswald's life was more settled and predictable than it had ever been. He had a permanent job, a home, a wife, and a child. His Atlantic crossings and other travels around the world had given way to a life ordered by class schedules and school terms. Yet inwardly he was as freewheeling and far-ranging as ever.

His letters to Biddy during days away from London reveal the set of his heart:

August 11, 1912:

> *I more and more realize that I am good for nothing saving as I can preach Him. Let us keep true to Him in our life. I have no sense of loyalty to anything but Jesus Christ.*

March 21, 1913:

> *I never see my way. I know God who guides so I fear nothing. I have never far-seeing plans, only confident trust.*
>
> *My mind still grows impatient at much of the success lusting desire of Christian workers. How many patrons had Jeremiah or the apostles! Alone for God is the greater calling of a man.*

The college provided a wonderful atmosphere for students but presented a challenge for Oswald and Biddy, especially with their daughter.

September 28, 1913:

> *Remember, Kathleen is God's gift to us, not someone we give to God. Do not allow the influence of the many loving women around you to turn your heart away from God's supreme*

> *call of us both with Kathleen to His service. As we strenuously keep Him first, He will bless us.*
>
> *I am scared at the possibility of spiritual declension in any of us along the subtle line of 'right.' Beware lest the cares of other things, the absorption in duties, should come in. Remember, none of the women around you these days quite understand God's relationship to us.*

As a husband and father, Oswald now felt different about his times away from the college. From the Perth Camp Meeting, he wrote Biddy in July, 1914:

> *Give my love to my precious little baby. I can scarcely bear to ask of her, she is so precious to my mind.*
>
> *I experience a great loneliness and a need of you. Not a grievous loneliness but a real loneliness. How few there are [with whom] there is any real comradeship since sudden ungenerous judgments of others seem to mar the minds of some of God's ripest saints. I am quite unincorporated into anyone or anything but you and my Lord Jesus Christ. Keep praying for me.*

Heavy rains forced the final meeting of the Perth Camp into the City Hall on August 2. Chambers preached from John 21:22 on the words "Follow *thou* me." He stressed the importance of obedience to God instead of constantly inquiring about the way we knew perfectly well. "What we need," he concluded, "is to begin to walk in the way we already know."

During the next two days and nights, an extraordinary amount of railway traffic rolled through Perth. Many trains carried only military men and equipment. People commented on it and guessed it had something to do with recent events in Europe. On the morning of August 5, the headlines shouted the awful truth, "BRITAIN AT WAR."

16
LAUNCHING ALL ON HIM

(1914–1915)

The war caught most Britons by surprise. Ominous clouds had gathered quickly over Europe after the assassination of Archduke Francis Ferdinand on June 28, but the trouble seemed far away. "If Austria-Hungary and Serbia have a scrap over it," Britons said, "that doesn't concern us." After all, the political weather in Europe was always stormy, and the next-door threat of civil war and secession in Ireland seemed a greater danger than the international jousting taking place across the English Channel. Few people were aware of the complex alliances and secret diplomacy that finally drew Britain into the war.

Suddenly, Oswald, Biddy, and the Bible Training College students were citizens of a country mobilizing for all-out war. Recruiting posters appeared everywhere, street meetings inspired patriotic response, and a month after Britain's declaration of war, men were joining the armed forces at the rate of thirty thousand a day. Many thought the war would end quickly and they would be home victorious by Christmas.

"Join now or miss out," many young men told themselves and their friends. Older veterans had seen war fever before and many of them sensed the prolonged agony to come. Without knowing it, the people of Britain were swept into the first modern military conflict to involve an entire civilian population.

In a matter of weeks, life in Britain began to turn upside down. People were called upon to sell their farm horses and civilian automobiles to the government. Even the bright red double decker buses from the streets of London were shipped across the Channel where they carried British troops to the front lines of battle. In addition, paper scrip replaced gold coinage, women entered the work force in munitions factories, transportation, and other jobs previously restricted to men, and houses along every street proudly displayed posters bearing a large red circle and the words, "Not At Home, A Man From This House Now Serving In His Majesty's Forces." Underneath the excitement and patriotic fervor, however, lay a pervading sense of uncertainty and fear.

In the September 1914 issue of *Tongues of Fire*, Chambers addressed the perplexities felt by many: "This question is on the lips of people today: Is war of the devil or of God? It is of neither. It is of man, though God and the devil are both behind it. War is a conflict of wills either in individuals or in nations, and just now there is a terrific conflict of wills in nations.

"Our Lord insists on the inevitability of peril. Right through His talks with His disciples, without panic and without passion and without fear He says, You must lay your account with this sort of thing, with war, with spite, with hatred, with jealousy, with despisings, with banishment and with death. Now remember I have told you these things that when they happen you may not be scared.

"We are not only hearing of wars and commotions, they are here right enough. It is not imagination, it is not newspaper reports, the thing is here at our doors, there is no getting away from it. War, such as the history of the world has never known, has now begun.

"Jesus Christ did not say: You will understand why the war has come—but: Do not be scared, do not be put in a panic.

"There is one thing worse than war, and that is sin. We get tremendously scared when our social order is broken up, and well we may. We get terrorized by hundreds of men being killed, but we forget there is something worse—sinful dastardly lives being lived day by day, year in and year out in our villages and towns . . . these are the things that produce pain in the heart of God, not the wars and the devastation that so upset us.

"Are the terrors that are abroad producing panic? You never saw anybody in a panic who did not grab for themselves whether it was sugar or butter or nations. Jesus would never allow His disciples to be in a panic. The one great crime on the part of a disciple, according to Jesus Christ, is worry. Whenever we begin to calculate without God we commit sin."

Daily life at the College continued to be bathed in prayer, but with new concerns. A half hour of intercession for the needs of the nation and men in battle now preceded the usual daily morning prayers together before breakfast. Oswald, always the first one there, played a favorite hymn of praise on the small organ as all the resident students gathered in the Lecture Hall to pray. Every Tuesday afternoon, the College met as a whole to praise God for His goodness and bring their needs before Him. During this time, the name of every resident student, past and present, was read aloud. On Friday evenings, the students now in missionary service were especially remembered in prayer.

Oswald's college report for 1914 noted with thanksgiving that among the former students, nine were serving as missionaries and two were in military service at the Front; six were definitely accepted missionary candidates and four had volunteered for the foreign field. He emphasized, however, that these opportunities for service were God's appointments, not his. "We undertake to find no sphere of labour for our students," he said. "Our duty is to see that this house maintains the honour of God and that each student is put into a right spiritual atmosphere. His clearly discerned will always follows."

Chambers believed this, but he was no stranger to the struggle of trying to gain a clear understanding of God's leading. It was not a matter of worry, but of sifting through competing calls to duty and discerning which one truly had come from God.

On December 31, 1914, Oswald and Biddy observed their usual custom of seeking God together for the New Year. They wrestled with the many possibilities. Should they stay at the college to continue the work of which he had dreamed for so long? If Oswald left, who would carry it on? What was his responsibility to the League of Prayer?

What responsibility did he have to his country? Should he volunteer for military service? The call was out for men from nineteen to forty. In a few months he would be forty-one. And what about Biddy and Kathleen? Would it be right to go away and leave them in God's keeping? How could he best love and care for them?

From his prayer journal: "Lord, I praise Thee for this place I am in; but the wonder has begun to stir in me—is this Thy place for me? Hold me steady doing Thy will. It may be only restlessness; if so, calm me to strength that I sin not against Thee by doubting."

The new year crept into a somber Britain. Too many men were dying in France for the holidays to ring with laughter and toasts for a happy 1915. As the church bells rang at midnight, Oswald and Biddy rose from their knees. God would lead them on His path, whatever it was, and it would be right. More than right, it would be filled with His joy and blessing. In the meantime, their task was to trust God and do the next thing.

At the college, Kathleen continued along her carefree way, wondering why so many grownups seemed to be sad. She provided regular comic relief so needed as students read grim newspaper headlines and pondered an uncertain future. When a meeting dragged on too long to suit her, she often gave her father's characteristic call to stand and be dismissed: From the back of the lecture hall, her tiny voice could be heard, saying "Shall we 'wise'?"

During the 1915 term, Chambers brought several guest lecturers to his Friday evening class on "Missionary Matters." Among them was the already legendary C. T. Studd, one of England's finest cricketers at Cambridge University and a noted pioneer missionary. Chambers had been a boy of ten when Studd first sailed for China to serve with Hudson Taylor. When Studd inherited a fortune from his father's estate, he gave it all away, choosing to trust God for his own needs. After years in China and India, Studd had gone to Africa in 1911. He was back in England, temporarily, until he could return to the Dark Continent. Two students, Jimmy Hanson and Philip Hancock, hoped to leave in a few months to serve with Studd's Heart of Africa Mission.

C. T. Studd sounded the call for Christians to enter the spiritual battle for the souls of men and women with the same courage being displayed on the battlefields of the Great War. "This can only be accomplished," he said, "by a red-hot, unconventional, unfettered Holy Ghost religion, where neither Church nor State, neither man nor traditions are worshipped or preached, but only Christ and Him crucified."

The war caused many Christians to focus on Bible prophecy and a preoccupation with the end times. Many felt that God's judgment had finally fallen on the godless nations of the world, and Britain was included.

Chambers, like Studd, viewed the grim realities of 1915 in a different way than the fearful or the doomsayers. Oswald's articles in *Tongues of Fire* show his growing concern to live aggressively for Christ during difficult days:

January 1915: "This war, while for a time it has made men in pain say petulant and unbelieving things about the creeds that are right in theory but utterly futile in practice, has at the same time prepared their hearts for the universality of the exclusive way of Christ. If He is the only way to the Father, it is a way that is open to any and every man, the way that knows neither Jew nor Greek, neither barbarian, Scythian, bond nor free, knows neither male nor female, nationality nor civilization. It is this glorious revelation which it is the duty and the privilege and the honour of us who are Christ's to proclaim with lip and life in impassioned zeal and earnestness in the closing phases of the dispensation in which we live."

March 1915: "A parenthesis is a sentence inserted into an otherwise grammatically complete sentence, and if you want to understand the author, pay particular attention to the parenthesis. God puts a parenthesis in the middle flow of our life, the life goes on before and after, but if you want to understand the life, read the parenthesis, if you can."

April 1915: "To the saints who know the end of things, it is not a time of separate aloneness, but of sanctified abandonment to God for intercession. Let us beware then of excessive brooding on our own personal whiteness, or as special coteries [cliques] regarding the Second Coming. Let us fling ourselves into abandonment on Him and intercede on behalf of the country we belong to that she may prove God's servant as well as God's instrument. Let us pray lest men look merely for peace instead of to and for God."

Oswald's own intercession led him to a momentous choice: "Lord, I have decided before Thee to offer for work with the Forces; undertake and guide me in each particular. I know Thou wilt, but I am fearful of my own precipitate judgment."

Even after the decision, his prayer journal chronicled an inner struggle filled with an uncharacteristic anxiety:

"How unrelieved my mind has been about the future, I praise Thee that this is not always so, or scarcely ever so. How there is nothing to hold to but just Thyself! Keep me from flagging and slacking.

"My mind is still vague regarding the way I am to take, Lord; so much has gone beyond my own discernment in this decision. It is not that I doubt Thee, but all is so completely shrouded.

"Lord, a vague desolation seems around my life, it is nebulous, I cannot define it. I have no misgiving over my decision for I have done what Thou didst indicate I should do, but still the sense of uncertainty remains. Touch this nebulous nimbus and turn it into a firmament of ordered beauty and form."

In a letter to his parents, he presented a more confident exterior:

B.T.C., May 24, 1915

My dear Mother and Father,

Florence will have told you of my decision to offer for the front as a chaplain, for 'first aid' spiritually. I wanted you to know as soon as I did myself. Nothing is arranged or even clear by any means yet, nothing but my decision before the Lord. I shall do my human best naturally, but as in many times in the past, I shall find God opening up the way. My mind is clear regarding God's call, the rest will 'fall out' or 'in' as He ordains.

Since the war began it has been a pressure on me all but unendurable to be here, but I know God well enough not to confound my own natural desires and impulses for His will or ordering.

At New Year time as Biddy and I waited before God, I said to her, 'Just look at my verse—'I am ready to be offered,' 2 Tim. 4:6, and we agreed before God that it was all right as He ordained. Since then the growing sense of God's pressure has been added until I became certain that it was time to decide, so I did, and told all whose business it was to know, and now I leave it. You see, in this way the idea sinks into people's minds like a seed thought, and they slowly grow used to it, so that there is no farewell meeting or anything like that, but just a simple slipping into the next thing almost unobservedly.

Biddy is just keen on the thing, and will never do anything but back me up, no matter what it costs her. Kathleen, what about her? Is it likely we would forget her or that He would? I am not several kinds of fools in one, I am only one kind of fool—the kind that believes and obeys God.

I got a grand word to my own soul on Sunday morning, Luke 10:1, 'Sent . . . before His face into every city and place, whither He Himself would come,' and again this morning with a quiet intimation unsought for by me, these words came to my remembrance: 'Nothing shall by any means hurt you,' Luke 10:19.

Now, Mother, just you take up your abode in John 14:1, and see Him work. These four years at the B.T.C. have been unique and blessed, and they terminate in a quiet, unobtrusive, splendid and final way. You will pray I know. I have a strong impression that the Y.M.C.A. Hut will be the plan adopted, but I do not know. However, He knows and I know He knows, and I know that I'll never think of anything He will forget, so I just go steadily on as I have always done, and He will engineer the circumstances.

Ever your loving son, Oswald

A few days later, his answer came and was recorded in his prayer journal:

"Lord, yesterday the Y.M.C.A. accepted me for their work in the Desert Camps in Egypt, and Thy word came this morning with great emphasis—'Sent before His face into every city and place whither He himself was about to come.'

"Lord, how I praise Thee for this College, it has been four years of unique loveliness, and now I give it up because I believe I do so in answer to Thy call."

The war had brought sweeping changes to every phase of life in Britain, and there was no end in sight. The Bible Training College would close its doors at the end of the term on July 14, 1915. For each one present it marked the end of an era, not just for themselves but for the League of Prayer, and for the nation. Everywhere people prepared for the inevitable disruptions ahead.

During the first week of June, the death of Duncan MacGregor took Chambers to Dunoon for the funeral of his long-time friend and mentor. The college at Kirn looked exceptionally beautiful with the flowering shrubs and trees in full blossom. As Chambers took his place in the lecture room for the service, a wave of emotion swept over him. It didn't seem possible that eighteen years had gone by since he first shook hands with MacGregor and knew he had found a unique man of God. On this morning in 1915, with his heart full of praise to God as well as the pain of loss, Oswald felt like his father had died.

He left quickly after the burial, promising Mrs. MacGregor he would return for a longer visit soon. Four weeks remained in the spring term at the B.T.C. in London, and he wanted to spend as much time with the students as he could. Crossing the Firth of Clyde as he had done hundreds of times before, he watched the familiar outline of the pier fade away and recalled a favorite line of poetry: "Our own are our own forever; God taketh not back His gift." He owed so much to "grand old Mac." He would miss him. How glad he would be to see him again in heaven.

A month later, with the emotions of life and death still close to the surface, Chambers gave a final talk to the B.T.C. students, concluding with these words of hope: "The saint who enters into the rest of God the Father and God the Son is, in the actual crisis of present conditions, under the control and inspiration of the Holy Spirit. So the words of Our Lord come to us with all the power of God—'Let not your heart be troubled: ye believe in God, *believe also in Me.*' "

Then he offered a final prayer: "We thank Thee that there is no Good-bye. We ask Thee that Thy Crown and Seal may be upon us every one until we meet Thee face to face. Amen."

Each person cherished a special memory of the days in the College. For some, it was the teaching of Oswald Chambers, but for most, it was the man.

Howgate Greenwood remembered the time Chambers approached him and said, "I believe you are rather hard up these days. I have just received a gift from a friend for God's work, and it is for you." With that, he handed the astonished Greenwood two pounds. How had he known?

Another student recalled walking with Chambers through a little country village when "he just very naturally stopped and prayed, asking for God's blessing on the village . . . so like what our Lord would have done when He was on earth."

The work of the B. T. C., although a small entity in London, could now be seen in its broader sphere of influence. During its four years of existence, 106 resident students studied, prayed, and lived under the powerful influence of Oswald and Biddy's example. By July 1915, forty of them were serving as missionaries, sixteen at home and twenty-four abroad.

From 1911 to 1915, the day students who attended lectures, wrote essays, and benefited from Oswald's instruction numbered more than 3,000. Hundreds of others had come to hear a single talk or a series without being enrolled.

The Bible Correspondence Course, begun a year before the College opened its doors, still provided systematic study for a far-flung and diverse student body of teachers, ministers, mothers, and working people. Oswald's sister Gertrude served as secretary, registrar, and one-woman post office for the 1,909 people enrolled. Every three weeks, she sent hundreds of lessons to students and received their papers, which Oswald personally read and marked. His comments usually consisted of two or three typed sentences of evaluation and a word of encouragement signed by his stamped signature in red ink.

An article in the August *Tongues of Fire* informed League members that the present phase of the Bible Training College was closed, and that a new expeditionary force phase was beginning.

"The great war and the desperate spiritual need of our soldiers have been keenly present with us night and day since the war began," Oswald wrote. "Also, the pressure of God's hand became so unmistakable as expressed by Isaiah, 'The Lord talked to me with a strong hand,' that after much prayer and waiting on God we made not only our requests, but our desires known with the result that Mrs. Chambers and myself, with little Kathleen, have been accepted for Egypt and the Dardanelles in the army camps, and we go out in October.

"We all realise at the College that this is the call of God, but we also realise that it is but an important episode, and 'if the Lord tarry' till the present war is over we expect to be again in this country for yet another phase of the Bible Training College.

"The B.T.C. in its present phase concludes as the College began, under the inspiration of God. We sincerely hope and pray that all friends will rally to the assistance of the president of the college, Mrs. Reader Harris, in keeping this place at least as a Bible Training Home during the war. Such places will be greatly needed as centres of real spiritual staying power."

A few months before, Chambers had struggled with how to fulfill his responsibilities to family, college, and country. Now God had answered his prayers in a way that blended all three in a new venture. Since much of Egypt was not technically a combat zone like the Western Front in France, the Y.M.C.A. agreed to his request that Biddy and Kathleen accompany him. Jimmy Hanson and Philip Hancock had put their missionary service on hold and had also been accepted for service with the Y.M.C.A. in Egypt. Katherine Ashe believed the military authorities would soon yield to her insistent demands that she be allowed to go, too. Chambers, as always, led by example, and these members of what he called "the B.T.C. Expeditionary Force" enlisted enthusiastically, hearing his call from God as their own.

Before the flurry of activity that would surround their departure, Oswald took his family and a contingent of friends to his beloved Yorkshire Dales. August brought much-needed days of rest in the picturesque village of Askrigg for the Chambers family and the many students who joined them. From their room above Jim Skidmore's antique shop, Biddy looked across the road at the historic parish church, built in the fifteenth century and roofed with lead from local mines. Its five-hundred-year-old name, St. Oswald's, was always a point of humor with their friends. Beyond the church the quiet road wound down a hill and a footpath led to the River Ure.

Chambers treasured the lush green hills of Wensleydale, where summer haying was done with hand scythes and pitchforks. Horse drawn sledges carried the rich crop from fields to barns. The prevailing silence of the dales ebbed and flowed with the noise of the wind and the bleating of sheep. He loved to walk the high moors where he could tramp for hours without seeing another person. Five miles above the gray stone buildings of Askrigg, he felt a million miles away from everything.

With Kathleen in a homemade canvas backpack, Oswald led daily hikes, picnics, and fishing expeditions into the countryside he called "my Heavenly Father's Dining Room." After building a fire and boiling the potatoes, without which no picnic was considered complete, Chambers led a prayer of thanksgiving for all God's gifts, especially "the leagues of pure air."

Sometimes, after the meal, he would still the conversation with a wave of his hand and point out the haunting songs of the summer birds—the "go-back, go-back" of the grouse, the cry of the curlew, and the single plaintive note of the golden plover. While others napped or searched for violets and wild orchids, Oswald donned his favorite wool hat and fished the clear, rushing waters for trout.

Each evening, the Chambers' cottage was open for Bible study and a time of prayer, while Sundays took him to the small churches of neighboring villages to preach.

From his prayer journal: "O, Lord, for the days of this holiday I praise and thank Thee—for the majesty of this crowded isolation, the leagues of moor, the radiant air, the tonic of naturalness, and the sweet tonic of spiritual instruction as I lie fallow to thy grace."

By September the holiday was over, the students were gone, and he was at work among the soldiers in the camps around Wensleydale. Too soon, the time of final preparations arrived. Late in the month, he took a last long walk in the hills he loved so well, and savored the fragrance of new mown hay. In a few weeks, he would exchange these green fields for a land of burning sand.

Askrigg, York, Sept. 25, 1915

My dear Mother,

I have my sailing orders for October 9th. I go first to prepare the way for Biddy and the students, this seems to me to be best anyway. It has been quite wonderful to me lately to recall the various texts of Scripture that have come to me peculiarly and in an intimate spiritual sense.

The very first of all the prominent ones was the one given me by Mrs. John Skidmore many years ago before I first went abroad. Isaiah 45:13, 'I have raised him up in righteousness, and I will direct all his ways: he shall build my city, and he shall let go my captives, not for price nor reward, saith the Lord of hosts.'

When the word came, 'Go ye into all the world,' I went, and truly He made 'all my ways' for they seemed certainly not mine or common sense.

I had thought to settle in Dunoon College, in Japan, in America, and in the B.T.C., but His way for me is 'the world.' Surely He hath made 'all my ways' and it has not been for 'price or reward,' saving that of building His city and setting His exiles free. And God has united Biddy with me in all these 'ways.'

Ever your loving son, Oswald

Finally, the day came for him to sail. He and Biddy said all their good-byes, shed all their tears, and prayed that God would have His way in their lives. He left her at the college and boarded a tram for the station. A few hours later, Biddy answered a knock at the door and found Oswald, smiling broadly. The sailing had been delayed for twenty-four hours.

The next day, with the pain of parting behind them, they bid each other a hopeful farewell, and this time, he was gone. They hoped to be reunited in a few weeks in Egypt, but it was wartime and circumstances often changed overnight. In typical fashion, he left behind a letter for Biddy:

> *You are bearing these days well. When you married me, I had no prospects, but just Him, and you had just me, and you loved me with a love that has been a shield and joy and a rampart of strength to me. Now God has given us our darling Kathleen and we go forth again.*
>
> *You have loved this place. It has been Bethel to you, a great joyous place and God's benediction . . . I praise God that His comforts delight your soul.*
>
> *I go forth without College and without students and without a calling, just to speak and be for Him, and you will go with me. Our years together have been radiantly blessed and now the few weeks apart will be radiant with His perfections. We will not sin against the disposition of the Holy Ghost by being even sad. God made the human heart and he knows it.*
>
> *How immensely glad I am that we are all so humanly His. I am actually hilarious now as I think of going. This is all by God's good and mighty grace. God has been unutterably good to me.*

Once again, Chambers was where he loved to be, on the sea, but this time it was different. German submarines lurked everywhere along the route from England to Egypt, and everything in their periscopes, including passenger liners, was a target. During the first half of 1915, the U-boats had sent thousands of tons of Allied shipping to the bottom of the ocean.

The *SS City of Paris,* normally a comfortable steamer, was so crowded with a wartime mixture of humanity that Chambers could scarcely find a place to be alone and pray. After a few frustrating days, he found the solution by crawling into a lifeboat. There he could spend an early morning hour with God, alone and uninterrupted.

Like many people of the time, he recorded each day in diary-letters and sent them to Biddy. These writings, combined with extracts of letters to friends, paint a picture of his days at sea:

October 12:

Do you know I have scarcely missed you, so completely and entirely have you been with me. The sense of God's presence is real and beautiful. The sense also is so entire that my going is of Him and His ways that although I cannot begin to discern what I am to do out in Egypt, I am not even concerned.

It was something of the nature of an earthquake to root up from London and the B.T.C., but where He leads we follow, and a joy it is, too. It is a great thing to be detached enough from possessions so as not to be held by them, because when called to uproot it is done with little real trouble, and one realizes how gloriously possible it is, without being heartless, to obey His injunction, 'See that you be not troubled.'

In any untoward or new circumstances, the thing to do is to just trust in Him with all the heart, and not lean to one's own understanding, and 'hang in' until one gets actually used to the new surroundings.

October 13:

The sense is strong in me today of the unutterable goodness and wisdom of God, and to me who possesses neither goodness or wisdom, He simply gives His own. Truly His will is the gladdest, finest thing conceivable. I am to speak at the Sunday evening service. My two cabin friends have promised to 'back me up' in my preaching; that means they will be there in the true spirit as comrades, God bless them.

From a letter to Gladys Ingram (Gladiolus), a B.T.C. student to whom he and Biddy were very close.

October 17—near Gibraltar:

Thank you for your letters and telegram. I love you to love me. I should be scared if you 'liked' me. Love is of God—like is of human dangerous-nature full of possibilities but full of pitfalls. I am glad you love Biddy: when I think of her I can but look into the face of God and say in my soul God is Good. These days I do not miss her, she is never away from me.

I am glad God let you know us because there is so much of unfortunate marriage that such an one as ours must be a good thing for you to know.

Be as much as you can with Biddy. Help her on her coming. Now I am going to write no more. God bless you Gladiolus! What we are is of much more use to God and our fellows than what we do. 'Consider the lilies' said Jesus our Lord. That is, do not get the 'actuality' fever; I mean this satanic idea of doing something. Be something ever as you are. I send you again John 14!

On the same day he wrote to Biddy:

Take the sea and the air and the sun and the stars and moon, all these are and what a ministration they exert! So often we mar God's designed influence by our self-conscious efforts at being consistent and useful.

Diary, October 18: My service last evening was well attended, I spoke on Matthew 11:3, 'Am I mistaken after all?' I had His liberty, thank God; my table turned out loyally. My Scandinavian room-mate impressed me by his remarks in broken English when he came into the cabin last night. 'Ah, I see, your jokes and light-heartedness plough the land, then you put in the seed. I feel in my insides that that is right.'

October 19: It is wonderful that I am not homesick for the B.T.C. This is of God, for the B.T.C. was the Gate of Heaven to us, yet He so profoundly called us out, and has so profoundly undertaken that it is just the most natural thing not to be there.

October 21: It is of peculiar interest to find men discover me to be agreeable, men of the tough and worldly sort, too, rough old sinners and sporting youths, they all unbosom without varnish their tales of woe and happiness and sin and sorrow and larks. Ever since I learned not to teach any consciously as an aim, men seem to come in many ways to me.

Lying looking over the magnificent moonlit pathway across the sea, my mind settled in to gratitude to God that I am going out under no denominational call at all, but with free scope to follow Him undeterred. This may sound loose, but it does not mean looseness, but rather the most delightful and strenuous concentration on Him.

They are beginning to call the life on board dull. My word! dull! with books and sea and mind and prayer, dull! It is teeming with endless and joyous interest. The vast expanse of sea is just great.

October 24: I do thank God for this voyage. It has been most delightful, and this lifeboat has been a real Bethel to me. It has come to be known now as my lifeboat. it has been a wonderful rest and tonic in every way, and now I go to behold His wonderful undertakings in landing, and in Egypt, and in the camps. It is a great charm not to know, but just to see Him unfold His purposes.

October 25: Glorious words in Daily Light today. Praise God for a safe good voyage and abundant peace and blessing every hour on board.

On an October day, eight years before, he had steamed through the Suez Canal and out of Port Said bound for home on the last leg of his journey around the world. Now, in the providence of God and the chaos of war, he was back. With great anticipation, he left the ship in Alexandria and boarded a train for Cairo.

PART 5

"We are not called to be successful in accordance with ordinary standards, but in accordance with a corn of wheat falling into the ground and dying, becoming in that way what it never could be if it were to abide alone."

— He Shall Glorify Me

17
THE Y.M.C.A. IN EGYPT

(1915)

Cairo, Egypt—October 26, 1915

William Jessop, Y.M.C.A. director in Cairo, dabbed the perspiration off his forehead and continued his search through the stack of file folders on his heavily laden desk. "Committees, Communications, Casualties . . . ," he muttered. Each folder could keep him busy for a week.

"Dardanelles . . ." He paused, unable to pass it by without thinking of the thousands of men living under constant artillery and machine-gun fire on the Gallipoli Peninsula. For the past six months, Australian, New Zealand, and British soldiers had been engaged in a bloody but futile attempt to dislodge Turkish troops from the strategic promontory overlooking the narrow waterway known as the Dardanelles. A victory there would clear the way for an invasion of Constantinople, but thousands of Allied deaths had purchased only a stalemate.

In August, Jessop had taken a troop ship six hundred miles to Gallipoli and risked his life to organize Y.M.C.A help for the soldiers. At Cape Helles, the awful suction and shuddering concussion of incoming artillery shells initiated him to life at the front lines. At Suvla Bay, he ran through the constant hail of sniper's bullets and machine-gun fire to distribute chocolate and cigarettes to the men in the trenches. He promised them a Y.M.C.A. hut, even if they had to put it underground. When he returned to the safety of Cairo, they remained to fight and die.

"Dardanelles," Jessop mumbled to himself. He set the file aside, determined to spend at least some time on it that day.

A thin file labeled PERSONNEL yielded the paper he sought. "Here," he said finally, extracting the page headed, CHAMBERS,

OSWALD. He handed the sheet with its attached photograph to his assistant, Stanley Barling.

"Chambers is due to arrive from Alexandria this morning," Jessop said. "Could you meet him at the railway station?"

Barling studied the photo and glanced at the particulars on the Y.M.C.A. form. "41 years old. Six feet tall, brown hair, blue eyes. Principal of a Bible College in London. Married, one daughter, two-and-a-half years old. Permission granted for family to accompany him."

"Are his wife and daughter with him?" Barling asked.

"No, he's alone," said Jessop. "No money for their fares just yet."

Barling studied the photo. There was something unique about the face, especially the eyes. *A rather penetrating gaze,* he thought, *even at a studio camera.*

"Bring him back here," Jessop said. "We'll show him around Cairo a bit and give him a day to get his feet on the ground. I think I'll ask him to take the work at Zeitoun."

Barling left the Y.M.C.A. headquarters and plunged into the sea of humanity outside. He walked in the street because there was no room on the sidewalk. On the street donkey carts vied for space with horse-drawn wagons, camels, and British motor ambulances. A young Egyptian boy balancing dozens of thin, round loaves of bread on a board atop his head weaved effortlessly through the same traffic that kept Barling in a halting gait of stops and starts.

"Oops, sorry," Barling mumbled after bumping into an old man who answered back politely in Arabic.

During his ten minute walk to the station, Barling passed an incredible diversity of people—Commonwealth soldiers, diplomats, British ladies in fine dresses, veiled Egyptian women, and barefoot children driving goats through the streets. He could stand almost anywhere in downtown Cairo and hear languages from all over the world. On the station platform Barling mounted a crate and scanned the diverse crowd spilling from the sun-baked, dusty coaches of the Egyptian State Railway. Finally, he spied a tall figure, smiling as he let the more agitated travelers elbow their way past him.

"Mr. Chambers," Barling called, waving his hat. Oswald acknowledged the greeting with a wide grin and began edging his way toward the young man who had hailed him. Barling called out again over the din, "Welcome to Cairo!"

That afternoon, over tea on the terrace of Shepheard's Hotel, William Jessop gave Chambers a summary of the situation. There were at least sixty thousand soldiers from every part of the British empire in camps, hospitals, and convalescent centers around Cairo. In the first week after the invasion of the Dardanelles began in April 1915, sixteen thousand sick and wounded men were brought to Egypt. The flood of casualties continued to pour in every week. Hotels, schools, and even an amusement park had been converted to hospitals, and still there was not enough room.

Cairo was surrounded by military camps so that on any given day, thousands of soldiers were on leave or in transit through the city. Jessop pointed across Kamel Pasha street toward the beautiful Ezbekieh Gardens. "Just beyond Ezbekieh," he said, "is the Muski, an ancient bazaar full of shops and vendors and everything under the sun. In a street named the Haret el Wasser is the most notorious red-light district in Cairo. The Australians and New Zealanders call it the 'Wozzer' and have had at least two riots there."

Chambers had already heard tales of "the First and Second Battles of the Wozzer."

"Hundreds of drinking parlors serve drugged liquor," Jessop continued, "and nearly two thousand prostitutes ply their trade among a community of pickpockets and thieves. Troops are easy prey and venereal disease is rampant. The Y.M.C.A. has opened a soldier's club in Ezbekieh Gardens and we hold nightly entertainment there, right on the edge of the red light district."

Chambers sipped his tea and tried to take it all in.

Military authorities were anxious to keep their men prepared for duty. A man with venereal disease was usually lost for the duration of the war, and often returned to the homeland in disgrace. Commanders looked to the Y.M.C.A. to provide activity centers and wholesome alternatives for men who were far away from the influence and restraints of home. But the Y.M.C.A. had a deeper motive than mere social service. Its three-fold emphasis of Body, Mind, and Spirit was centered on bringing men to a personal faith in Jesus Christ. From its beginning in the mid-nineteenth century, the Young Men's Christian Association firmly held a two-fold purpose: "To unite those young men who, regarding Jesus Christ as their God and Saviour according to the Holy Scripture, desire to be His disciples in their doctrine and in their life, and to associate their efforts for the extension of His Kingdom among young men" (Y.M.C.A. Paris Resolution, 1855). The military gave great cooperation and encouragement to the "Y.M.," but did not fund its activities or provide its basic supplies. Jessop began his outreach to troops with a hundred dollars given by friends in Cairo. Since then, contributions and needs had raced ahead, with needs always in the lead.

Missionary pastors along with workers from the Egypt General Mission, Church Missionary Society, and the American Presbyterian Mission threw themselves into work with the soldiers. The Rev. Samuel Zwemer and Canon Temple Gairdner visited hospitals and never refused a request to speak to the men.

Chambers found the whole situation intriguing. Cairo assaulted his physical senses with enticing aromas from streetside cafes and the eerie Muslim calls to prayer from countless minarets. Spiritually, the challenge of taking the gospel to several thousand men in a busy military camp seemed almost staggering.

He longed for the day Biddy and Kathleen could come, but quickly encountered the erratic circumstances of war in which rules and regulations changed by the moment. Before he left England, travel permits to Egypt for civilians were available, and now conflicting orders seemed to be issued every day.

Diary, October 26: A conference of workers took place this morning. I listened and wondered how God was going to engineer circumstances for Biddy to come and work with me here, but we shall see. God always performs wonders.

The next day, Jessop and Chambers took a tram for the six-mile jaunt northeast from Cairo to Heliopolis. From there they set off on foot through the soft sand for a mile to Zeitoun (zay TOON), where the sprawling Base Detail Camp of the Australian and New Zealand forces surrounded the small missionary home and compound of the Egypt General Mission. "I'd be grateful if you'd work among the men here," Jessop said.

That night Oswald wrote Biddy to encourage her, and perhaps himself: "It will be wonderful to see how all His ways will become plain and exquisite. My heart has been at the lowest ebb as it looked more and more like mad impossibility to get you out here. But I am sure God is just marvelously undertaking."

"This [area] is absolutely desert," Chambers recorded in his diary, "in the very heart of the troops and a glorious opportunity for men. It is all immensely unlike anything I have been used to, and I am watching with interest the new things God will do and engineer."

It didn't take long to tour the Y.M.C.A. "facilities," which consisted of one large structure known as a "hut." Common to camps throughout Egypt, the hut was a seventy-foot by forty-foot wooden frame, covered on the outside with "walls" of matting, made from native rushes. Inside, benches to seat four hundred stood on a floor of desert sand. At one end stood a raised platform and at the other, there were two small rooms for the Y.M.C.A. "secretary," and his assistant, if he could find one.

The Y.M.C.A. provided free writing paper and pencils for the troops and distributed other items supplied occasionally through the Red Cross or military sources. In the canteen, tobacco, post cards, stamps, and refreshment items were sold at a minimal cost. Social and spiritual activities in each camp were determined by the secretary.

Oswald's predecessor at Zeitoun had taken a negative approach by plastering the hut with rules, regulations, and instructions. "Don't swear in this hut" and "Whoever borrowed my pen, return it now." The low ebb of spiritual influence was indicated by a small notice saying: "A short prayer meeting will be held in the Secretary's cubicle each evening at 8:45." Everyone knew it never took place.

Chambers strolled through the place, removing the signs and personally greeting the men writing letters at the tables. The first evening at 8:30, he mounted the platform and announced in a ringing voice that prayers would be held in the hut in fifteen minutes. He was giving them due warning so they could leave if they didn't want to pray. Everyone left except Atkinson and Mackenzie, two soldiers on convalescent status who had been assigned to help Chambers. Oswald held prayers with the two of them in the main part of the hut, not in the back room. The next night one or two others stayed for prayers, and within a few days, the numbers began to grow.

A few days later, Chambers announced a week-night religious service, something he had been told would not work with these men. But on Thursday, November 4, only a week after he arrived at Zeitoun, four hundred men packed the hut to hear his talk titled, "What Is The Good of Prayer?" For three-quarters of an hour, he spoke to an unusually attentive audience about the change prayer brings to our lives so that we may change things. Many of the men present that night were Australians, soon to be thrust into the insane slaughter at the Dardanelles.

Watching the men write letters home that evening was especially moving for Chambers. It drove him to intercessory prayer. "The unbearably pathetic side is never absent for long," he wrote. "These men go to Gallipoli on Monday and certainly half will never return, and they know it. I never get used to the going-off scenes and do not hope I ever shall."

Chambers had strong convictions about observing the Lord's Day, so on Sundays he closed the canteen and allowed nothing to be sold. Other secretaries said the men would never stand for it, but Chambers found that expressions of appreciation far outweighed negative reaction.

Diary, November 8: The early morning hours of prayer are unspeakably fine. I go over the camp and the men, and never cease to ask God to charge the atmosphere of the Hut with His Spirit, and that prayer is answered in the certain restraint on language and conduct. I cannot convey what a fathomless rest this intercession on behalf of the men is. Now I go into the day watching God's great ways again.

Prayer Journal, November 9: Lord, this day be the restraining One in the midst of these thousands of men; many of them are godless—Thou didst die for 'the ungodly.' Cause them to turn to Thee.

Diary, November 10: Last night two lads came in and we had a good time dealing with God, they came beautifully through to Jesus Christ on Luke 11:13. I have put their names on the War Roll, a register in which men's names are put down as they come into the light.

The great concert and boxing night has come and gone, about 1,200 men and marvelous behaviour, there was not one item of coarseness in the whole proceedings, for which I do praise God for it is all of Him. The uniqueness of asking God's blessing on a boxing bout! Phil. 4:6 It is just these sordid actualities that make the right arena for Our Lord's Reality. I am devoted to the plain rough human stuff as it is, and it is glorious to know that the reality of God's presence is but increased by things as they actually are.

Back in London, Biddy, Kathleen, and Mary Riley had received money from friends to cover their one-way voyage to Egypt, but awaited word from Oswald before booking their passage. Communication was slow and capricious. Letters might take ten days or three weeks to arrive. If a ship went down, thousands of letters were lost. To a person waiting for news from loved ones, the destroyed letters could seem more tragic than the torpedoed ship and the people killed.

Biddy knew that the military regulations were in a constant state of flux. The problem was not leaving England but being allowed to enter Egypt once they arrived. There had been cases of people without entry permits being detained at Port Said and forced to return to England on the next available ship.

On November 17, Chambers reached a momentous decision. "I have decided to write today for Biddy and Miss Riley to come right away," he noted in his diary. "I got two wonderful verses this morning about the matter for which I thank God. Mark 9:8 and Psalm 37:4."

Along with his instructions to Biddy to come as soon as possible, he wrote: "I have had a great and blessed time before God in prayer this morn. It came so clearly that in all ventures for God I had to go in faith and now I do the same. I have never far-seeing plans, only confident trust. On the top of those very billows which look as if they would overwhelm us walks the son of God!"

Two days later he received permission from Mr. Swan of the Egypt General Mission to build a bungalow within their compound. It would provide housing for Oswald's family and a home-like place of hospitality for soldiers outside the hut. Without money in hand to pay for it, or wife and daughter there to occupy it, he pressed ahead.

Each day Chambers moved through the compound, talking with men, ordering supplies, arranging meetings, and overseeing the details of the bungalow's construction. The November sun lacked the fierce heat of summer, but it was still intense and a far cry from a drizzly autumn day in London. He wore khaki trousers held up by wide suspenders (braces), a long-sleeved khaki shirt and tie, and a topee (sun) helmet or cloth service cap. A horsehair fly whisk rarely left his hand. After a month at Zeitoun, his face was nearly mahogany in color.

Diary, December 1: A cold and beautiful morning, I had a fine time with my [Bible] portions and prayer list.

I have just seen the foundations of my bungalow, it is just fine. I went over the foundation of each room and had a fine time of dedicatory prayer, committing the whole house to God for His purpose.

Diary, December 3: As I walked through the lines tonight, alone in this mighty desert, under the serene dome of sky and the wonderful stars, I realized again the unique sense of the presence of angels. I noticed it repeatedly the first time I went abroad. It is quite distinct from the certainty that God is guarding, this is the beautiful sense of angel presence. Anyway that is how it strikes me and I thank God for it.

December 9: I discovered something that was a deep joy this morning. I took a cup of tea to Atkinson and Mackenzie this morning at 6:15 (for the first time), and found at Atkinson's head a copy of my *Discipline of Prayer.* I said nothing, and later on he said, 'Mackenzie must have been surprised to see me on my knees praying, I have not done such a thing for twenty-four years.' That launched us. He said, 'It is all you, and your life anyway. Do you think God will hear me if I pray?' I gave him Luke 11:13, and deeply rejoiced. He has been won purely by prayer, he's well educated and sarcastic, but he's won, thank God.

Biddy, Kathleen, and Mary Riley sailed from England on December 12 aboard the *SS Herefordshire.* A frustrating delay had kept them from traveling on a ship that departed a week before. In Biddy's purse she carried an envelope from Oswald with thirteen folded, numbered scraps of paper. Each contained words of encouragement and a love-note, one for each day of the voyage. If all went according to plan, they would be in Egypt for Christmas.

In mid-December, the ill-fated Dardanelles campaign came to a close with a wholesale evacuation to Egypt. Many of the men who survived returned sickened by the slaughter they had seen and disillusioned with a God who could allow it to happen. A large number of these battle-weary Australian and New Zealand troops returned to Zeitoun camp.

Diary, December 22: The day arrives, both Christmas Day and Biddy's arrival. God be praised. They have only just come in time for I understand that no more women are to be allowed to land in Egypt.

December 24: The exact day of Biddy's arrival is still uncertain. The bungalow looks really fine, but for the first two nights Mr. Jessop has most kindly offered us the use of his flat in Cairo, as the E.G.M. missionaries will be using the bungalow during their Christmas convention.

Tonight's sunset is the most angry and grand I have yet seen out here.

December 25: Christmas morning, Hallelujah! The morning is simply exquisite. At two this morning, a most superb moonlit night, the military band played Christmas hymns and carols, and it is not in my power to describe the solemn and inspiring and moving beauty of the music in this atmosphere of war and death and desert, it was one of the most memorable experiences of my life.

But what a night! I had scarcely written down the words about the sunset when it began to rain. Whew! Everything was drenched, and the accumulation of sand on the hut streamed down like mild and annoying treacle [molasses] on everything, beds and tables and Xmas decorations. This morning everything in my hut is sopping. However, the sun is up and all goes grandly.

On December 26, Oswald traveled by train to Port Said to stay overnight and meet Biddy's boat in the morning.

December 27: The whole day has been a wonder of excitement. We got on to the Herefordshire at 7 a.m., they all looked radiantly well. I write baldly, but God knows it was a cup running over.

On December 29 Chambers joyfully noted that Jimmy Hanson and Philip Hancock, former B.T.C. students, had arrived from England for Y.M.C.A. service with him at Zeitoun.

He continued in his dairy:

Nothing could equal the way Biddy and Miss Riley have faced the work and new life, and Kathleen has fitted in as naturally as the sun. It was 'it' to see her playing in the sand with Mrs. Swan's children (grand folks, the Swans) in the shelter of the compound.

This evening a man came and gave me 100 piastres saying that he was now a Christian and wanted to give me this for putting up a text in the hut, Luke 11:13.

Chambers soon had a key phrase of the verse lettered on a banner stretching the width of the platform: ". . . how much more shall your heavenly Father give the Holy Spirit to them that ask him."

Diary, December 31: Well, here ends the most devilish and ruinous year that has ever been, yet in my personal experience one of the finest and mightiest years of my life, God be praised. Here I am all after the desire of my heart, in the centre of a great military encampment, and Biddy and Kathleen and Miss Riley here with me. Hallelujah!

18
WAR WORK

(1916)

Oswald posted a large map of Egypt inside his Y.M.C.A. hut at Zeitoun and often paused to study it in detail. It encouraged his prayers for the work among the troops, and also helped him gain a broad perspective of this land, so full of historical and geographical significance.

The city of Cairo sat astride a geographer's line of 30 degrees north latitude—roughly 1,800 miles above the Equator. To the north, the fertile Nile delta spread out like a fan, ever-widening for a hundred miles to the Mediterranean Sea. Apart from the delta and the Nile's thin ribbon of floodplain south of Cairo, Egypt was boundless miles of sere, sun-blasted desert.

Fifty miles due east of Cairo lay the southern entrance to the Suez Canal, a key factor in Britain's hopes to win the war. The one-hundred-mile canal linked the Red Sea with the Mediterranean and shortened the journey from India to England by six thousand miles. British control of the canal, opened in 1869, ensured swift troop movements from Australia, New Zealand, and India.

In 1916, Cairo's population of some 700,000 was packed into a staggering density of 21,000 people per square mile. Allied military troops who were camped within a fifteen-mile radius of the city numbered nearly a hundred thousand more. From the Y.M.C.A.'s hub in Cairo, it sought to serve the men in permanent military camps that spread out like spokes to the far western desert, south along the Nile, and eastward to the edge of the Sinai Peninsula.

Chambers found the Egyptian setting fascinating, especially in his personal study. "I am reading two very different but entrancing books out here," he wrote to a friend. "One is the Book of Deuteronomy and the other is The Arabian Nights. The former was enacted within less than fifty miles of this spot, and the other was written of Cairo in the fourteenth century. I am a great believer in atmosphere, and this Eastern atmosphere is most conducive to an understanding of these books."

As a Y.M.C.A. secretary, Chambers had a basic pattern to follow in meeting the physical needs of the soldiers, but great latitude in addressing the recreational and spiritual dimension of the work. When he told a group of fellow secretaries that he had decided to forego concerts and motion pictures at Zeitoun in favor of Bible classes, they predicted an immediate exodus of men from his huts.

What the skeptics had not considered was Chamber's unusual personal appeal, his gift in speaking, and his genuine concern for the men. To keep from disturbing the soldiers who used the Y.M.C.A. hut for relaxing and writing letters in the evening, Oswald erected a tent nearby in which he held nightly classes on Biblical Psychology. Soon, the men in the three-hundred-seat tent outnumbered those at the writing tables in the larger hut.

Reports began filtering in to Y.M.C.A. headquarters that soldiers whom no one could accuse of being religious turned out night after night to study the Bible. The missionaries and Y.M.C.A. secretaries who dropped by Zeitoun for an evening visit were astounded to find it was true.

Several times a week Oswald traveled to hospitals and convalescent homes around Cairo, where he brought a message from the Bible and talked with individual men. The plight of a sick or wounded soldier in Egypt was far different from that of a man who fell in Europe. Some trenches of the Western Front were little more than a hundred fifty miles from London, so a soldier wounded in a morning battle in France could sometimes be in a hospital in England by evening of the same day. A sick or wounded trooper in the Mediterranean theater of war stayed there for treatment and convalescence until he was returned to his unit.

On January 27 Chambers took Theo Atkinson, a former opera singer, to a service at Cairo's Bulac Hospital. After singing for the men, Atkinson told of his conversion to Christ at Zeitoun and how radically his life had changed in the past few weeks. "It was a moment to live for," Oswald wrote that night, "one of those supreme moments of life that shine as an immortal memory."

Chambers saw many men like Atkinson who came to faith in Christ and wanted to grow. "Instruction is certainly the crying need among these men, and not the habitual evangelistic cry for Gospel meetings," he noted. "There are so many 'saved' souls waiting instruction, and they take it with great zest."

"There is no difficulty at all in getting men to 'decide' for Christ, they do it readily," Oswald's diary continued. "However, I more and more deprecate the counting of cases, and prefer the soaking method of teaching God's word, providing an atmosphere of prayer, and then making a definite issue of will."

In February he was asked to teach a Bible class one night a week at Ezbekich Gardens in the center of Cairo. "What a sight it is there," he wrote. "The men sit in the roller-skating rink, there is a vast open space for speaking under the grand Egyptian night, and you speak from a brilliantly lighted cinema platform. Atkinson sang and Bessie Zwemer played, and after I had spoken on Luke 19:19, Atkinson sang 'Nearer My God to Thee' and then gave his testimony. This work in Ezbekieh Gardens is an opportunity of opportunities."

The immense military melting pot brought men from every corner of the British empire to Egypt, renewing Chambers' contact with friends from years before. One night a man from Askrigg who spent five months in the Dardanelles came to the class at Ezbekieh. "It was a delight to meet him again," Oswald recorded. "He tells me that I fished in his favourite bits in the becks!" [pools in the river].

When the Y.M.C.A. planned a simultaneous evangelistic mission throughout all the military camps in Egypt (March 23–April 2, 1916), they turned to Oswald as a man who could clearly articulate the gospel of Christ to the troops.

On March 23, he left Cairo by train and traveled a hundred miles northeast to Ismailia, near the midpoint of the Suez Canal.

Diary, March 24: I am now in Mr. [Ashley] King's home after having had a most absorbingly interesting day in Moascar Camp. These two, Mr. and Mrs. King, are absolute gold.

The evening meeting was a great one, Atkinson sang and gave his testimony. Ted Strack was there also, and Guy Morton; in fact, I cannot begin to tell the multitude of 'kenned' [personally known] men who came. We had some magnificent decisions, and I would not allow singing or even bowing of heads, but just told them to come out before all their comrades if they meant business, and out they came.

March 26: Never will I forget this evening service. I spoke on 'Will Ye Also Go Away?' Many decided, but the unique thing was that I knew I never would see many of the men again in the flesh. The crowding round afterwards, and the handshakes and farewells were all manly and fine and well understood. Some of the men walked with me to the limit of the camp, and then I went out over the bridge into the Eastern night, under the vast vault of starry sky, amid the strange loud croaking of frogs and the otherwise silent night, then the lonely challenge of the sentry, 'Who goes there?' a few words of friendly good night, and I came on, a deep paean of praise in my soul and a quiet joy. Again I say, thank God for my Moascar [Camp] mission.

The next day, Chambers traveled south to a large camp at Suez, guarding the southern reaches of the canal. "We had a famous meeting tonight," he noted in his diary. "It is a great treat to see Tommies again after so many months with Colonials."*

Chambers gave himself unreservedly to ministry among the soldiers, but at the same time, he seemed to have an uncanny sense of his need for diversion and rarely passed up an opportunity for adventure and learning. In company with two local Y.M.C.A. secretaries, he ventured into the bleak and forbidding Mummy Mountains.

March 29: We left at six o'clock this morn. on donkeys and have just arrived here, after three hours scorching ride into the heart of these mountains. We came up a river bed, wild and fantastic and silent to an awful degree, when the torrent is running it must be appalling, for the boulders are strewn around in a wild manner. We were stopped by an Arab outpost on a large white camel, he allowed us to pass with many courtesies. Coming back we came across a spring of water welling up through the desert sand, a most unusual thing. We were seven hours in the saddle, and the sun was an unveiled scorcher all the time. At night we drove out a long way to the Tommies' camp and held a meeting, the finest of this series, great and good."

His final mission took him to Wardan, in the western desert.

---

* *Tommies*: a nickname for British soldiers. Tommy Atkins = G.I. Joe. *Colonials*: a nickname for Australian and New Zealand troops.

Diary, April 1—Wardan: It was a grand meeting tonight, thank God, a full gathering, the tent was crowded out and rows deep all round outside. Afterwards I went a short ramble in the glorious desert night before turning in and came on a concert party in full swing. It was superb singing, a choir of Welsh men, and it was wonderful to hear the singing in that silent desert night.

April 2: I am spending a lazy and luxurious morning with my English Mail and the Times, Spectator, British Weekly, etc. This afternoon I meet the recent converts and talk to them and have my final service tonight. God is certainly very wonderful in His working with the Secretaries here.

Chambers concluded his meetings, feeling enlarged by his travels and encouraged by the growing scope of his ministry among the troops. On April 3, he noted in his diary: "I return to Cairo today, it has been a wonderful and refreshing time from the presence of God, and has convinced me yet more firmly that what the men require, and what they will come for, is instruction in Christian matters, much more than the old form of evangelistic services."

His euphoria, however, was short-lived. Back in Cairo, Chambers was "interviewed" by British military authorities regarding his status as a Y.M.C.A. secretary. Recent anti-war statements by three British secretaries had led to their arrest by enraged military authorities, and to a threat that all Y.M.C.A. secretaries would be sent back to England and required to enter military service.

In the midst of the uncertainty, Chambers noted in his diary: "The reading in 1 Samuel 8 struck me impressively, viz. that in any dilemma produced by providential circumstances, the temptation is to yield to ordinary common sense rather than wait for God to fulfill His purpose. God's order comes to us through the haphazard."

To Biddy, he said of the situation: "Let us keep very near Him and wait."

The wholesale reassignment of Y.M.C.A secretaries never materialized even though the possibility left many of Chambers' friends quite unnerved. In contrast, he never seemed disturbed by it, sticking resolutely to his unspoken motto in every circumstance, "I *refuse* to worry." Without anxiety, he welcomed each day and its developments under the sovereign hand of God.

In the rigid atmosphere of a military environment, Chambers' flair for the spontaneous and carefree pervaded his relationship with Biddy and Kathleen. When a bit of extra money appeared, he would quickly sweep the two of them off to Cairo for a dinner at Groppi's restaurant or tea at Shepheard's Hotel. He took great delight in buying Biddy a new hat or having Kathleen's hair washed and curled in the beauty shop at Shepheard's.

He would freely ask for contributions to build a hut or feed the soldiers but rarely mentioned his own financial needs. A diary entry early in 1916 provides an unusual glimpse at the approach he and Biddy took to money:

> And now what am I to say regarding the Speke Hall people and the many others who have sent money out for the B.T.C. bungalow? The whole cost is £78. God bless all the givers, as I know He does, for their generosity.
>
> Really the receiving of money has been most wonderful. I have not had one penny of salary, and yet everything I have asked for has come. However, I always feel Our Lord's caution in Matt. 7:6 in talking about this matter, for it has been, through a long spell of years, an amazement to find how few even of God's real children believe me when I have spoken of money matters, they imagine I have a supply other than I say. But never have I had, and if any saint should read this, take courage and never be sore if other saints cast doubt on you.
>
> (This is a private matter but it may be useful. When Biddy and I married we determined before God we would never talk of money matters before anyone, nor ever use the phrase 'we cannot afford it,' and God has undoubtedly blessed that decision. For so many have their intercourse with God rudely corrupted by the perpetual plaint of chronic impecuniousness. It is to my mind more of a shame to mention money in the way one so often hears than many another thing considered more shameful. Now this is a betrayal of myself. I feel like the sentiment in 2 Cor. 12:11).

The next day, his diary continued:

> I went to see Mr. Jessop about various matters, and was astounded at his information that Mr. Yapp had sent word from England that I was receive £100 per anum. This struck me very forcibly as only a day ago I had noted in my diary my views on money matters, and here a profound alteration happens, so we thank God and go forward. Anyway, it will greatly facilitate doing more things.

Life in Egypt was full of other "profound alterations." A sandstorm on April 13, 1916, ripped the meeting tent at Zeitoun from bottom to top and collapsed the center poles. A week later, a massive troop movement completely emptied the surrounding military camp of its thousands of men. The Y.M.C.A. huts, thronged by men a few days before, now stood silent in the sand. Kathleen surveyed the empty compound and asked in wonder, "Where have all the soldiers gone?"

In mid-May, Jessop asked Chambers to return to Suez and temporarily lead the work there in a camp of twenty thousand Tommies. Biddy and Kathleen stayed behind in the home of missionary friends at Zeitoun.

Diary, May 17—Suez: How wonderfully beautiful are the providential ways of God. Here I am, far from Zeitoun, and now I have the opportunity of saturating this great Hut with prayer, and then watching to see how God will work. I am strangely and devoutly thankful to be here, and to know, too, of Biddy's unselfish joy in my coming. She would rejoice if she could see the opportunity of this place.

May 18: The day has been busy, and all to the accompaniment of a blinding sandstorm. This is real camp life, much more so than Zeitoun, absolutely in the wild. I thank God for this chance in a rough and ready soldiers' camp. I am asking God for great things here spiritually.

The men always found Chambers available for personal conversations and quite unlike most clergymen they had encountered before. If a soldier huffed, "I can't stand religious people," Oswald often said, "Neither can I." With that settled, they could talk about Christ and how it changed all of life to know Him.

May 19: It is now 10 p.m. and it has been a busy and enjoyable day. I found many lonely lads, hungry spiritually. One lad from Manchester told me how fed up he was with his former life, what would I advise him to do? That gave me my opportunity with him, and the opportunity is all the time.

May 23: A most wonderful sunrise, great and inspiring. The splendour of these sunrises is unique indeed, the glow of the light on the mountains opposite is of the 'Ancient of Days' order. All the noises of the camp are stirring and fine, the men are astir at 4 a.m., the movement of horses, the bugles, the whirr of aeroplanes, all makes this life a real delight to see somehow. The men are unlimited in their gratitude for the Y.M. hut.

I am finding that an eminently assisting way to pray is to ask God to give me His wisdom for the day, so that I might remember all the practical actual matters in accordance with His astute wisdom, instead of my own human cunning. This by no means implies that everything I do will be right, but it does mean that if I keep in the light as He is in the light, I need not do any unwise thing at all.

On May 24, he noted Kathleen's third birthday and the next day, the sixth anniversary of his marriage to Biddy.

In early June, he was summoned back to Cairo and asked to open a new work at Ismailia, on the Suez Canal. Because of recent fighting in the Canal Zone, Biddy, Kathleen, and Mary Riley needed military permits to join Oswald. He would go ahead while they stayed in the Swan's house at Zeitoun and waited for the permits to be issued.

Even though the fighting in Europe showed no sign of ending soon, thoughts of life back home after the war entered everyone's thinking. Oswald had always believed that he and Biddy would return to London and reopen the Bible Training College. Soldiers frequently expressed their desire to study under his leadership once the conflict finally ended.

But just before leaving for Ismailia, he received a letter closing that door, but opening his mind to new possibilities for the future. The letter from Mrs. Reader Harris, usually filled with news of friends and the League of Prayer, began with a different tone. She was grateful for all his past service but needed to clarify the League's present position and future plans. The League had given up its lease on 45 North Side, Clapham Common, and had no plans to reopen a residential Bible Training College after the war. For the present, they wished Chambers to continue conducting the Bible Correspondence Course from Egypt and send articles, along with personal news to *Spiritual Life*, the new name of the *Tongues of Fire* magazine.

Oswald read the letter carefully to be sure he understood what she had said then showed it to Biddy. Yes, it was very clear.

In a letter to a friend, Chambers said, "Mrs. Reader Harris has written me wishing me to consider my career with the Pentecostal League finished . . . it is very clear that she or some connected with the P.L. are afraid that I may persist in claiming some support from her and the League. I am really glad that such a decision has been arrived at, although I am sorry that Mrs. R.H. has had to write it to me, I mean for her sake, but I am now honorably dismissed."

The same mail contained a letter from C. T. Studd, asking Oswald to visit his mission stations in Africa before returning to England after the war. "This must be prayed about," Chambers wrote.

The letters from Mrs. Harris and C. T. Studd sparked his thoughts of days to come. Might God want him to start a Bible college on his own after the war, unconnected with any sponsoring organization? His practical friends would say it was impossible. *Of course it is,* Chambers thought. *Only God could do it.*

In a letter to a friend he said: "I am blazing before the Lord because I believe He has told me to start a B.T.C. of my own untrammeled. He will send me students. My heart and head and hilarity are swelling with expectations and joy at the prospect of a great new venture in His name, a Bible Training College on a much bigger scale than the previous one, always B.T.C., Better To Come."

What he might do after the war remained a matter of conjecture. His advice to others facing uncertainty had always been, "Trust God and do the next thing." The task at hand for him was to leave the scene of his successful work at Zeitoun and start from the ground up in Ismailia.

The night before Oswald's departure, he and Biddy closed the bungalow, took a last walk around the deserted huts at Zeitoun, and said good-bye, not knowing when they would see each other again. They agreed to look past the pain of separation and thankfully embrace this new opportunity to serve. Early the next morning, Chambers boarded a crowded train for a slow, sweltering journey to Ismailia.

During his seven months in Egypt, he had discovered that Y.M.C.A. work demanded mobility, flexibility, and adaptability. When the troops moved, so did the Y.M.C.A. The war was a terrible thing but it had brought an incredible opportunity to reach men for Christ. Even so, Oswald felt things might change dramatically much sooner than anyone thought.

Diary, June 8: The reading in 2 Kings 7 brought back with renewed confidence my prayer that the war would end by an act of God, and end this year, verse 2 is just it—"If the Lord would make windows in heaven, might this thing be?" this is not so much an expression of ridicule or unbelief as the pagan sense of futility in expecting such a thing.

But the windows were opened in heaven, and the incredible thing happened.

19
BROKEN BREAD AND POURED OUT WINE

(1916)

Oswald said of Ismailia, "This little town fascinates me with its unique beauty." It attracted British military commanders and tens of thousands of troops because of its strategic position near the midpoint of the Suez Canal. Turkish attacks launched from the Sinai Peninsula in 1915 and early 1916 had failed to penetrate British defenses on the historic waterway, but protecting the canal was still considered a top priority.

Oswald's first job in the sweltering summer heat of Ismailia was to build a Y.M.C.A. hut. As foreman of the project, he located and purchased materials, hired Egyptian workers, and supervised their efforts. A shortage of carpenters sent him to the officer in charge of a nearby British detachment to see if he could spare two men for several days. Benches, tables, and counters were built from scratch. In two weeks, it was finished.

By late June the relentless sun turned the desert sand into a daily inferno. Mid-day temperatures inside a bell tent reached 130 degrees Fahrenheit. Outside there was little or no shade. The allotted one gallon of water per man per day fell far short of human craving to slake the intense thirst.

Flies that hatched in the waste of thousands of horses and other animals drove some men to near insanity with their annoying presence on everyone and everything. A man in camp was considered unarmed without a fly whisk. At night hordes of insatiable mosquitoes emerged to feed and spread malaria. When the military ran out of mosquito netting, soldiers wrote their families with desperate appeals for life-saving, mind-saving parcels from home.

One soldier described the mental and physical toll of desert life: "Few people know, unless they have experienced it, what a climate such as that of Egypt can mean. The effect of the climate and of the historic atmosphere of Egypt is psychically appalling to certain temperaments, and to those who are spared this, there is yet the continual sapping of the physical forces by fever and the resultant lowness of par which makes it difficult to fight moral or mental battles."

Chambers rarely wrote home of the harsh conditions of life in the desert. He shared the same climate and difficult living conditions as the troops, but the very things that brought others low seemed to breathe new life into him.

A summer diary entry said: "Sun! I have been considering it. One cannot conceive of such sun unless one has summered in Egypt. It is the only power that makes this land possibly habitable. It is fierce, appallingly so, but fascinating; my own experience is that desert life is productive of intense vitality and energy, not of langour.

"There is much exhaustion amongst the secretaries in the work along the Canal, and I realize how certainly God keeps us well for His own purposes. It is not an effort to be well, we are all well really and it is a cause for profound thanksgiving."

Diary, June 21—Ismailia: Another eloquent dawn, clear leagues of air right from the eternities of God. I am greatly enjoying some sermons of Dr. John Hutton's entitled 'The Fear of Things.' Here is one fine bit—'It is the lonely calling of each one of us that we fall not out of contact with God . . . It is laid upon each one of us, and it ought to be a happy responsibility—it is our whole work of faith, to take up the obscure tasks within ourselves which we know must be attended to if we are to live on happy terms with Jesus Christ our Lord.'

Each day he hoped the military would issue the permits for Biddy and the others to come. There was no reason for them to delay. But each day he was greeted with official silence. For nearly a month he labored without his family in Ismailia until finally, on July 1, he received a cable from Barling: "Cheers, meet the 9:20 train."

On the crowded railway platform, Kathleen walked cautiously until she saw her father, then she was off in a headlong dash into his waiting arms. How she had missed him! She clung to him as he embraced Biddy and greeted Mary Riley. Then the happy foursome jostled their way to a waiting car.

Over supper that night, Oswald told the women of a new idea he was going to try the next day, Sunday. The canteen would be closed as usual, but the men were invited to a free tea between two and five in the afternoon. A friend had given him five pounds to get the project rolling.

The next afternoon, the men came in droves, consuming huge urns of tea, coffee, and cold drinks along with mountains of cookies and cakes. Biddy and Mary Riley worked endlessly behind the canteen bar, assisted by several soldiers and Egyptian helpers. It appeared that nearly four hundred men had come for the first tea.

When word of Chambers' free teas reached Cairo, the Y.M.C.A. supplies manager caught the first train for Ismailia to voice his strong objections. "If you have a 'free' tea," he told Oswald, "the men are going to expect it in all the huts. Y.M.C.A. policy says refreshments must be sold, not given away."

Oswald listened and then explained his desire to observe the Lord's Day and still serve the soldiers. If the men wanted to help with the cost, there was a small contribution box in the hut, but he would not ask them to pay. After talking with Chambers and hearing reactions from the men, the Y.M. official not only agreed to allow the free teas, but said he would contribute five pounds if Oswald could find four others to do the same. "I promptly got two who were listening," Chambers said, "and the others will follow."

His diary chronicled a summer that marched along, each day filled with people and the common elements of life.

July 19: It is a strange experience to sit in this hut in the still midsummer heat of Egypt and remember my B.T.C. days. It is full of contrast and interest and of implicit things, and I just live in the last verse of the last Psalm. 'Let every thing that hath breath praise the Lord.'

July 24: An extremely beautiful morning. Kathleen and Miss Riley are just off to their marketing. Fancy shopping in London at 6:30 a.m.!

July 27: The Bible class goes well, several of the men are making enquiries about becoming B.T.C. students at the close of the war, we shall see.

August 8: I commenced the new series in Biblical Ethics tonight with very fine results. I find the men are always keen on this subject, it deals with so many problems from a fundamental standpoint and is productive of real thinking on their part.

The feature of features just now is my new orderly, he has the innocent face of a baby hippopotamus or embryo gargoyle, occasionally a flash of keen humour, and he issues his orders in his coarse 'Glesgy' [Glasgow] voice. The first time he appeared behind the counter, Kathleen said in her clear voice, before a hut full of men—'Daddy, why doesn't that soldier smile at me?' This morning when I went down, his greeting, without a smile on his lugubrious face, was—'Wait till ye see the ants in the trifle.' Miss Riley puts things away in the ice chest overnight and the ants had discovered something good!

August 20: The question class was a particularly important one, a Unitarian asked many vital questions and we had a time of keen profit. In discussion afterwards, someone remarked, 'I had no idea such thoughts occurred to men's minds.' I am afraid this is the case with a great many, they exclude from themselves a knowledge of what the men actually think.'

August 21: Today the Australian Stationary Hospital men leave for Alexandria and then England. These men have been the mainstay of my class, and we have become very attached to them. One said the other night, 'It has been worthwhile enlisting to come to these classes.'

August 23: In reading this morning I came across a stirring phrase in II Cor. 1:14—'I am your source of pride (as you are mine) on the Day of our Lord Jesus" (Moffat). I think if I have an ambition, it is just that—to have honourable mention in anyone's personal relationship to our Lord Jesus Christ.

August 31: At family prayers the Psalms seem to take on great and new meaning, and the men listen with that genuine elemental reverence that is to my heart of more value than anything more formal.

September 2: I have not noted much lately the most characteristic thing in the work here, viz. the continual talks with the men about their own spiritual condition, I find them most communicative on these matters.

After a demanding three months in the Canal Zone, word came from Jessop that the camp at Zeitoun was being reopened as a military school of instruction. Chambers should make plans to return within the next two weeks.

Just before leaving on September 18, Chambers wrote: "It has been a great few months in Ismailia, easily the finest bit of work we have done together yet. The testimonies of the men have been as the wine of life, and it has been quite affecting to say good-bye to them all and to the E.G.M. missionaries. Again I would like to pay tribute to the real saintly goodness of these missionaries."

The days of moving back to Zeitoun allowed time for a rare holiday in Alexandria. For ten days Oswald and Biddy exchanged oppressive desert heat for the invigorating sea breezes of the ancient city founded by Alexander the Great. Kathleen frolicked on the sand while her mother and father watched the breakers roll in off the deep blue Mediterranean.

But the greatest treat of all was the presence of three former B.T.C. students just arrived from England. Eva Spink, Gladys Ingram, and Gertrude Ballinger had come on special permits for Y.M.C.A. work with Katherine Ashe in Alexandria. No one was more delighted than Kathleen at the prospect of having her friends from the B.T.C. close by. No one except Philip Hancock.

Up the line on the Palestinian front, Hancock could hardly contain his excitement at the news of their coming. A year before, he had volunteered for Y.M.C.A. service, leaving Gertrude Ballinger in God's hands. And now the Almighty had brought the woman he loved to Egypt.

Back in Alexandria, Oswald treated all the ladies to an exotic Egyptian meal and assured the new arrivals that they would fall in love with the city. Beneath his lighthearted exterior, he prayed they could bear up under the demanding work and the relentless pace set by Miss Ashe. He would do all he could to encourage them.

The loyalty of these ladies to Chambers sprang from his genuine love for God and for them. Their relationship also mirrored the strong bond between Oswald and former students of the Bible Training College. In Eva Spink's personal diary, she often called Chambers "my beloved captain," a feeling shared by many others of following a courageous leader into battle. He always walked ahead but not beyond them in a shared adventure of service to Christ.

The way in which Oswald co-labored equally well with men and women may have stemmed from the high regard in which he held his mother. From Alexandria, he wrote to Hannah on her seventy-sixth birthday:

> *My dear Mother,*
>
> *God bless you on your birthday. How everything that touches you in my mind and memory is a benediction of blessedness. All that formed my ideas of women (and I have great ideas) is from you.*

> *And in these years as I have grown older, I have perceived with awe and adoration how much I owe to my Mother. My life with Biddy and Kathleen has been made blessed by the motherly kindness of you, 'my own native mother,' in those earliest days.*
>
> *And now that evening is greatly on you, there will be a most beautiful transfiguration on you and in you.*
>
> *Ever your loving son, Oswald*

A few days later it was back by train to Cairo through the familiar green of the Nile Delta, where the twentieth century was still a stranger in Egypt. Families cultivated their fields with the same triangular hoes pictured on the walls of Pharaonic tombs. Water buffalo turned ancient wheels to irrigate fields just as they had done for thousands of years before men invented steamships, airplanes, and machine guns.

When the war first began, Oswald had written an article on "God's parentheses" and the significance of His seemingly haphazard scrambling of human plans. If this war was a parenthesis in his experience and that of the world, Oswald intended to study it well and live it fully, to discover the mind of the Author.

Oswald, Biddy, and Kathleen returned to Zeitoun in October 1916 to find the situation much different from the one they left four months before. Their Bungalow and the Y.M.C.A. huts were unchanged, but instead of a traditional military camp with a permanently assigned unit, the area around the E.G.M. compound was now home to the Imperial School of Instruction. Every six to eight weeks a new contingent of several thousand men arrived for military training classes as those completing the course returned to their units.

Oswald quickly assessed the situation and adapted to meet the changing needs. He built a large, mat-walled Study Hut for evening Bible classes and erected a huge sign boldly announcing a series of talks and discussions on "Religious Problems Raised by the War." It was a new venture, but he felt confident that God would open the way with the men as He had in the past.

By day the men drilled in the desert, fired machine guns, and plotted artillery trajectories. At night and on Sundays they were free to visit the Y.M.C.A. huts. The soldiers' brief stay at the school presented Chambers with a more transient audience than before, but it expanded the number of men he touched from hundreds to thousands.

Diary, October 18: This morning I have been the round of the Huts. It is a memorable experience to go over all the ground where I was a year ago when I first came out to this vast camp, with not an inkling of how to proceed, and in looking back what gracious and wonderful memories there are. It is just a Te Deum of praise to think of the men who today thank God for His salvation, and in the heart of those days Cumine, Atkinson, and Mackenzie remain as a most precious memory. God bless them.

October 26: I am praying that the new B.T.C. hut may be the centre of a deep spiritual awakening amongst the men.

October 27: A proposition comes from Miss Ashe that I go to Alexandria to lecture each Wednesday. This comes with interest as I am being planned for Sundays at Ezbekieh now instead of Wednesdays; so I shall have five nights at Zeitoun, one at Alexandria and one at Ezbekieh, and in this way the number of men I shall be able to talk to is enormously increased.

Oswald knew the weekly round-trip journey from Zeitoun to Alexandria would be physically as well as spiritually taxing. After getting to Cairo and fighting the inevitable chaos in the main railway station, it was still at least a three-hour journey to Sidi Gaber, just outside Alexandria. However, Chambers considered it a prime opportunity with men as well as a chance to encourage Miss Ashe and the three young women from the B.T.C. serving with her.

In the face of increasing demands on his time and energy, Chambers stringently maintained his early mornings alone with God. A double-fly bell tent pitched outside the bungalow gave him an open air study for daily Bible reading and prayer. By 6 a.m., he was in the tent, awaiting the sunrise, which he described as "a daily poem of eternal worship, a ritual of aesthetic beauty indulged in before God."

His autumn reading centered on the book of Job.

October 28: Job 23 is surely the classic of deep woe rolling out across the very universe: "Oh that I knew where I might find Him!" All through the book of Job there is a heartbreaking devotion to God in the midst of inexplicable complexity of sorrow. I feel growingly sure that Job is the Book of consolation for the sorrow-tossed and bereaved and broken by the war. Not only is the voice of human suffering expressed here better than anywhere, but the very breath is drawn in the fear of the Lord, and the heart is strong in the hope that grades higher than faith (1 Cor. 13:13).

Oswald's morning hour with God was the only undisturbed portion of his day. From breakfast until late at night, people and projects kept him in a blur of activity. His diary, typed and mailed home to family members by Biddy, offered only an understated glimpse of his demanding schedule, and it never mentioned being sick, even when he was.

October 31: The morning has passed away busily with final touches to my B.T.C. hut and other matters.

He had neither time nor inclination to record the "other matters," which included supervising a crew of Egyptian workers building mud brick kitchens and a food storehouse. Several soldiers spent their days of leave making rock-lined pathways to the various huts. Chambers himself was often found with bucket and brush in hand white-washing the rocks along with them.

In the midst of the daily work, he and Biddy maintained their focus on people. When Gladys Ingram received news that her brother had been killed in France, she came at once from Alexandria to Zeitoun, where they welcomed her into the bungalow and their daily lives. Along with times of listening and prayer, they took her into Cairo for lunch at Groppi's and organized a moonlight excursion to the nearby Pyramids of Giza and the Sphinx.

Oswald and Biddy felt the pangs of grief each time a man they had come to know fell on the field of battle. On November 6, Chambers noted: "We have a letter from a New Zealand friend telling us that Ted Strack has been killed. And so Ted Strack has 'gone to be with Jesus.' That is just how he would have put it, without the slightest affectation of piety. Ted Strack was a rough beauty of nature and of grace, a fearless, lovable little saint. Thank God for every remembrance of him, all round me just now is the evidence of his handiwork in our little bungalow garden. So they are gathering one by one."

Strack, like many other soldiers, had visited Zeitoun at every opportunity. Just before being sent to France, he spent his last hours of leave working in the hot sun to finish the flower bed and paths around the bungalow. Chambers opened his prayer notebook and wrote beside the young man's name as he had by so many others, "With Christ."

The Sunday free teas had proven so popular in Ismailia that Oswald inaugurated them in Zeitoun. Thus the workload for Mary Riley, Biddy, and their few helpers increased dramatically. Soon a weekly crowd of five to seven hundred men thronged the hut, consuming the fried eggs, sandwiches, and cakes that provided a delicious taste of home.

Biddy insisted that every table have a clean, white tablecloth and a vase of freshly-cut flowers. It was her special touch and a way of welcoming the men to this giant desert dining room in her "home."

Contributions from League members and other friends in England funded the enterprise so that it was offered free of charge to the troops. Many men were surprised when the tea concluded without a sermon from the secretary. Too many times, soldiers had found free cakes and tea were the bait in a "gospel trap." Chambers didn't believe in that approach. "They came to eat," he said, "not to hear a sermon. There's a meeting later tonight if they want to stay and hear someone preach."

After the free tea, Oswald was off to Cairo for his weekly meeting at Ezbekieh Gardens. When he returned, there might be a dozen soldiers with him, having eagerly accepted his invitation to the evening meal. Sunday supper rarely started before 9 p.m., and all who came usually stayed for family prayers. With Oswald playing a small, foot-pump organ, they sang together, especially the evening hymns that Biddy loved so well. Few needed to look at the Y.M.C.A. hymnal to sing number 494, "God Be With You Till We Meet Again."

Both Oswald and Biddy believed strongly in the ministry of hospitality. The bungalow at Zeitoun provided more than a place for them to live. "If you have a house," Chambers said, "the next thing the Bible counsels is hospitality—'given to hospitality' (Romans 12:13). When we try to economize, God puts dry rot in us instantly. When we have the lavish hand, there is munificence at once."

The bungalow was their home and it was open to all. "God keeps open house for the universe," Oswald was fond of saying. When soldiers, missionaries or other Y.M. secretaries came unannounced for a meal, they knew a warm welcome awaited them. Biddy and Mary Riley never knew for certain how much to prepare, but there was always enough.

Rev. Douglas Downes, a Church of England chaplain working in Cairo, became a frequent visitor and close friend of Chambers. Downes described the supper parties at the bungalow as "taking place with such hilarity as might have shocked the respectably religious into believing what the Jews believed of the Apostles on the Day of Pentecost!"

The bungalow was a touch of home where little Kathleen reached out in innocent love to men long-separated from their wives and children. With a large bow in her sun-bleached hair, she roamed the compound and the hut, calling soldiers by name and sharing whatever she had with them. They, in turn, doted on her and kept her supplied with pets of every description—rabbits, kittens, and puppies. Her special friend, Peter Kay from Australia, gave her a small donkey to ride. Kathleen shared her parents' love for all God's creatures.

Occasionally, a man, lonely for his own little ones, sat outside her window at night just to listen to her bedtime prayers. Some of her favorite soldier-friends tiptoed in after family prayers to watch her sleeping and give her a good-night kiss before sprinting back to camp before the sounding of "Last Post."

Oswald and Biddy's few private moments together came most often after the men had returned to camp, and the two of them took a short walk into the desert under the stunning night sky. Often Oswald would lift the sleeping Kathleen gently from her cot and carry her along. If she slept, he and Biddy could talk alone for a few moments and unburden their hearts to each other and to God.

They encouraged each other by walking individually with God and finding His grace sufficient to meet their needs. Together, their lives intertwined into a cord of shared ministry that was stronger than either could have woven alone. Each day brought a never-ending stream of people whose emotional and spiritual needs were usually far greater than their need for food. Yet a cup of tea and one of Biddy's homemade cakes served on a tablecloth outside the bungalow was often the key that unlocked a cynical heart and opened long-stopped ears to hear the gospel during Oswald's teaching.

And just as she had at the Bible Training College in London, Biddy attended almost every one of Oswald's classes at Zeitoun. With Kathleen tucked in bed under the watchful eye of Eva Spink or Mary Riley, Biddy often slipped into the back of the hut just before Oswald began to speak. Seated on a wooden bench, her pencil flew over the pages of her stenographer's notebook, recording in shorthand every word he said. During the hour of his message, thoughts of the next day's meals or of the letters she needed to answer were banished along with her own feelings of physical weariness. As she wrote, she listened with her mind focused on Oswald's direction and his meaning. During his closing prayer, she slipped out and moved toward her next task.

Knowing the price Biddy paid to keep "open house for the universe," Oswald freely expressed his appreciation. Whenever he was gone for a night, she found a letter or note tucked under her pillow.

November 15—Zeitoun: Do not let your heart be troubled. I know, I think, just how you feel about yourself during our haphazard existence out here. The feeling of futility and incompetence is not a bad one because it comes near His beatitude—Poverty in brain and body and heart is blessed if it will drive us on to His fathomless resources. If not it ends in wounded vanity and brutality and a sense of being thwarted.

When I consider how completely and nobly you have foregone all quiet civilised influences that other women have and have been living a literal hand to mouth existence all transfigured by your great love for me and Him, I must bow my head in dedication and say God bless thee!

As 1916 drew to a close, Chambers reflected on the past year and made note of his own fallibility in discerning the mind and plan of God.

December 9: There is an interesting puzzle in my mind concerning the intuitions born in communion with God. For instance, I had such a joyous confidence that the war would end this year, but there is no apparent likelihood that it will. It is just another indication of how little we dare trust anything but Our Lord Himself. Again, there are intuitions born in the same way splendidly and wonderfully fulfilled. It makes it clear that the Holy Spirit must be recognized as the sagacious Ruler in all affairs, and not our astute common sense.

Christmas Eve 1916 fell on Sunday evening, Chambers' regularly scheduled time at Ezbekieh Gardens. The beautiful park in the center of Cairo was jammed with soldiers longing for a touch of home. A report of the gathering, published in *The Sphinx* weekly, said: "Mr. Oswald Chambers' address on the subject 'Has History Disproved the Song of the Angels' was a convincing defense of Christianity; he was listened to with rapt attention, and much appreciation by the audience, soldiers and civilians alike."

It seems extraordinary that *The Sphinx,* usually focused on prominent diplomatic and social figures in Cairo, devoted as much space to the Ezbekieh service as to the annual gala Christmas party at Shepheard's Hotel.

A week later Oswald closed the year with a watch-night service, again at Ezbekieh Gardens. His subject was "Finish 1916" and on a large blackboard he wrote these words: "The Irreparable Past—Sleep On Now. The Irresistible Future—Arise Let Us Be Going. Matt. 26:45–46."

At midnight he turned the blackboard over to reveal:

1917, A great New Year to you all
"And God shall wipe away all tears," Rev. 21:4

20
IN HIS PRESENCE

(1917)

The New Year stormed in with such violent rain that on January 2, 1917, Chambers posted a sign outside the study hut: CLOSED DURING SUBMARINE MANOEUVRES! It temporarily replaced the previous notice which said, BEWARE! THERE IS A RELIGIOUS TALK HERE EACH EVENING. "Apparently out here," he wrote, "no one prepares for rain, so when it comes we are like the earth, patient and absorbent."

In his thoughts and prayers for the days ahead, several possibilities appeared:

Diary, January 7: I am to give six more lectures at Alexandria, then if it can be arranged I would like to visit all the centres in Egypt before returning to England, or going on to Palestine, if developments take place in that direction.

At the time, the British army was stalled in the northern Sinai after taking the town of El Arish just before Christmas. Everyone expected that sometime during 1917, they would mount a massive attack and try to take Palestine from the Turks.

January 22: There seems every prospect that I will be going round all the camps in the Canal Zone and into Palestine, I hope, speaking to the men and seeing things for myself.

January 29: My mind is ever ruminating on our return to England in April, and I await the final touch of conviction about it that will cause me to say—this is God's order.

January 30: The committee have asked me not to think of leaving in the spring as they want my kind of work to continue. This needs praying about, but we shall see it all right when the time comes.

Oswald and Biddy concluded that the Y.M.C.A. committee was right and, for the time being, they were exactly where they should be. If America entered the war, as many felt sure it would, that might turn the tide in Europe and help bring the conflict to an end. There was certainly no shortage of spiritually needy men in Egypt and the response to their ministry at Zeitoun grew day by day.

In mid-January Oswald began holding a Sunday morning service at the Aotea Convalescent Home for New Zealand soldiers. After walking a mile through soft sand to Aotea and then another mile back in the sun, he spoke for the usual communion service at Zeitoun. Afternoon at the American Mission in Cairo and the evening service at Ezbekieh rounded out his normal Sunday schedule—preaching at least three, and often four times. In the midst of constant giving out, he treasured his rare opportunities to receive from others.

Diary, February 3: This afternoon I went into Cairo and had a most absorbing time with Dr. Rendel Harris and Bishop and Mortimer. It was a season of pure intellectual and spiritual pleasure. The Doctor was memorable in his estimates of the men we talked of—Dr. Forsyth, Dr. Denney, Dr. Robertson Nichol, Dr. David Smith and Dean Inge. The thing that 'keened' me up was that his scholarly estimate verified my own personal views. It was all nutriment to my very bones.

Another great encouragement came when Eva Spink and Gladys Ingram arrived from Alexandria to work fulltime at Zeitoun. Biddy and Mary Riley eagerly welcomed their friends from the B.T.C. days in London. Jimmy Hanson, Chambers' right hand man for many months, continued his flurry of activity at Zeitoun as a jack-of-all-trades who could repair almost anything.

Besides Chambers' associates working at Zeitoun, other former B.T.C. students occupied strategic positions with great ministry opportunities. Thirty miles north of Cairo, at the busy Benha railway junction, Miss Ashe and Gertrude Ballinger operated a Y.M.C.A. hut right on the train platform. Every day they served hundreds of troops in transit whose trains stopped there. On the front lines near Gaza, Philip Hancock served as Y.M.C.A. secretary among the men who would spearhead the coming battle for Palestine.

Diary, March 4: This morning I am filled with a sense of quiet wonder at the way things have transpired and that the 'B.T.C. Expeditionary Force' should really be altogether here now. 'This is from the Lord; and it is marvellous in our eyes.' There is an all-alive expectancy over the next thing God will allow circumstance to precipitate.

Oswald's diary entry for Monday, March 26, is typical of the busy days filled with an endless round of people:

> The Saturday evening class was peculiarly satisfactory. Three Australians, really way-back Scots, came in and questioned me. These rough 'old dogs' were acquainted intimately with Calvin's 'Institutes,' Pascal, Coleridge, Hugh Miller, Thomas Guthrie, Thomas Boston and the Bible. Altogether it was the most delightful question class I have had.
>
> In the morning Kathleen and I went to Benha to see Miss Ashe and Miss Ballinger. The hut [there] is the nucleus of any amount of possibility. They are really roughing it more than any of us, and, as usual, are appearing no end 'bucked' [encouraged] with the very difficulties.
>
> Sunday was a full and glorious day. The Aotea Home service was a fine season, the subject being 'The Blind Spot,' Mark 6:20. The Communion service here was also a great time, I spoke on 'Spiritual Auto-Suggestion,' 2 Cor. 11:3. The afternoon was busy with the free tea, and in the evening I went to Ezbekieh where the service was peculiarly vigorous and fine, and we had quite a swarm of men to supper afterwards.

When a break in the schedule came, Oswald rarely let it pass without planning a special event:

> Good Friday, April 5, 7 p.m. The Pyramids
>
> This is now our fourth visit to the Pyramids. As we came flying along in the motor from Cairo, moment by moment the familiar went in the fascinating colours of sunset, and now it is completely unfamiliar and ancient and Egyptian, and the most gorgeous of moons is rising higher and higher into a faultless blue night. As we left Cairo we were enthralled in noticing the moon rising over the Mokattam Hills, it had that 'unperspectived' effect (to coin a word) of the Egyptian twilight where everything looks like a perfect pre-Raphaelite decorative painting, rather than a modern landscape picture.
>
> We are now sitting at the foot of the Great Pyramid, the moon is beautiful to a superb degree over a deep veil of mist and all around is silence, great lofty invaluable silence everywhere. We are now by the Sphinx; it is noticeable, as Pierre Loti points out, that the moonlight brings out the features of the Sphinx which in sunlight seems for the most part a defaced mass of stone boulder. The swinging ride home at night was a glorious remembrance.

Biddy's roles of wife, mother, and hostess in the bungalow were each a full-time job. In addition, she helped prepare and serve the Sunday tea for the men, and carried on a growing correspondence with friends at home and people they had met in Egypt. Every day she found time to write at least half a dozen letters, each with a bit of personal news and a word of encouragement from the Scriptures.

Once a month she transcribed, typed, and mailed one of Oswald's talks as an article for publication in the League's magazine in England. And every time Oswald spoke at Zeitoun, she recorded his message in shorthand. Occasionally she accompanied him to the Aotea Home on Sunday morning and took notes of the talk there as well. For students of the Bible School Correspondence Course, Biddy prepared typed lesson summaries from Oswald's longhand notes. No one had any idea where she found time to do all that as well as type his daily diaries in multiple carbon copies and send them to family and friends.

The idea of putting some of Oswald's sermons into print originated ten years before, when he was visiting America. The Revivalist Press in Cincinnati published two of his sermons in pamphlet form in 1907. The League of Prayer published little besides the writings of the late Reader Harris, and printed only one pamphlet by Chambers, a sermon titled *Death to Self: Christian or Pagan*?

Throughout 1911 at the B.T.C. in London, Biddy took verbatim notes of Oswald's lectures on Biblical Psychology. Because of interest expressed at God's Bible School, she sent the notes to Cincinnati where the Revivalist Press gladly published *Biblical Psychology* as a book in 1914. The next year, the Revivalist Press published Oswald's *Studies in the Sermon on the Mount*.

In the months just before the B.T.C. closed in 1915, Oswald's friend Rae Griffin and several students had urged Chambers to put some of his lectures into print. Two booklets, *The Discipline in the Cure of Souls* and *The Discipline of Peril*, were published in May 1915 with *The Discipline of Prayer* being made ready for print. All profits from the sale of these booklets were designated for student scholarships at the Bible Training College. When Chambers left for Egypt, Rae Griffin took over the booklet venture, with any net proceeds promised to the B.T.C. work in Egypt.

Chambers had great respect for a keen mind well-expressed in print. He often quoted some of Reader Harris's last words: "Probably the most lasting of all preaching is with the pen." Oswald maintained a free literature table in the hut with League of Prayer materials and a few of his own booklets. If men wanted to contribute toward further printing they could, but no charge was ever made. His goal was to spread greater understanding of the Word of God.

Oswald's autumn 1916 reading and meditation in Job resulted in a month-long series of evening talks in the Zeitoun hut beginning in March 1917. When he finished the series in April, Biddy set to work typing her shorthand notes. His messages had spoken so clearly to the needs of soldiers, missionaries, and Y.M.C.A. secretaries, Biddy saw great value in putting them into print.

With summer coming on, Oswald started construction of an information hut for the soldiers and an underground room he called a "dugout," where he and Biddy could work and find refuge from the oppressive midday sun and heat. The roof of the dugout above ground resembled a miniature fort and became a favorite gathering place in cooler hours of early morning and late evening.

A free-standing wooden roof now covered the Bungalow, shielding the house from the direct rays of the sun. On one side of the roof, a wide, sloping trough was positioned to catch any precious rainfall and channel it into barrels below. His earlier notation about being unprepared for rain had not been forgotten.

Chambers believed that if physical improvements were not made and new touches occasionally given to the huts, they would come to reflect slovenly care, which would be unpleasing to God. "A grave defect in much work of today," he said, "is that men do not follow Solomon's admonition, 'Whatsoever thy hand findeth to do, do it with thy might.' The tendency is to argue, 'It's only for so short a time, why trouble?' If it is only for five minutes, let it be well done."

But no matter how well prepared the buildings were, there was no adequate protection from an Egyptian sandstorm.

May 18: Today is awful. Last night about sundown the wind began to rise, and it rose and rose until at 1:30 a.m. it sounded like a veritable hurricane . . . all day it has been a terrific wind filled with sand, and the heat of the nethermost pit. Everything is covered deep and dense with sand, we eat sand, drink sand, think sand, and pray sand. These women folk are just no end of an admirable crowd, and I can assure you it takes some vitality, morally, physically, and spiritually to be cheerful in weather like today. All the morning long there were crowds of men streaming into the hut for cool drinks, they were grateful to get in any kind of shelter from the wind and sand.

Oswald considered it a privilege when his friend the Rev. Douglas Downes asked him to give a series of talks at the Dermatological Hospital in Abassia. The patients, all venereal cases, had been neglected for some months while the Y.M.C.A.'s scarce human resources were channeled to other hospitals. Many people saw the men with venereal disease as "moral lepers" with self-inflected "wounds." Chambers went expectantly, glad of the opportunity to talk to these men of the salvation and healing presence of Jesus Christ. To free Oswald for the ministry at Abassia, Biddy taught the Thursday night classes at Zeitoun.

In summer Chambers usually rose by 5:30 a.m. to have his time alone until everyone met for prayers at quarter past seven. Breakfast followed, then a full morning of work until noon. After the meal until three o'clock, everyone, including soldiers in camp and Egyptian workers, rested through the hottest part of the day. Following afternoon tea in the bungalow or the dugout, men thronged the huts until they closed at 10:00 p.m. During the evening class from 7:30 to 8:30, the canteen closed so soldiers and workers could attend Oswald's class.

Word filtering back from the front lines in the northern Sinai pointed to an autumn offensive into Palestine. Y.M.C.A. philosophy called for it to "follow the troops," and some informal discussion had taken place on what that might mean for Chambers and other secretaries around Cairo. The final decision lay with the military authorities, but the Y.M. was ready whatever the request.

On July 24, Chambers made an uncharacteristically long and personal diary entry:

This is my birthday, my 43rd. It has been a glorious day in all ways, very hot but psychically very fine, and as it was a summarizing time for me, I am going to put down the results of the summary as I wrote it to two of my intimate friends. The first was a restatement of beliefs:

Foremost, that Redemption, and not Rationalism, is the basis of human life, and that on that basis, spirituality is the reality of mind and conscience and feeling at one with Jesus Christ in a 'spontaneous moral originality' of relationship.

Second. That the 'soul saving passion' as an aim must cease and merge into the passion for Christ, revealing itself in holiness in all human relationships.

Third. That the Holy Spirit must be recognized as the sagacious Ruler in the saint's affairs, not astute common sense.

Fourth. That organization must be seen to be scaffolding raised by the organism, and must never be allowed to take the place of the organism.

Fifth. That a scheme of socialistic propaganda [teaching] is about to be enacted on a universal scale with a mixture of astonishing good and atrocious bad, and until this has had its vogue Our Lord will not return, that is, if the past fairness to human schemes which God seems ever to have exhibited, is anything to go on.

The other is rather intimate autobiography, but I will put it down:

There comes to me growingly a sense of the 'externals' of things. Perhaps the plunging horror and conviction of sin in my early life not only disrupted my art calling and all the tendencies of those years, but switched me off by a consequent swing of the pendulum away from external beauties of expression in form and colour and rhetoric, and made me react into the rugged and uncouth and unrefined. But now I seem to have the experience Ruskin refers to—his grief at realizing the loss of his appreciation of the beauty of an English hedgerow, and his sad wonder if he would ever have the old emotions back again; then his recurrent joy and bounding delight when he found it all came back with redoubled force in later life. That perhaps states it.

The beauty of form, of expression, of colour, all the fleeting features of the immense external fields of life, are again delighting me marvelously. The old delight is back in a glorious edition de luxe, as it were. It is no longer an individual delight but a personal one, without the lust to possess, and without the forced detachment of the spectacular, yet with all the complete delight which possesses a child's mind in things. My inner career at the beginning was heavy and strong, and even lurid and very agonizing in the earlier phases; latterly, austere and peaceful, and now it is merging into a joy which is truly the receiving of a hundredfold more.

By mid August, he and Biddy were proofreading the last pages of his talks on Job, before sending them to the Nile Mission Press in Cairo. He chose the book's title from a favorite line of Browning: *Baffled to Fight Better.*

Oswald's heavy speaking schedule necessitated reusing many of his sermons. His diary records dates, places, and message titles, presumably in an effort to keep from repeating a talk to the same audience. On Sunday, August 26, at the Aotea Home, he preached a new message with the striking title, "A Poetical View of Appendicitis" with Jeremiah 8:11 as his text: "They have healed the hurt of the daughter of my people slightly, saying, Peace, peace; when there is no peace." That morning, Chambers gave his audience this spiritual application: "That is the perpetual peril at all times, relieving present pain by a temporal fictitious cure, when what is needed for an effectual cure is a surgical operation." There is no evidence that anyone considered it unusual at the time, but in months to come, it would seem almost prophetic.

While Oswald's diaries reveal a man full of health and enthusiasm, photographs taken during this time show his face weathered and lined with fatigue. His sunken cheeks appear in marked contrast to his appearance two years before. Friends often expressed concern when he refused to rest during the midday heat and left the compound to visit men in hospitals.

In the past four months, he had had only five days off during a brief holiday at Damietta. He and the others at Zeitoun had taken those days only because the American Mission needed the E.G.M. compound and their bungalow for a conference. With Jimmy Hanson away for three months in England to be married, Oswald's responsibility for everyday tasks had greatly increased. Characteristically, though, his diary and letters were full of praise for the hard work of others:

> August 25, 1917. 4:30 p.m. Items Hut
> Surely no work ever had such devoted women as these here, nothing seems to daunt. Here is Woodbine [Gertrude Ballinger, just recovered from a near fatal illness] back again at Benha with Miss Ashe who has had an arduous time of it, and these here [Zeitoun] at it.

In addition to their other duties, Biddy, Miss Riley, and Eva Spink had just agreed to provide daily meals for twenty-five officers stationed in the nearby camp.

Chambers' diary continued:

> There are no dangers or heroic footlights to reveal matters of devotion of a rare stamp, but let anyone bear in mind the peculiarly arduous conditions of the climate here and remember that these women have had exactly one week's respite in the summer while the missionaries take two months in the year, and one will be able to gather a way of estimating the service of these faithful women, who would certainly have been among those in the New Testament of whom it is recorded 'they ministered unto Him of their substance.'

To Mrs. Hobbs, Biddy's mother, he wrote:

> *As for Biddy I love her and I am her husband*
> *but I do not believe it is possible to exaggerate*
> *what she has been in the way of a Sacrament*

out here—God conveying His presence through the common elements of an ordinary life. The letters she has received from mothers and wives and sisters and fathers and brothers are in themselves a deep testimony to a most unconscious ministry of wife and mother and woman.

Of the other women, what can I say. Never I think did any man have such a unique privilege as I have had in being associated with such women.

He continued with appreciation for Mrs. Hobbs and Dais, Biddy's sister, who had been so faithful in sending letters and books while enduring the food rationing and shortages in Britain, which had not touched them in Egypt.

At times I wonder if my words can be of any use to people who have been and are in suffering that I cannot imagine. They may say, 'Well what does he know of it all?' I know nothing but I do know that He is completely able for any strain any human being may be put to.

I think surely we will be Home to England next year. What a joy it will be to come back and see and be with you again. I am longing to get back, and contradictory though it seems after what I have just said, I have much burning to say and preach. . . .

I have been supernaturally protected by God's providence. Perhaps what He has taught me in these wonderful desert days may yet be uttered in the cities of men.

Chambers' diary continues the same tone of present contentment and expectancy for the immediate future:

September 3: The evening class was still fuller yet, and some fine private conversations issuing. As Biddy and I walked out again tonight in the desert under the glory of the waning moon, the wonder and the greatness of the time God has given us out here came again, also the sense of His protection so wonderful and complete.

On September 4, he wrote to his brother, Franklin:

Hanson is now en route to England or Heaven—as the submarines permit! Hancock

> *is at Gaza. Miss Ashe and Miss Ballinger are at Benha Station. All the other B.T.C. workers are at Zeitoun. Their work is beyond praise. I am like the figurehead—they do the work and I get the nominal praise but they do everything.*
>
> *There is every prospect of my going up the line some while later at the appointment of the Y.M. Administrative Council as a sort of co-ordinator of the Y.M.C.A. out here. The equipment is very quaint and modern. Boots, water bottle, sleeping tent, gas helmet and gumption. I shall fascinatingly enjoy it: mostly after El Arish, it is dugouts in the sand. However this is some way ahead yet.*
>
> *The religious side here is a great and big thing still growing. A blackboard talk every night at 7:30 and this has grown to outside the hut as well as inside. And three meetings on Sunday. Aotea Home 9:30 a.m., Zeitoun 11 and a big meeting in the Canteen at 7:30 Sunday evening.*

September 14: Again it is a lovely morning, the sun rose in a real marvel of glorious light. Each sunrise here looks as if it were a new thought of God, and makes me think what delight the Creator must have in thinking them.

I think I ought to give some notice in the diary of our animals, they are real adjuncts to the compound and especially to Kathleen's world. First, there is the donkey, he has a very reputable stable inscribed 'Eshat el Homar' (Hut of the Donkey); alongside is the rabbit hutch, but alas no rabbits, John Silence (of whom more anon) killed both, at least we suspect so.

Then Patsy, prime favourite, a perfect delight of a small black and tan collie, the very doggy incarnation of good temper, gentleness and splendid spirits. He is full of the most eminent sagacity and doggy good humour, lavishly fond of Kathleen, very spunky and no end of a sport. In fact he fills in Tweed's place like no other dog I ever had. He is splendidly loyal and comrady and a favourite with everyone. Each night after the class he goes for his run in the desert with Biddy and myself. We are taking care of him for Mr. Downes.

And then the cats—first the four kittens whose gambols and friskings are endlessly entertaining, and another Persian kitten which lives at the cash desk with Gladiolus mostly. And then John Silence, the presiding silent genius of the compound. He is a big cat, strong, jet black, panther-like, and completely devoted to the compound like a phantom. We have tried to get rid of him because he is quite wild and untamed, but he always comes back, silent and affectionate and dominatingly persistent. Certainly he is unlike any other cat I have ever known. These are the abiding compound pets, there are many other stray ones, tortoises, chameleons, lizards, and Kathleen's doves and pigeons, but they are safely housed in Mr. Swan's dovecote and are a very aristocratic assemblage.

A special tiny hut built for Kathleen served as a playhouse. Her toys, dolls, and favorite things, supposed to be kept in her hut, were usually found all over the compound, where she generously shared them with others. For every journey, long or short, she carried a weird collection of odds and ends, all of which she considered essential. The opening of Kathleen's "kit bag" became a regular feature at Zeitoun, during which soldiers expressed the greatest interest as she lectured on the merits of each item.

While life went on in Egypt, the British Army was poised at Gaza, with a railroad and water pipeline stretching behind them back to sources of supply. General Allenby had requested the Y.M.C.A. to attach secretaries and workers to each casualty clearing station in the battle area once the advance began. Their job was to help with physical aid, encourage the wounded, and pray with the dying.

September 20: I received the welcome news yesterday that I must hold myself in readiness to go up the line soon now.

On September 21, Biddy wrote home:

"My dearest Mother and Dais,

There have been two odd mails in this week but no letters from home yet. I am sending off a diary, and this is only a note as I want to try and get the diaries up to date, and as I am a month in arrear, I'll have to hurry up. We have got the Correspondence booklet ready and dispatched to Gertrude [Oswald's sister], and I am very glad that it and Job are done and we can soon look forward to seeing them in print and being read.

"There's a real chance of Oswald going soon for the Y.M. have undertaken the work of the clearing stations once the fight begins, it can't be long postponed now or the rains will be on them and make fighting impossible. All the secs. from here are to be ready to go any minute, and I think Oswald could catch the next train!

"He will go with an American doctor, Dr. Deaver, a delightful man and he'll be a fine companion, and of course it's essential to have medical knowledge as well as the other kind of help. So when you read of the 'taking' of Gaza in the papers you'll know that he'll be up amongst the wounded men and mighty glad he'll be too to be there. I don't suppose it will be too long at a time as of course they are only temporary [at] the clearing stations till they get sent off to the various hospitals. We shall carry on here as well as may be, rather like walking about with your head cut off! but we'll do our durndest all the same.

"A very nice Padre has started to take a Weds. evening service here, setting Oswald free for Ezbekieh again, he had a great time this Weds. and lots of the old ones gathered round. The Padre is very Scotch and at the end asked if anyone wanted to ask a question at him! It made me smile.

"Well, I shall be led into writing a long letter and I mustn't stay to do that. Friday is generally a busy day and we have about 18 hospital men to tea. It is a boon to have it cooler, the air is delightful now and one can begin to enjoy being in the sun! though its still blazing and fierce at noon.

Yours lovingly, Gertie."

Although rumors abounded concerning the start of Allenby's advance, no word came for Oswald to leave. On September 24, he began a new series on Ecclesiastes in the evening classes at Zeitoun. His diary chronicled the days of waiting, filled with people and God's blessing on the whole enterprise at Zeitoun.

September 30: What testimonies we have from time to time, all spontaneous and unsolicited. A man came to see me yesterday and his story was simple and splendid, and such an evidence of God's working in the haphazard. Some months ago he had been sent from hospital to the School and was lying out in the cold over against the wall the other side of the compound. He was a very heavy drinker, really drinking himself to death. We began our family worship and the hymn struck him, and the Spirit of God got hold of him, he came to the Devotional Hut classes, took stock, prayed, asked God to give him the Holy Spirit, lost all appetite for drink, threw up his smoking. He found smoking harder to give up than drinking, but he thought of Abraham giving up Isaac and was ashamed of himself, and pitched his cigarette case over the wall and has never smoked since, or had the desire for it. All this without one word to anyone, just by the Spirit of God. He has written from hospital telling me how he was saved, and asking would I put new heart into a mate of his who had just lost his mother.

Chambers' personal study in the autumn centered on the minor prophets, especially Hosea.

October 3: Hosea 14 is a great illumination for the parable of the prodigal son, especially verses 1-5. The magnanimous generosity of God's mighty joy in restoration when once backsliders return, no vindictiveness, no back memories, just great vast new beginnings, with the past as a fine culture of character for the present. V 9 is searchingly fine, 'For the ways of the Lord are right, and the just shall walk in them.'

October 5: The class was good and as large and keen as ever, and the night is now a supreme glory of moon and stars. Many men came to say good-bye as they are off up the line. I am told I must wait a little longer before going up.

October 7: A gem of an experience came after the evening service, a soldier came to see me under deep compunction of conscience, and after a talk we knelt in the deep and glorious moonlight at an old sun-bleached form in the compound and he transacted business with God on Luke 11:13, confirmed by 1 John 5:14-15, and his witness was undoubtedly John 14:27, 'My peace I give unto you.' One never gets used to the unspeakable wonder of a soul entering consciously into the Kingdom of Our Lord. It was a great joy to experience it all again.

October 17: I certainly find Dr. Forsyth's The Christian Ethic of War the greatest book I have read for many a year. Wherever the next phase of the BTC is formed in God's providence, this book shall undoubtedly be the text-book of the Christian Ethic class.

Oswald returned from his Wednesday night meeting at Ezbekieh feeling ill and spent a sleepless night suffering from intense abdominal pain. He assumed it was some kind of stomach bug, but it kept him in bed all the next day. His only diary mention of any difficulty was "lack of opportunity to write."

For three days he had no appetite and was unable to sleep, except in fitful minutes of sheer exhaustion. His face was drawn in pain and frequently he could not suppress his audible groans. The constant pain in his side ranged from a dull hurt to an aching throb.

On Sunday, October 21, he lumped three days diary together, writing:

As there is every prospect of my going up the line shortly, it is time some of these saints got broken in to taking the classes, so Biddy took the class Saturday night and the service this morning, which was peculiarly radiant with His presence. This evening Mr. Swan is taking the service.

By Tuesday, October 23, Oswald felt a little better, but prevailed on Mr. Swan to take all the evening classes for the coming week. During the day Chambers rested, read, and moved about as he was able. He resisted all suggestions of going to a hospital for an examination. Allenby had just launched his long-expected offensive against Gaza and Beersheba, and the battle was raging. He would not take a bed needed by wounded soldiers as they were brought back from the fighting in Palestine.

October 28: It is two years today since I began in this region, in the old hut, Zeitoun II, with Atkinson and Mackenzie and Cumine. In the early morning the passing of an Eastern night before the dawn brought out all its characteristics, limitless silver, grey-black shadows, dim white walls, violet blue skies. There is no idea of distance, and it is a thing to be witnessed.

Biddy took the morning service in the Devotional Hut, she has what we in Scotland mean when we speak of a 'lift' or an inspiration, her subject was Romans 12:1.

We had many people to dinner, Woodbine among them. Cross of the Remounts turned up, thus we are kept always in touch with many men.

The next day, Monday, October 29, the pain returned with such searing intensity that he allowed himself to be taken to Gizeh Red Cross Hospital. A resident surgeon immediately performed an emergency appendectomy, which was termed "successful." Biddy made plans to stay in the hospital and give Oswald round-the-clock care. Word from the hospital reached the camp at Zeitoun in time for the evening class, where scores of men knelt in the sand to pray for God's hand of healing on their spiritual "officer in charge," O.C.

For a week, Oswald gained strength and appeared to be recovering well. On Saturday, November 3, Eva Spink's prayer journal noted praise "for Thy keeping of my beloved two [Oswald and Biddy] in bringing him through safely."

The next day he suffered a serious relapse from a blood clot in his lung. He rallied from it only to be hit with another more serious attack the next day. As he drifted in and out of consciousness, Biddy clung to the verse God had impressed on her: "This sickness is not unto death."

The attending nurse tried to deal honestly with Biddy about the gravity of the situation. "There's no way he can recover," she said gently. "It's best to face it and be prepared for the worst."

Incredibly, Oswald came through it and began regaining strength again. Biddy felt sure a visit from Kathleen would cheer him, so friends brought the bright-eyed four-and-a-half-year-old with a huge ribbon in her hair to the hospital. Biddy took her to Oswald's bed where he managed a smile and a greeting.

"Hello, Scallywag," he said, and could say no more. Kathleen knew her Daddy's voice and his pet name for her, but she hardly recognized the man in the bed. He was so sick, so frail, so unlike her father had ever been before. She told him a story of the animals at Zeitoun and gave him a kiss before the nurse insisted the visit must end.

For another week Oswald fought back and gradually regained strength until Tuesday, November 13, when without warning he began to hemorrhage from the lungs. The next day he improved slightly but the attacks resumed during the night. At seven o'clock on the morning of November 15, he died.

Biddy left the hospital, numb with shock, and made her way to the Zwemer home just around the corner from Groppi's Restaurant. The thought of dinners at Groppi's with Oswald ambushed her with a fresh wave of pain and loss. A knock at the door brought Mrs. Amy Zwemer, who wrapped Biddy in her arms and gave her the gift of quiet listening and tears. Samuel, just back from the Far East, joined them as they committed Oswald to the glorious presence of God and waited together in prayer.

The words of Psalm 142:7 came to Biddy powerfully out of the silence: "Bring my soul out of prison, that I may praise thy name: the righteous shall compass me about; for thou shalt deal bountifully with me."

Before returning to Zeitoun, she jotted names of people for William Jessop to cable as soon as he could. Her mother and Dais must know, Oswald's father and mother, Mrs. Reader Harris, Franklin in Perth, and Arthur in Harrow. They could send the word round to others. The message?

"Oswald in His Presence."

On the day Chambers died, Allenby's forces advanced to within three miles of Jaffa, the biblical seaport of Joppa.

A journalist's dispatch from Palestine, printed on November 15 in the *London Daily Telegraph,* seemed to sum up the final battle Oswald had fought and won that day in Gizeh Red Cross Hospital. The London paper proclaimed:

"These Scots, who have borne the brunt of the work for the last two years in Egyptian desert warfare, are daily adding to their magnificent record. Nothing they have done in the past is equal to the present grand advance."

21
THE WORK GOES ON

(1917–1919)

Biddy would have preferred a simple burial, but the soldiers asked if they could honor Oswald their way. In their minds, he had given his life for them just as surely as a man who died in battle. Biddy knew Oswald would not want any pomp, but he had loved these Territorials and Tommies deeply. They should have the chance to commemorate the life of the man they loved as one of their own. She prayed that instead of mourning, God would give them all a sense of triumph.

Almost all military burials in Egypt took place on the day of death. Hospitals had neither time nor facilities for embalming, and next of kin were usually thousands of miles away. Funerals were most often a short graveside service attended by soldiers from a man's unit.

In Oswald's case, the funeral was delayed a full day in order to make arrangements for burial with full military honors. The cortege would leave from Gizeh Red Cross Hospital on the Nile's west bank and wind its way across the ancient river through the narrow streets of Old Cairo to the cemetery for soldiers from Britain, Australia, and New Zealand. Officers from the hospital asked if they might carry the casket from the gun carriage to the grave. A hundred other soldiers volunteered to march as an escort.

The crowd that gathered for the service was a cross-section of Cairo. Soldiers in uniform from half a dozen countries stood beside men wearing frock coats and holding top hats in their hands. Doctors, nurses, and men from hospitals and convalescent homes around the city came to say good-bye to the man who had so often cheered them by his visits. British ladies in long dresses took their place alongside Egyptian businessmen and servants. Mahommed, the lift operator from the Y.M.C.A., stood with head bowed next to Sidrak Effendi, foreman of the native workers at Zeitoun.

Many were asking "Why?" With modern medical facilities so close at hand, it seemed such a needless death. "If he had been at the front line," people said, "it would be understandable, but he was just outside Cairo. Why had he waited so long to seek treatment? Why hadn't someone recognized the symptoms of appendicitis earlier and insisted he get help? Why had he worked so long without rest, depleting his physical reserve to almost nothing? Why hadn't God overruled and spared a man so needed by his family and others?"

Biddy knew all the questions and had heard all the answers, helpful and trite. She knew what Oswald would say, and she often smiled when recalling his words and emphatic tone of voice. She could only pray that the Word of God in her dazed mind might find its way to touch the aching emptiness in the pit of her stomach.

Biddy, Kathleen, and Eva Spink left immediately after the funeral and boarded an overnight train for the four-hundred-and-fifty-mile journey to Luxor. Kathleen quickly fell asleep as night came and the train trundled south along the Nile. In the darkness, Biddy laid her head on Eva's shoulder and wept with great heaving sobs. Those left behind packed the hut at Zeitoun on Sunday night, November 18, for a memorial service. Into the crowd of nearly a thousand, each individual brought memories of an unusual man.

The Matron of the Aotea Home closed her eyes and saw Chambers walking toward the home every Sunday morning. Once, he arrived in a blinding sandstorm on a day she was sure he could not come. Her own belief in God had been shattered by the maimed bodies of men until Oswald's messages, week by week, caused her to see the loving compassion of Christ.

George Swan of the Egypt General Mission recalled the earnest man who had asked to build a bungalow in the mission compound two years earlier. Chambers was always innovating, always expanding in his own life and in his work with the men.

And how he loved children, especially his and Biddy's little "flower of God." Swan pictured his own son David, Kathleen's age, splashing together with her in the bathtub and playing in the sand. "I'm going to be a doctor and Kathleen's going to be a nurse," David often proclaimed. "When we grow up we're going to be married and be Mr. and Mrs. Jones." Swan wondered how anyone could bear death without children and without faith in God.

Gladys Ingram wondered how she could possibly get through the song Biddy had asked her to sing without crying. But from the first notes of "Jesus Triumphant" to the end, her voice was strong. For those who knew nothing of the Bible Training College in London, she told of the days before the war and then how they had all been led to Egypt. She had no time to tell of Chambers' faithful letters encouraging her to stay true to Christ in the face of overpowering temptations. She would never forget his most frequently written phrase to her, "Be absolutely His!" and his characteristic light-hearted signature, "Yours ever, Father Hicks."

The testimonies included soldiers whom Chambers had led to Christ and Sidrak Effendi's appreciation for Oswald's good teaching and his gentleness with him and all the Egyptian servants.

They all rose to their feet and sang their hope of meeting again, "When the roll is called up yonder I'll be there." And they wept in sorrow and joy as Private Kendle sang with deep feeling:

> On the Resurrection morning,
> Soul and body meet again,
> No more sorrow, no more weeping,
> No more pain.

When the service was over, they dispersed under a canopy of dazzling stars into the dark Egyptian night, their footsteps muffled by the sand. They all left, as Stanley Barling described it, "in a reconsecration of our lives to the Master he loved and obeyed without question above everything else."

The next day, the Personal and Social column of *The Egyptian Gazette* included news of The Sultan, the British Under Secretary for Agriculture, postings of high ranking military commanders, and the death of Oswald Chambers.

That same afternoon, far away in Luxor, Biddy sat alone on the deck of the *Ibis*, watching the ancient columns of the famous Luxor Temple grow dim in the gathering twilight. Down below, Eva Spink read Kathleen a bedtime story so Biddy could have a few moments alone. Samuel Zwemer had arranged for the three of them to spend a week with Mr. and Mrs. Phillips, American missionaries who used the boat for village outreach on the Nile. The Phillipses were gracious hosts and ready tour guides who also respected Biddy's need for time alone.

A felucca with its tall mast and single sail glided past silently. Biddy recalled their last holiday together at Damietta in August. Oswald had hired a felucca for a trip to Ras el Barr, where one branch of the Nile merged into the Mediterranean. She could hear his laughter and words of praise for the scenery as they sailed up and down the river. Was he really gone? Kathleen seemed to comprehend it so much better. Her father was not here, but There. He seemed every bit as real to her There as he had been here. "Don't forget," she often told Biddy, "Daddy's quite near you." Her childlike confidence in God allowed her to believe genuinely that it was just fine for her Daddy to be with Jesus.

Biddy walked to the bow of the boat and looked across the broad Nile. A faint afterglow outlined the hills rising behind the Valley of the Kings. The pharaohs buried there had sought a guide across the river of death to immortality on the other side. How much more Oswald knew now of life than he had ever known before!

The last words she had heard Oswald speak came back to her powerfully in the twilight quiet, "Greater works than these shall he do, because I go unto my Father."

"I felt as if God were there in Person by my side, actually speaking the words to me," she later wrote. "Instantly everything that had seemed to shut one in to the immediate present lifted, and again there was 'the land of far distances' and the assurance came, dimly at first, of a work yet to be done for Him."

Throughout the week, passages of Scripture came back to Biddy with renewed comfort and meaning. When they first faced the prospect of Oswald's going to the front in Palestine and the others carrying on the work without him, God's word of encouragement to Biddy was Joshua 1:5–6, "As I was with Moses, so will I be with thee: I will not fail thee, nor forsake thee. . . . Be strong and of a good courage."

"I wrote the promise down, together with others," she recalled, "and it was a wonderful experience to re-read the words later and realize how much more God had meant in giving the promise than one had ever dreamt.

"Through all the days of the illness and its crises, the word which held me was, 'This sickness is not unto death, but for the glory of God,' and there were times when it seemed that the promise was to have a literal fulfillment. But again God had a fuller meaning."

Each morning the words of *Daily Light* and the Psalms seemed to be especially for Biddy, Kathleen, and "Sphinx." For a week they enjoyed the completely different surroundings, saw the sights of Luxor, and began to heal. Samuel Zwemer's eighteen-year-old daughter, Bessie, was in Luxor during Biddy's visit. She was deeply shocked and disillusioned by Oswald's death. For two years she had provided piano accompaniment at Oswald's Ezbekieh meetings in Cairo. From this vantage point she had watched his spirituality spread among men who seemed impossible to reach with the gospel. The two shared a love of music as well as a friendship and partnership in ministry. His jokes had sent her into gales of laughter during her mother's famous Friday afternoon teas in the Zwemer home. She could not understand a kind, merciful God taking such a radiant man who was so vital to the life of the men in Egypt.

One night, Bessie and Biddy were sitting in deck chairs on the *Ibis* talking about Oswald. Bessie glanced toward a table and was astonished to see Oswald sitting there, "as natural as ever, though seemingly more radiant." She heard him say, "Bulger, [his nickname for her], let not your heart be troubled. It's all right, you can't understand God's ways but get down into His love. Don't lose your grip. Be radiant for Him."

Bessie turned to Biddy and asked excitedly, "Did you see him here just now?" She described the vision. Biddy replied that she hadn't seen it, but didn't doubt that her young friend had. For days Bessie pondered the experience, wondering if it could have come to bring her back to faith in the goodness and love of God.

After a week in Luxor, the Wilkinsons, friends of Bessie Zwemer, invited Biddy and Kathleen to their home at Wasta, some sixty miles south of Cairo on the Nile. For another week they enjoyed gracious hospitality and beautiful surroundings with people who had been greatly influenced by reading some of Oswald's sermons.

In late November, Jimmy Hanson arrived in Port Said from England and was stunned to learn of Oswald's death. After a day at Zeitoun, he came to Wasta to be with Biddy and talk about the future. What was God leading them all to do? Jessop had asked Biddy if she and the others would stay on at Zeitoun and continue the work. She felt it was the only thing to do but struggled with the seeming impossibility of carrying it on in Oswald's "radiant" way. "Anything less than that," she said, "would not be worthwhile."

On the evening of November 30, Biddy and Kathleen arrived back at Zeitoun. They stood for a time at the entrance of the compound, looking at the familiar scene—the huts, the groups of soldiers, and at the far end, the bungalow with men and women gathering for the suppertime fellowship and family prayers. Everything looked just the same, and yet all was so completely changed.

The words of *Daily Light* that morning came back to her, "My peace I give unto you . . . My presence shall go with thee."

They walked across the compound into a chorus of greetings and hugs. Kathleen was delighted to be back home with her friends. Biddy knew it was the place for her, too, and believed that one day at a time, God would show her how to pick up the pieces and go on.

The evening classes resumed with the men being told that it was no longer a situation of "teacher and taught," but they would all learn together the truths of God. Two nights a week they studied Oswald's book *Biblical Psychology,* one night in the gospel of John, a Saturday evening prayer meeting, and the remaining services taken by Padre Watson and other chaplains.

No one pretended that it was the same without Oswald. But as much as they all missed him, they accepted the new situation and went on. Biddy took the Sunday morning service every other week, alternating with others of the "B.T.C. Expeditionary Force." The men continued to throng the huts for the free tea and faithfully attended the evening classes.

In the weeks following Oswald's death, Biddy received scores of letters from soldiers, missionaries, and friends at home. Each person voiced a sense of loss along with deep appreciation for Oswald's impact on them. Each day more letters arrived, and it appeared hopeless to think of sending a personal answer to them all.

While leafing through Oswald's Bible, she found a letter written in October to former students of the Bible Training College. She had it printed and mailed as a New Year's card to their B.T.C. family scattered around the world.

> *To all former students of the Bible Training College we send a message of good cheer, and a hearty reminder that the 'B.T.C.' still stands as our watchword, viz. 'Better to Come.'*
>
> *Let us watch and pray, taking these words to mean keeping ourselves by spiritual concentration heedful of the true source of our life—our relationship to Jesus Christ, which is but the reminder that the Best is yet to be.*
>
> *Let me recall to your remembrance our unity of spirit in the days now gone. Such a union, unless it is seen to be in Him and for His purpose, easily sinks into a sentimental episode. Our union is not so much a union for work or for any organization, as a union out of which Our Lord can 'help Himself.' Never mistake organization for the organism; organization is a great necessity, but not an end in itself. To live for any organization is a spiritual disaster; to use organization without abusing it is the only aim of our union.*

> *Our main idea should be to remain where our business or calling or location finds us at the time, allowing God to shape our circumstances as He providentially may.*
>
> *In the immediate days after the war we may meet together again, or we may not; we may have another passing organization of the B.T.C., or we may not; but whatever transpires, it is ever 'the best is yet to be.'*

The letter addressed the need to communicate with one group of friends but had no relevance to the soldiers they had met during the past two years. One day in early December, Jimmy Hanson showed Biddy a folder of clippings from the League of Prayer magazine. Each one was a sermon of Oswald's. "Wouldn't it be great," he said, "if we could print one of these as a leaflet and send it to the men in Egypt and France?"

The suggestion seemed to answer the dilemma so perfectly that Biddy enthusiastically agreed. They sifted through the articles and selected "The Place of Help," a message on Psalm 121 that Oswald had dictated to her during their honeymoon in the Catskill Mountains. The sermon was eagerly devoured and requests poured in for more.

On January 5, 1918, Biddy wrote to her mother and sister: "God's seal has so signally been put on the work in every way just as it was when Oswald was here. It's such a delight to send the books around and hear from the men how keen they are to get and read them. Three sermons are under way by now."

Baffled to Fight Better was back from the printer, and free copies were sent to men all over Egypt. When the men found there was no charge for the books, they voluntarily gave money to help with further printings. Dr. Zwemer sent a hundred copies to missionaries as New Year's gifts. Biddy was gratified, feeling that the printed word was simply an extension of the ministry Oswald's teaching had begun.

In February an attack of jaundice sent her back to the Wilkinsons' home in Wasta to recuperate. The trip itself was enough to cause a relapse. A balky Y.M. car caused Biddy, Kathleen, and Mary Riley to miss the fast train from Cairo. After waiting for an hour at the station, they took a slow train that took three hours to travel the sixty miles. Then they endured a storm-tossed crossing of the Nile at Wasta.

On February 11, a few days after arriving, she wrote home, reveling in her improved health and the quiet home atmosphere and gracious hospitality of her hostess. "Mrs. Wilkinson says she can never show her gratitude for the difference it has made in her life to read Oswald's books. She says everything is different now and it seems to be what she has been waiting for for years. It confirms me so much in the assurance I have that I am to go on getting everything I can printed. It will be like casting bread upon the waters and we'll know someday all it has meant in people's lives. I am more and more grateful to have the work to do. I feel like John that the world couldn't contain the writings if I were to get all my notes printed."

For a month Biddy had the luxury to do little more than eat, sleep, walk in the garden, read, and answer a growing mound of mail. The days with no pressure and responsibility gave her new opportunity to come to terms with Oswald's death.

To her mother she wrote on February 14: "I do love you to say how near he seems, the sense of that as well as the wonder of the life he's living (for it must be all we can imagine of 'life and joy and far, far more') grows increasingly.

"Bishop Moule in writing of 'with Christ which is far better,' says it means better than the earthly at its very best, and in that way is so true of Oswald for he sort of lived to the utmost, and it gives one an idea of what the 'very far better' must be for him and the thought is always with one that that life is for us too when God's time comes. It makes each day of the 'in between' time so full of significance. Oswald always used to say, 'Lay out each day as you do a sovereign and spend the hours for Him.' "

Again, to her mother on February 21: "I went up on the roof at sunset time and there was a glorious view of river and trees and hills and the Psalm for the morn had been the wonderful 121st, and in the quiet and peace of it all God again lifted my eyes right onto Himself, and I recalled the Daily Light words 'ye are dead and your life is hid with Christ in God.' It made me realize how really we are one with those already in His presence. They seem to live on with us and we seem to share in their life too, and there is no separation."

The first leaflet sermon sent out in December 1917 was followed by one each month until July 1918 when William Jessop asked if the Y.M.C.A. could take over the responsibility of the monthly printing and distribution. For each of the next ten months, the Y.M. printed ten thousand copies of one of Oswald's talks given in the Zeitoun Hut, and sent them to every camp in Egypt, Palestine, and France.

George Swan of the Egypt General Mission once dubbed Oswald "the apostle of the haphazard" because of Chambers' emphasis on discovering God's will through what he called "the haphazard circumstances of life." Biddy and Oswald had always talked of literary work "together" and with his death, the dream had died. That had been a wrenching surprise, a shock of such surpassing pain that for a time Biddy despaired of her future. Now it seemed that the whole enterprise of printing his talks had sprung up out of nothing into a growing conviction of God's purpose for her.

During Biddy's visit to the Rev. Douglas Downes' hut near Alexandria in late June, he told the men about Oswald and his printed sermons. "They took all the sermons Mr. Downes put out," she wrote home, "so this will be another centre. Many opportunities of distributing the sermons have opened up here. At the Y.M. they have asked for a number. Every day the circle widens and I do see it all being done in the spontaneous way that marked every bit of Oswald's life.

"More and more I see the truth of what he said, 'The one right thing to be is a believer in Jesus Christ.' To me he is always that preeminently."

During the sweltering summer of 1918, Biddy divided her time between serving soldiers in the canteen at Zeitoun and typing sermons and writing letters in the dugout. She wrote to her sister on August 31:

"I am just getting ready another sermon, 'What's The Good of Temptation?' and it certainly will be the very best yet! I am glad I feel that about each one. The next one should be out today, 'Is Human Sacrifice Redemptive?' and that is specially good. It's fine to have to get one out regularly every month.

"I feel as if I will never come to an end of my wealth of notes. I just gloat over the College store when we get back. *The Sermon on the Mount* is in hand being reprinted, and I have got the calendar of sayings all ready, and shall send Gertrude [Oswald's sister] a copy of it next week so that she can have them printed in England also. I feel as if that is going to mean a lot to many, I know you will like the idea.

"Then the next book will be *Shadow of an Agony* that is in the process of retyping just now. I find how much benefit I have got still from my old legal days, I mean getting into the habit of perfecting a thing by typing and retyping, and I am glad to have had all the experience of those other days.

"We are quite slack in the canteen today, considerably over 1,000 men went away this morning and so far none have taken their places, but we hear of 1,500 to come from England into the Administrative Unit, that's what they call the place where the R.A.M.C. (Royal Army Medical Corps) men are turned into infantry, much to the general dislike!

"This is most assuredly our spot until we get orders to quit. You can imagine what a strength and even joy it is to be here and carry on Oswald's work and to so continually see a harvest of his life and teaching, and more and more I do feel that he is still part of it. As he said in 'The Dawn of Eternal Hope,' we can live the actual life in the light of eternal realities, and that is just what it seems to be here. And just as one knows the presence of God so I growingly realise Oswald's presence, and so continually some word of his own comes with all the power and bracing that it ever did when he spoke, and I feel there is only one way to go on just praising God for the reality of the unseen things, and for the work He has given us to do.

"I know too how very much I owe to your prayers and the prayers of so many, those words in Hebrews, 'find grace to help in time of need' seem to be true not only for oneself in prayer but as one prays for others, and I am certain that is where much of my grace comes from.

"Living with Oswald and seeing his faith in God and knowing that 'by his faithfulness he is speaking to us still' is the secret of life these days, and I feel as if it will be overwhelming to one day see what God has wrought, and one will only be sorry not to have trusted more utterly. So just go on praying and believing and we will surely find that God is doing His wondrous things all the time.

"Kathleen is sitting under the verandah 'reading.' She has done some scrubbing and some needling! The Weaver boys have gone away so she has no playmates till David [Swan] returns in about three weeks. Mr. Swan has returned and has his meals with us while the house is being painted. We always have some 'odd' ones in to meals, and for a few nights. They do so appreciate being near a home.

"These days are very hot and it's the damp time of year when the Nile is rising, and the sun is very fierce. Another month will see the hottest time over though and the summer has gone wonderfully quickly.

"You'd be surprised how we miss the sun if it happens to be a cloudy morning, we feel quite odd till the sun blazes again! So I don't know how we will get on in Blighty [soldier's slang for England]. I shant mind trying it all the same!"

On November 11, 1918, the Armistice in Europe brought the war to an end. But while an army can be deployed into battle overnight, it takes months to bring it home. An army of occupation stays until the lines are drawn and the politicians are satisfied the borders will not be violated. After orders to demobilize orders were finally issued in Egypt the Y.M.C.A. still had plenty of work left to do.

In January 1919, Biddy accompanied Eva Spink and Gladys Ingram to Cairo station to tell them good-bye. Both were engaged to be married and thrilled to be on their way home to England. Almost as they left, Jimmy Hanson's wife came from England, finally permitted to join him after their marriage sixteen months before. Faithful Mary Riley of the early B.T.C. contingent remained at Zeitoun, recently rejoined by Katherine Ashe, back from a time of duty in a hostel in Jerusalem. Philip and Gertrude (Ballinger) Hancock, now married, were at Ismailia. Political unrest and an uprising among the Egyptians in early 1919 further delayed the slow demobilization process. Men longing to go home languished in camps with little to do except "hurry up and wait."

At Zeitoun the weekly classes and services continued as usual, with constantly changing faces. Along with new men, old friends from the early years in Egypt were reassigned to the Imperial School of Instruction, bringing them back for a time.

In late April Biddy and Kathleen took a ten-day trip to Jerusalem. In spite of the abundance of "authentic sites" and religious relics on display, Biddy remarked that being in the places where Jesus walked enabled her to enter "a little more into what it cost for Him 'to keep open house for the Universe.' " Kathleen enjoyed dipping her foot in the Pool of Siloam and pronouncing herself "healed," but flatly refused to accompany Biddy on a final day trip to Hebron. "No more tombs!" was her word for the day.

By the time they returned to Zeitoun, more friends had left for home. In June, Biddy and Kathleen, along with Mary Riley and the Hansons, received a sailing date, and final preparations began in earnest. The last member of their "family" of soldiers who had labored so tirelessly in the work at Zeitoun left for demobilization just before they did.

Each was glad to go and sad to leave. They would leave behind more of themselves than anyone could know. Oswald's grave still bore its wooden cross with his name, the date of his death, and the words "Superintendent Y.M.C.A." At the foot of the cross lay a Bible, carved in stone, given by Peter Kay, the rugged Australian soldier who had found Christ through Chambers. Its pages were open to Luke 11:13, "If ye being evil know how to give good gifts to your children, how much more shall your heavenly Father give the Holy Spirit to those who ask him."

"On our last day," Biddy wrote, "we went out to Old Cairo, to the place from which one is never far in spirit. And in the beauty and solitude which reign there, we thanked God for all the knowledge of Himself that had come to us during the years in Egypt; we offered Him praise for all that we had heard and seen concerning the Word of Life; and we thanked Him for the abiding fellowship with the one who had lived before us the Great Life of believing in Jesus Christ."

PART 6

"There will come one day a personal and direct touch from God when every tear and perplexity, every oppression and distress, every suffering and pain, and wrong and injustice will have a complete and ample and overwhelming explanation."
— Shade of His Hand

22
MY UTMOST

(1919–1926)

Kathleen kept her face pressed to the window from the moment the train left Southampton. "It's so green," she kept repeating in six-year-old amazement. "Will Grandma and Aunt Dais meet us at the station? Do you think they'll recognize me? Where are we going to live?"

Biddy and the others in the compartment took turns responding to the endless stream of questions and comments. It did seem strange to be back in England after three and a half years away. The countryside looked beautiful with the trees and flowers at the height of their summer glory.

The war had not touched the land here, but the people who worked it were as deeply scarred as the shattered forests and trench-lined fields of France. Every home and family in Britain had lost someone in the Great War. Rationing of food and fuel still persisted in the aftermath of a conflict that had taken the lives of nearly a million men from the British Empire. In the war-ravaged countries of Europe, the toll of soldiers and civilians was an unthinkable fifteen times greater. Even after massive relief efforts, starvation, exposure, and disease still claimed lives on the Continent every day.

A small group of family and friends met the train and hustled everyone off for a cup of tea and hours of conversation. The August issue of *Spiritual Life* magazine reported the event for League of Prayer readers under the heading, "HOME AGAIN!"

"Everyone will be very glad to know that Mrs. Chambers and Kathleen, accompanied by Miss Ashe and Mr. and Mrs. Jimmy Hanson arrived home from Egypt on Thursday, July 3rd. The notice was short, and many who would have liked to have been at Waterloo [station] did not hear in time, though the few who got the good news gave them a very warm welcome. They all looked fine and well, with a touch of the real Eastern complexion, while Kathleen has grown from a kiddie in arms to a little slip of a girl, all sun-bonnet and smiles, and so like her daddy.

"The news soon spread, and quite a crowd of Zeitoun men came up to see them at the Polytechnic on the Sunday afternoon following their arrival. Mrs. Chambers spoke for a few minutes, emphasising the need for us all, through the joy and strangeness of coming home, to remember the abiding things of God, and to put Him first in everything. She has now gone to the country for a week or two.

"Future plans are uncertain, but we all know that there is first God's Plan to be lived, and we can safely leave everything to Him, 'carefully careless' of it all."

Following the initial round of welcome gatherings, Kathleen and Biddy moved into a small London flat with her mother and sister. Kathleen dressed like a proper British little girl, but she had the heart of an untamed bedouin. From the freedom of roaming the compound at Zeitoun, she had entered the confined space of a few rooms where her grandmother's breakable things could not be touched. Loud talking and singing were out of the question. Even Biddy's daily typing proved to be too much noise for the ailing Mrs. Hobbs. Everyone endured for a few months, knowing all along that a change had to be made.

Everywhere Kathleen turned there seemed to be a new rule or regulation. When she passed a green grocer's shop on the way to school, she reached out for a banana or an orange as naturally as she had done in the canteen at Zeitoun. Once Biddy discovered the inadvertent thefts, she asked the grocer to keep a running tab, which she paid weekly. In the meantime, she tried to orient Kathleen to a completely new culture.

Eric and Gladys Ofverberg's flat in the North London suburb of Finsbury Park was no bigger than Mrs. Hobbs', but they were young and had a three-year-old daughter of their own. They shared a deep friendship with Biddy because of their contact with Oswald at Speke Hall and evening classes at the Bible Training College.

"Come live with us," they said. "We don't have anything breakable that isn't already broken." For most of a year the two families blended together, sharing what they had. Eric worked for Westminster Bank while Biddy was sustained by occasional gifts of food and money from family and friends.

The days were filled with visits from former B.T.C. students, League of Prayer friends, and men they had met in Egypt. All expressed their hope that she would continue publishing Oswald's messages and eagerly awaited each new issue. Many days, a small gift for "the work of the books" arrived, enclosed in a letter from a friend.

She continued to focus on getting Oswald's words into print and could now work from the rich store of notes taken during the Bible College years. The small amount of money received from any sales went toward further printing projects. Biddy took nothing for herself and Kathleen.

Oswald's sister Gertrude had served as home secretary of the Bible Correspondence Course during the Egypt years and handled reprinting of the earliest sermons in England. Gertrude, like all of Oswald's sisters had never married. Now, from the family home in southeast London, she fulfilled requests for books and helped answer mail. After Hannah Chambers' death in 1921, Gertrude continued to care for her father, Clarence, until his passing four years later.

After almost a year with the Ofverbergs, a friend wrote Biddy about a cottage for rent in Yarnton, just north of Oxford. For only five shillings a week, it was worth a look. Kathleen was eight and they needed a home of their own. The cottage turned out to be primitive but livable. Their New Year's card for 1922 bore the address of Ivy Lodge, Yarnton.

They had no electricity, no running water, a coal fire for cooking, and an outdoor toilet. Much of each day for Biddy was spent in the never-ending tasks of cooking, keeping house, and doing laundry. Still, she made time to sit at the typewriter and transcribe her shorthand notes. In 1922 *The Psychology of Redemption* took its place alongside five previously published books. With each new printing, she made corrections and alterations, striving for the clearest presentation of Oswald's words.

Their cottage belonged to a large manor house inhabited by a prosperous Oxford businessman, his wife, and sister. The wife, confined to a wheelchair by crippling arthritis, frequently drank herself into angry rages. She shouted and swore, railing against everyone and everything she thought responsible for her confinement and pain. Sometimes, late at night, while Kathleen slept, the man servant from the manor house would rap quietly on the door of the lodge, saying, "Mrs. Chambers, the lady of the house is asking for you."

Biddy would dress quietly, then follow him to the house, where she would sit for an hour without saying a word as she listened to the woman vent her torment. When the bitterness and blasphemy had run their course, Biddy would approach the woman, kiss her forehead gently, and say, "God bless you. Sleep well."

Major John Skidmore, Oswald's close friend from League days, paid Kathleen's fees to attend a good school in Oxford. Each morning the man of the house drove his pony and trap to work in Oxford, and beside him sat Kathleen, his honored guest on her way to school.

In 1923 their next adventure in living took them to a large, eight-bedroom house at 200 Woodstock Road in Oxford. The owner sold it for a pittance and agreed to leave his furniture, ponderous and ugly as it was. As a frustrated inventor of toilets, he also left a wildly conceived and constructed water closet, resembling some kind of brass-railed throne. Kathleen found it all very amusing and inconvenient.

Biddy took the large house in Oxford to earn income as a licensed lodging-house keeper for university students. With four men as resident boarders, she provided them with breakfast and supper during the week and full board on weekends.

At 6:00 a.m. every day she was up with her teapot and Bible, often filling a notebook page with her shorthand prayers. Before preparing breakfast for the students, she left a cup of tea on the stand next to Kathleen's bed and awakened her with a kiss. Then she cooked and served the morning meal. With everyone off to school and the morning dishes washed up, she retreated to a small basement room lined with books and boxes.

She lifted the dust cover from her immaculately kept typewriter and began to transcribe her notes from the sermon class at the Bible Training College. She hadn't finished two sentences when a knock echoed down from the front door. Without hesitation, she replaced the dust cover and made her way upstairs.

Two hours later, a worried friend from up the road was on her way, fortified by tea, homemade cakes, and the satisfaction of having poured out her trouble to someone who cared and prayed with her. "Give to all who ask," Biddy said to herself as she picked up her shopping basket, "and the Lord will look after who comes to ask."

After her daily trip to the green grocer, the butcher shop, the bakery, and the mercantile for canned goods, she might complete the laundry and cleaning before preparing the evening meal. Perhaps after that she could return to "the books."

Miss Ashe would be back soon for one of her prolonged stays, and that meant a whirlwind of activity. Biddy loved the devoted, white-haired lady, but her domineering presence overpowered all other plans. Miss Ashe's concern for them, like a thick wool blanket, was welcome when wrapped around their shoulders, but smothering when held over their heads.

In 1924 a new edition of *Shade of His Hand,* Oswald's last talks at Zeitoun, was published by Alden and Company in Oxford. Biddy appreciated their fine work and mentioned to them that she was working on a new book, a collection of daily readings gleaned from all of Oswald's talks. "When you have it ready," they said, "we'd like to see it."

The problem was getting it ready. She needed three hundred sixty-five portions, each on a single theme, each complete in itself and not more than five hundred words long. Before she could make the selections, there were hundreds of talks she must transform from verbatim shorthand notes into typed copy.

What was it Oswald used to say? "Do your work; don't let your work cling to you. The latter impedes you while the former expresses you." So she would begin, and each day work with the time and energy God gave. When people came, she put them first.

In the midst of it all, she didn't want to neglect Kathleen, now a headstrong girl approaching twelve. When the students paid on time, it provided just enough to live on, never enough for new clothes. Biddy could do without indefinitely, but it hurt her to see Kathleen so distraught over being unable to dress like the other girls at school.

More than once, the efforts of well-meaning, but insensitive people precipitated a crisis. A well-dressed lady would come by and leave them a box of clothing. "I'm sure you can use these," she would say to Kathleen, giving her a pat on the head. When the lady was gone, Kathleen would stare in disbelief at the worn out, soiled, ragged clothes.

"What do they think we are?" she would shout, hurling the detested dresses and frayed blouses across the room. "I wouldn't be caught dead in these!"

Biddy would wait until all the clothes had been thrown and all the frustration had been aired before trying to comfort Kathleen. "They don't understand," was all she could say. She didn't expect her young daughter to notice that she had no new clothes herself. Some day it would be clear to Kathleen and that would be soon enough. Biddy had the same needs as any woman, but her wants were on an entirely different plane than most.

After nearly three years of painstaking work in moments stolen from her lodging-house duties, Biddy had compiled the book of daily readings. There seemed only one title appropriate for it, one of Oswald's most repeated watchwords—*My Utmost For His Highest*.

Biddy herself was the editor and publisher. With gifts from friends, she paid for the first edition to be printed by Alden in Oxford. She was responsible for distribution and wisely involved a large London firm, Simpkin, Marshall, Hamilton, Kent and Company.

Biddy was forty-four when she wrote the foreword in October 1927:

"These daily readings have been selected from various sources, chiefly from the lectures given at the Bible Training College, Clapham, during the years 1911–1915; then, from October 1915 to November 1917, from talks given night by night in the

Y.M.C.A. Huts, Zeitoun, Egypt. In November 1917 my husband entered God's presence. Since then many of the talks have been published in book form, and the various sets of lectures from which these readings have been gathered will also be published in due course.

"A large proportion of the readings have been chosen from the talks given during the Devotional Hour at the College—an hour which marked for so many of the students an epoch in their life with God.

" 'Men return again and again to the few who have mastered the spiritual secret, whose life has been hid with Christ in God. These are of the old time religion, hung to the nails of the Cross' (Robert Murray McCheyne). It is because it is felt that the author is one to whose teaching men will return, that this book has been prepared, and it is sent out with the prayer that day by day the messages may continue to bring the quickening life and inspiration of the Holy Spirit."

She signed only her initials, "B.C." Nowhere in the book did it mention her name or her work of taking shorthand notes, typing the talks, and merging paragraphs from three different messages into a coherent reading for a single day. The author was Oswald Chambers. She was a channel through which his words were conveyed to others. That was her way.

23
WORDS FOR THE WORLD

(1927–1966)

My Utmost was eagerly received by readers of the earlier books and soon found its way to a wider audience. People who had never heard of Oswald Chambers were taken by these powerful words that seemed to have been written the very morning they read them. Biddy sent scores of free copies to friends and missionaries around the world.

In 1928, Biddy moved from Oxford to London to help Dais care for their mother, now in seriously failing health. They all lived together in a small house at 40 Church Crescent in the lovely north London borough of Muswell Hill. Knowing that Kathleen needed a different environment in which to flourish, Biddy arranged for her to continue her education in Scotland and live with Mr. and Mrs. Guy Morton, long-time family friends. Guy had met Oswald and Biddy while serving as a soldier in Egypt and deeply appreciated their ministry to him. Having their daughter join his family was a personal joy, and his way of saying "thanks."

The Mortons lived in a beautiful home in the Ochil Hills of Clackmannanshire County, northeast of Stirling. Every afternoon before doing her homework, Kathleen took the family dogs, two Labradors, and walked up to a tiny cabin to have tea with an old sheepherder. Often she arrived as he serenaded his flock with his bagpipes. Soon she understood why her father loved Scotland so much. For six years she attended Dollar Academy, which provided an excellent education in a setting she greatly enjoyed—three hundred boys to one hundred girls.

As much as Biddy missed Kathleen, she wanted her to grow and develop independently, not tied to her apron strings. She hoped the Mortons' home would help nurture her daughter during these important years and help fill the void of having no father.

The success of *My Utmost* created great interest in Oswald's teachings, and Biddy continued to give herself to "the work of the books," as she always referred to her calling. From month to month, the receipts from sales provided just enough to produce new books and keep the previous works in print. When a printing bill came in the mail, it seemed to be closely followed by money from a bookseller or distributor. Biddy accounted meticulously for every shilling and still took nothing for her work.

Her greatest joy came from relationships—letters and visits from the "family" forged together at the B.T.C. and in Egypt. Every day brought news from another part of the world. Gladiolus and her husband Vyvyan Donnithorne were now missionaries in China. Sphinx had married Stephen Pulford, a soldier she met at Zeitoun, and he was now a Vicar in the Church of England. Jimmy Hanson ran a Methodist mission in the most dangerous slums of London's East End. The Hancocks were in Persia, and other beloved friends were scattered around the globe.

In the early 1930s, a group of friends gathered around Biddy to share responsibilities in the growing complexity of the book work. Percy Lockhart, best man at their wedding, chaired an informal committee that included Oswald's sister Gertrude, Biddy's sister Dais, Rae Griffin, and L.R.S. Clarke, a former soldier from Egypt.

Each meeting brought news of further interest in the books and translations into new languages. When the balance sheet showed a positive result, the committee did what Biddy would never do for herself by voting to pay her house rent and taxes, as well as providing a small salary for her work and a gift for an annual holiday. She in turn kept the committee on track when the business considerations threatened to overshadow the ministry. When a fee was received for translation rights, she always moved that the money be given to a missionary and usually suggested a name. When the committee questioned the number of books given away, she reminded them that their mission together was not to sell books, but to help people.

In 1932, with the help of the Rev. David Lambert, Biddy launched the *Bible Training Course Monthly Journal.* A primary purpose was to maintain ties with former students of the B.T.C. who were now serving as foreign missionaries. The *Journal* contained previously unpublished messages given by Oswald at the Bible College in London along with personal reports from former students. Soon the circulation of the *Journal* reached 700.

With the *Journal,* as with the books, Biddy's set purpose and strong determination carried the day in every committee decision. When the *Journal* began operating at a loss and subscriptions dropped, the committee wanted to cease publication. Biddy quietly but firmly reminded them that the missionaries in remote areas looked forward to it each month and that alone was enough for its continued existence. She was never overbearing on any issue, but she was never timid in speaking her mind.

About this time, close friends finally persuaded Biddy to compile a book about Oswald. For the past fifteen years, she had been content to let his books speak for themselves, but so many new readers asked questions about the man himself, she took it as God's leading to move ahead. *Oswald Chambers: His Life and Work,* published in 1933, presented Chambers through his diaries, letters, and the recollections of family and friends. Compared to *My Utmost,* sales of "The Life" were modest and caused Biddy to wonder if she had done the right thing. But steady demand led to an expanded second edition in 1938.

The death of Biddy's mother and the quite unexpected marriage of her sister at the age of sixty brought the sale of the house at 40 Church Crescent and a move in 1938 to nearby 29 Woodberry Crescent. Kathleen had returned to London and completed her nurse's training at King's College Hospital. The house was always filled with her friends. In the midst of hosting weekly Bible studies and keeping an open house for all, Biddy invested long hours at her typewriter, still working from her store of shorthand notes to bring yet another book into being.

By this time, nearly fifty letters a day came to Biddy asking about the books and the man who wrote them. The volume of mail caused the Muswell Hill post office to set apart a separate "pigeon hole" for Biddy. One letter addressed to "Mrs. Oswald Chambers, London," was delivered to her with no delay.

When war engulfed the world again in 1939, demand surged for Oswald's books. His words spoken in the huts of Egypt fell on listening ears of people thrust into "the shadow of an agony." For a time it seemed that the war would bring an undreamed of expansion for the work of the books. And then the unthinkable happened.

In September 1940, the German Luftwaffe launched a devastating campaign of nightly aerial attacks that became known as the London Blitz. On December 29, Simpkin Marshall's book warehouse, near St. Paul's Cathedral, was hit by incendiary bombs causing a fire that raged out of control for two days. The entire stock was destroyed by the blaze, including 40,000 copies of books by Oswald Chambers.

Six months before, Biddy and the book committee had decided, after lengthy discussion, that in accordance with the teaching in the books, the stock should not be insured. If a fire should occur at Simpkins, no claim would be made. Now, their bank balance of £250 in January 1941 could not come near replacing the enormous quantity of books lost in the Blitz. With that, it appeared "the work of the books" had come to an end.

In her typical way, Biddy remained unperturbed. When news came of the burned books, she put down her teacup, turned to Kathleen and said calmly, "Well, God has used the books for His glory, but now that is over. We'll wait and see what God will do now." As the bombs continued to rain on London, she found strength through quietness and confidence in the Almighty. God was in control, and He would make His way plain.

One of Oswald's abiding concerns had been to heed God's ruling and never keep an enterprise going just because it was doing well. That attitude of trust had enabled them to clearly see God's hand in the closing of the B.T.C. when the war came. Oswald had often said, "When *God* finishes something, it must be finished."

The loss in the bombing was soon tempered by bits of good news. Word came that all the books in German had been bought by friends and were safely in Switzerland. A printer in southwest England wrote saying that he had the plates for several books and could reprint any time. People kept asking for Oswald's books, and Biddy decided that evidently God was not yet finished with this work.

At home her commitment to hospitality continued through the war years and beyond, even when a progressive loss of hearing made conversation very difficult for her. The house in Muswell Hill was always crowded with visitors, and Biddy, as usual, frequently exchanged her service at the typewriter for her ministry of the teapot.

One afternoon Kathleen popped in for a visit to find her mother and three neighborhood children sitting in the back garden during a downpour. They were laughing hilariously as the water ran off their rain hats into their teacups. "Whatever are you doing?" Kathleen yelled out the door.

"Mrs. Biddy said we could have a tea party outside this afternoon," one of the children replied, "and so we are!"

When the cat ate the fish Biddy had laid out for dinner and extra guests arrived unexpectedly, she searched the pantry for an alternative and sang, "Praise my soul the King of Heaven." When everything was back to normal, she would declare it so by saying, "There we are, praise the Lord, all nice and straight again."

Biddy rarely had a twenty-four-hour period in which it appeared she had accomplished something great for God. But the total of her days added up to a towering achievement of published works and human kindness. The *B.T.C. Journal* continued for eighteen years. Before she died in 1966, fifty books bearing her husband's name had been published along with thousands of booklets, seed thought calendars, and leaflet sermons. Every morning, people around the world opened a small book they called *My Utmost* to help set their sights on God for that day.

Like Oswald, however, her life centered on people, not publishing. The work of the books took its place in the larger context of lovingly giving herself to Christ and "to all who ask."

One evening, not long after the Second World War, a group of seminary students arrived unannounced at 29 Woodberry Crescent and, of course, Biddy invited them to stay for supper. They seemed awed at being in the home of Oswald Chambers' wife and talked only of theological issues related to "the great man" and his books. All through the meal Biddy felt the atmosphere was stuffy and formal, not at all what it should be around the table in her home.

To the astonishment of her very serious guests, Biddy looked at thirty-five-year-old Kathleen and said, "Why don't you see if you can spit a cherry seed clear to the top of the overmantle." Knowing exactly what her mother was up to, Kathleen whooshed a tiny projectile toward the target. Ping!

"It was close, but fell short of the top," Biddy said matter-of-factly. "I don't suppose any of these young men could do better."

Almost without thinking, a would-be bishop spat a cherry stone nearly to the ceiling, followed by scores of others from his competitive friends. The room erupted in laughter and Biddy smiled with satisfaction.

"Oswald would enjoy this," she thought. "There we are, praise the Lord, all nice and straight again."

Ping!

THE POEMS OF OSWALD CHAMBERS

LONDON

(July 6, 1892)

Sad heart, why art thou weary
  With anxious strivings drear?
Thou hast no cause for sadness,
  No cause for restless fear.

Thou longest for Thy Master,
  Then cease and be at rest;
For shall not He who made thee
  Know what for thee is best?

WAIT

(July 7, 1892)

Cease from disquietude,
Fret not, this is unto thee a preparation time;
Thou must be made in likeness unto Him thou wouldest serve.
Wait, the diamond must be cut ere from its tiny facets
Flash the glory of the sun's pure ray.
Rain must descend,
Else from yon dull grey bulb springeth no sweet perfumed flower.
Be silent upon God, thy time for service has not come;
Patience, this waiting trial is by Him who loves thee sent;
Be still—He knoweth all, thou knowest that His will is best.

FRAGMENT

(London, January 13, 1893)

Weariness! yet not of sadness,
'Tis thy unceaseful deeps, O soul!
Immortal! Not here, but yonder
Thou'lt be unstayed—
Hush! The Master sayeth, "Peace."

FRAGMENT

(January 27, 1893)

Envy! Dire hateful fiend, begone!
Thou'st nought in me, once to God's heart
Of might; Love has me tak'n—for Him
Alone I live. Offspring of hell,
Thither betake thyself, nor 'sturb
My peace again.

EVENING

(March 23, 1893)

Blest eventide!
Thrice welcome is thy hush of stealing peace;
Effort hath wound me round with weariness.
My thoughts high on ambition's youthful wind
All day have flown, but now thy still flood
Findeth me tired, e'en whilst within my soul
Yearnings unutterable, full with cravings
For something unknown, still very real
Doth deep o'erwhelm—Lo! the Master cometh!
Farewell, sweet twilight, thou hast borne me safe
Unto a bosom than thine own more dear
Wherein a Saviour's heart doth loving beat.

Father, I am so wearied with my task,
So weak I am and oh so tired tonight.
Please lift me in Thine arms and give me rest;
Yes! Father give me rest, 'tis Thee I want.
Dear blessed Jesus, now I'll go to sleep,
Then when the morning breaketh, Thou'lt still be near.

MENTAL DEPRESSION

(London, April 29, 1893)

Depressed and weary sank the mind in gloom,
Gloom deep as night in which there is no moon;
 Times rushing down its darkening cloisters past
 Conflicting thoughts, unhindered, blast on blast,
Until the very brain did shriek and rave in turn,
Reason's control in madness by it spurned.
 Sudden it ceased, one mighty wrench, then fled
 And stillness o'er the whole its silence spread;
Whilst from the fullness of the immortal soul
Deep tender music did its charm unroll.
 Lifting the burden from the anguished heart
 Sent forth its floods and healed the inward smart;

So! in the midst is heard the Saviour's voice,
Soulfully sweet, inviting to rejoice;
And there resounds divinely full and free,
"Sad, weary heart, be still and come to Me."
Soon in the soul the sound of quiet rest
Breathes real and low and draws us to His breast,
Where Jesus, looking in our faces smiled,
Soothes us to sleep because He loves His child.

STRANGE LEADINGS

(London, June 23, 1893)

Real human sympathy is sweet and good—
Sweet, because it calmeth as the evening,
Good, because its sweetness stayeth, e'en when
The heart that gave it lieth hushed in death.
But times to heights beyond most mortals' ken,
Or to unfathomed depths before unknown
The soul is tak'n and there o'ercoming will,
Rushing forth, reveal such fearsome wonders
That the body, sinking 'neath the greatness
It doth hold, seeketh human sympathy
And findeth none, and heavy, groweth sad.
But One alone doth know the yearning drear
Of such a soul, for He hath led it there.

SOLILOQUY

(London, June 24, 1893)

O soul, will I always be thus perplexed
At thy great deeps? Or will in after-life
A time arise when I shall understand
And thy great fullness sound? Are other souls
Too big for them? If so, why do they laugh
At my perplexity? Are all men's souls
Alike? Does everybody understand
The deepness that o'erwhelmeth me? Do all
Know what it is to have such might unlocked,
That strives with power against this mortal clay,
Straining to rise above all bands and bars
Unhindered, and at each struggle wring
The life with pain? Is such the life of all
And yet will no one sympathise? and I
So small, so puny in their eyes that they
Can only be amused at me? It cannot be!
Did Christ hew straight through the hard face of sin
A path for such a puny thing? Nay! Nay!

For man, and I'm a man. Then, soul, be still
And wait; thou know'st that yonder thou wilt be
Expressed—Strain not this mortal tenement
So high, else it will break. Yet if thou must
Remind me of "Hereafter," then unlock
Thy depths such time as night enshrouds the earth
That none may know; but help me to learn
When others smile to smile, when weep, to weep.

A SKETCH

(Perth, September 1, 1893)

Mysterious morning mist, so dense and frail,
Slowly stealing, tenderly white and pale,
Weirdly clinging, concealing in thy shrouds
Reflections perfect, clear of woods and clouds,
Rendering the distance indistinct and strange,
Changing to mystery all within thy range.

Rifting, lifting, scattering in the breeze,
Fading, dissolving, dying 'mid the trees,
Lost in thyself forever as the sun
Flashes his splendour in the river's run.

BROOKLET

(Perth, September 4, 1893)

Tiny, lowly little brook—whispering low,
Dimpling o'er thy pebbly bed, sparkling so.

Pretty, modest little brook—hid away,
Murmuring secrets to the grass all the day.

Living, lovely little brook, cool and clear,
To the birds and grass and flowers, oh so dear!

Sweet, unsullied little brook, dazzling pure,
Richest green to pass by thee is secure.

Tiny, precious little brook, singing low,
Dimpling o'er thy pebbly bed, sparkling so.

MYSTERY

(October 7, 1893)

O restless soul,
Some unseen, unknown, incomprehensible
Power doth crush me to utterance;
I'm weary, savagely weary with thinking

Expressionless, unfathomable thoughts,
And yet, I must write or speak—
But what to say, what to write,
What to think! I know not—
I crave, I long, I yearn, I stretch
After something as yet unknown,
Something human, not divine, to love,
A friend to pour my soul out to—
My whole being—and be at rest.

FRAGMENTS

(London, November 10, 1893)

Undone. Great deeds, precious principles and true,
Fallen far, far short of, striving, struggling,
Battling. Almost — — gone!
Heartsick and weary. Undone! Undone!

And these must pass away and be no more
Into the huge deep hush of Past.
How fond the heart is tremblingly reaching
For what once was, now is not!
Re-entering on itself, sinks pained,
More silent and more deep to live.

Wasted time! Bitter torturing memory!
Work, overwork, and work again after
Drowneth not the bitterness of wasted time
Unrecallable and unforgettable.

FOR FRANCES RIDLEY HAVERGAL

(London, November 1893)

Poet divine!
My heart is full of love,
My thoughts well in my throat and melt in tears
When seeking to express the power thy words convey.
Thou hast a soul that wraps round mine sweet peace,
That tells me all I need and gives it me;
Thy sweet, cool hand is oft upon my brow,
Thy holy purity inspireth me.

When sadness o'erwhelmeth me, thou art sad,
And sadness mingled giveth sympathy.
When joy shines bright, thy joy shines also,
And rejoices with me—Whence comes this power?
Methinks thou hast been on the mountaintop
And in the valleys. Aye! and through the dark

Thou hast been to the green Hill far away,
And there thy life melted into His, thence
As a ripple from His smile thou'rt come. Hail!
All Hail! the blessing of thy soulful words.

And now thou'rt on the breast of Jesus Christ
Perfectly good—thou knowest now the way
Thou traversed here, but if thou wert still here
I'd long to see thee, clasp thy hand, and pray,
Speechless from love because thou knowest me.
Mayhap strange unto thee things thou wrotest
Might have appeared, but He who knoweth all
Guided thy hand. Thou'rt happy, God be blest.

Nearer to Jesus hath thy poem led
A soul perplexed by thought for him too great.
If thou, O Poet, can behold us here,
O pray that I may like thee be good
And humbly learn of Jesus, that His life
Be manifest in my life and work, and glorified
Even as He was in thine.
Then when morning breaketh, and away
Flee all the shadows, may I grasp thy hand,
Look into thy face, and call thee sister.

FRAGMENTS

(London, December 16, 1893)

Unappreciated! Great thoughts,
Greater imaginings, Music—all executed.
Patience waits—dies—unappreciated.

Myself. Pure, terrible, high,
Vile, sensual, devilish,
God-like, Devil-like—A man!

The silent, thoughtful clouds moved o'er the moon
That fitful shone, and silver tipped their shades.
Distant the church bells murmured sweet, the breeze
Breathed low—one star peeped through and shone unmoved.
The trees stood weirdly still, all things were hushed,
The whole soothed, like the dew earth's breath. A Soul!

INSANE

(December 26, 1893)

Insane!
Thus man proclaimeth the poetic—
Rhymes, jingles of all words, may not be sane,
But Poetry? those motions of the soul
Expressed inadequately in words—never!
That dew descending on the heart—insanity?

Music—insanity?
Only if sanity be that hard, dry,
Mechanical monotony of so-called *fact*.
But if that mechanical monotony of fact
Be but as the organ case, what then?
The appreciation of the music insanity?

Man! who is man? there's One, his creator,
Who gave those divine essences we call
Music, Poetry, Art, through which God breathes
His Spirit of Peace into the soul.

Mechanical monotony of so-called fact
Whereby we in this clay do exist—
God gave this too, and lo! death and His judgment
Descends on him who ignores this means sent
For existence here
Whilst training for existence hereafter.

Likewise,
On him who calleth those divine breathings
Puny and unreal, God comes in judgment,
Shutting his eyes to all the beautiful,
His ears to the altogether lovely,
His mind to the pure and noble.

Man, beware!
God is a Spirit,
And they that worship Him must worship Him
In Spirit.

THE BEST

(London, December 29, 1893)

Nearer than Home and than dearest,
Nearer than near or than nearest;
Nearer than breath,
Nearer than death
Is the sweet spirit of Jesus.

Dearer than all that is nearest,
Dearer than dear or than dearest,
Dearer than sight,
Dearer than light
Is the communion with Jesus.

EMANCIPATION
(London, December 29, 1893)

Away from the world and the cruel,
Away from the day and its strife;
Away from the sad and the joyful,
Away from the struggle of life.

Away through the high hush of midnight,
Away from myself am I borne,
Away to the region of music,
Where the beautiful ever is worn.

Like a strange eager thing, half-frightened,
Like the rushing of wind held back,
My soul, yearning, longing was waiting,
Strained intensely, as held on a rack.

Far away, now so near—now so far
Came a presence so painfully dear;
Away burst my soul from its longing,
Away burst my heart from the fear.

Home from those wayward wanderings,
Home from that cold foreign clime,
Home, to the arms of "Our Father,"
Where I am all His and He's mine.

REQUIESCAT IN PACE
(London, January 24, 1894)

At Rest
On the dear, cold breast of Death,
In the silent calm of the grave,
Where there's no more need for breath.

At Rest
The wearied eyes are sleeping,
Never here to wake again,
In peace is the body steeping.

At Rest
From itself and its neighbors,
From the ceaseless moan of the poor
Lies the body, from pain and from labour—
At Rest.

PARADOX
(London, January 29, 1894)

Crushed!—it filled with patience,
Wounded!—it beamed with love,
Wearied!—it mounted upward,
Up to the great life above.

Weak!—it grew with greatness,
Feeble!—it rose with strength,
Fitful!—it heaved majestic,
Heaved to calm peace at length.

This is the constitution,
Opposites always combined,
Of body, soul, and spirit,
Limited—undefined.

"AND AFTER THAT"
(London, February 2, 1894)

At last, from the cold, dark gloom of the grave,
From the fetters of death that held it slave,
A soul came forth alone.

Silent it stood on eternity's shore,
Silent it gazed at the gloom stretched before,
And silent remained.

Till, like the howl of a storm through a glen,
Till, like the shriek of demoniac men,
It cried and then fled.

On through the rush of that strange solemn sight,
On through its waylessness speeded the flight,
Whither, it knew not.

Dreariness, dreariness, sameness and same,
Weariness, weariness, painful and pain,
O desolate flight!

Worn out it sank, and sinking swooned away,
Deathlike and helpless, despairing it lay
Unconscious of its doom.

Slowly it there beheld a visage sad,
A face so awful, yet with anguish clad
The features of the Past.

LONDONERS

(April 4, 1894)

Busy, driving, rushing Londoners,
Driven, palefaced, wiry blunderers,
  Striving ever,
  Praying never,
Busy, driving, rushing Londoners.

Thoughtless, flippant, godless Londoners,
Tricky, grasping, cruel plunderers,
  "Doing" ever,
  "Done by" never,
Thoughtless, flippant, godless Londoners.

Tired out, weary, haggard Londoners,
Beer-sopped, feeble, worn-out conjurers,
  Struggling ever,
  Resting never,
Tired out, weary, haggard Londoners.

Silent, lifeless, buried Londoners,
Death and Time have proved true sunderers,
  Gone for ever,
  Remembered never,
Silent, lifeless, buried Londoners.

TWILIGHT

(London, June 2, 1894)

The pale blue sky,
Tinted clouds pass by,
Weary breezes blow,
And the sun is low.

The day is done,
Children cease from fun,
Merry laughter stops,
And the night tide drops.

Angels come and go,
Flying to and fro,
Soothing weary flesh,
With soft hushful rest.

All unseen they move,
Wondrously they soothe,
Dropping perfect peace,
When our strivings cease.

PIS ALLER
(Elie, August 12, 1894)

The deep, deep sea,
The silent, silent sand,
The dark, dark rocks
By evening breezes fanned.

The pale, pale sky,
The patient, patient light,
The strange, strange clouds
Wait thoughtful for the night.

The cold, cold life,
The craving, craving soul,
The deep, strange breath—
These viewing find control.

WRITTEN ON THE TOP OF A BUS IN LONDON CITY
(10:30 p.m., November 2, 1894)

In the stillness of the night
Comes a spirit weirdly walking
In the cold electric light
Of the silent city stalking.

Never halting on its way,
Ever silent, never speaking,
Ever haunting till the day,
Never turning from its seeking.

There are yearning, weary sounds
As of angels sadly weeping,
Always with it on its rounds
In a strange and awful keeping.

With the passing of the years
Stays that spirit weirdly gliding
Through the silent night of fears,
Seeking mortals who are hiding.

CHIAROSCURO
(London, November 17, 1894)

Through the mist the light is streaming,
Streaming softly, streaming slow,
But the shadows still are dreaming
In the sad, dark vale below.

Through the night the stars are singing,
Singing sweetly, singing low,
But our cloudland stops them bringing
Their sweet singing down below.

Through the life sweet love is streaming,
Streaming softly, streaming slow,
But the shadows still are dreaming
In the sad, dark heart below.

Through the night are angels singing,
Singing sweetly, singing slow,
But our cloudland stops them bringing
Their sweet singing down below.

MY STAR

(London, December 19, 1894)

Pure and divine
There shines a lovely star;
It dwells and moves afar,
But it is mine.

Bright lovely star,
Through clouds and mists alike
Still streams thy holy light
Nothing can mar.

Unresting shrine,
I love thee, precious star,
Though now thou mov'st afar,
Surely thou'rt mine!

DE PROFUNDIS

(London, January 22, 1895)

Hush! there comes the sound of weeping
Of my spirit vainly seeking
Through the passions that are sweeping
Another sphere.

And its great tears ever falling
And its pained voice ever calling
Rack my life with fears;
Never can I live in gladness,
Never can I turn from sadness,
But must dwell in tears.

Only when this life is ending,
And my spirit is ascending,
And the God-life with it blending,
Can they cease.

PATIENCE

(London, February 27, 1895)

Be patient.
The landscape breathes it to the whispering breeze,
The night tide sighs it through the silent trees,
The pale moon prints it on the heaving deep,
The goodbye sings it when we fall asleep.

Be patient.
The poet breathes it through the woodland glade,
The lover sighs it in the heart's deep shade,
The furnace tells it to the molten gold,
The holly pricks it through the winter's cold.

Be patient.
This life doth write it with a painful hand,
This spirit weeps it in a foreign land,
This madness shrieks it through each fitful storm,
This death replies it by its cold, cold form.

Read patience written by the hand of God,
Live patience, cheerful 'neath His chastening rod.

UNTITLED

(London, February 27, 1895)

Irritated, torn, and stung
By a madd'ning melancholy;
Peace and patience from us flung,
Restless yearnings have begun,
All is emptiness and folly.

O God! O God! these yearnings of the mind,
Craving vainly for what they cannot find,
Stay in their sad career.
Listen with patient ear,
O Thou Divine!

UNEMPLOYED
(London, February 27, 1895)

We are the unemployed,
By want of work annoyed,
Of rest and peace devoid,
That's why we rave.

We have got minds that think,
But thoughts and passions link
To drive us to the brink—
Oh, dire despair.

We have got hearts that cling
To every holy thing,
But want of bread doth bring
Intensest hate.

We knew the love of some,
Now starved to death and dumb,
Whose spirits often come
And pain our hearts.

We feel our need to pray,
But hunger rules the day;
Starvation shrieks its sway:
We must have bread.

O God, our ranks are thin,
Our children's eyes are dim,
And must our women sin
To gain us bread?

O rise, great God, at last
Ere reason's from us cast
And revolution's blast
Blacken our name.

DECISION
(London, March 8, 1895)

At last
The fog has lifted,
The clouds have sifted;
My soul, which drifted,
Has been uplifted
Into the light.

At last
The call's descended,
Power with it blended,
My soul's ascended,
God has transcended
Mortal night.

At last
Ambition's breaking
From all that's shaking,
The thirst it's slaking,
The good it's taking
Is divine.

At last
I am contented,
Though thought demented
To have consented
And not repented,
To take this course.

INADEQUATE
(London, March 15, 1895)

Frantic the billows of the spirit surge,
Thund'ring their fury in a loud, long dirge,
Crashing an ocean on a mortal life,
Crushing its beauties in an awful strife.

Ebbing it sobs along life's tearful strand,
Trailing dead seaweed in its quivering hand,
Heaving grief's silver on its mighty deep,
Rising the moonbeams as they fall asleep.

Sometimes the spirit breathes in quiet rest,
Sometimes love sails across the peaceful breast,
Sometimes the life must sink its golden sand,
Sometimes the spirit owns God's Spirit-hand.

MUSIC MISSION
(London, March 16, 1895)

Oh, the fierce delight of playing
When the soul's too strained for praying,
While the mighty spirit's slaying
Every feeble thing.

Hurling through the passion's thunder,
Storms of music burst asunder,
Drowning agonies thereunder,
Seize the soul with raptured wonder
At their might.

Everything stands still and listens,
And the life with new power glistens,
Sweeps the soul in glad submission
To its rest.

LOVE'S CROWN

(London, March 25, 1895)

On love's head meet many crowns,
But earth's crown of thorns it presses,
And its pain-points it caresses,
While life's wrongs love sure redresses,
While our ills love truly blesses,
And our thirst love's mercy drowns.

EFFORT

(London, April 16, 1895)

Speed on, immortal coursers of the soul,
Ages before thee as behind thee roll;
Fly, to the impulse of my spirit bred,
Fly, by God's spirit be thy fire-hoofs led.

On through the surging clouds of error go,
Deaf to all cries and shrieks of cowardly woe,
Vainly! determined strength, immortal sight,
On through the gloom and reach truth's holy light.

Heed not the terror of the mighty storm
That sweeps around thee wreathed in awful form;
Pant for the quiet of eternal peace,
Strive in the conflict till the conflict cease.

Turn from the singing of the siren stars,
Pass by their beauty, for their beauty mars,
True to the heart that pants and strains with thine,
Faithful in love, till love and light combine.

Speed, for the mighty power has seized thy rein,
Speed, for no effort now can be in vain;
Fly, through the noontide of our finite sun,
Fly, till the chastening of thy race is run.

Gain through the finite night infinite day,
Hear at the dawnlight God's great Spirit say,
"Welcome, brave coursers from man's finite fields!
Welcome, My mighty power thou now shalt wield!"

DUTY

(Edinburgh, January 27, 1896)

The moon shines cold through the leafless trees,
The mists dream pale and low;
The weird wails pass of the restless breeze,
The clouds move strange and slow.

We wait through the cold of gloomlight land,
Our souls weep tears of pain;
We wait for the grasp of God's right hand,
Oh say, do we wait in vain?

No! dawnlight breaks o'er the sullen hill,
The way lies clear and plain;
And God's right hand grasps the swaying will,
And duty smiles again.

MULTA GEMAUS

(Edinburgh, February 28, 1896)

I'm worn with this too hard existence,
The pain of a restless strife,
The strain, the pull, the persistence
That's needful to live this life.

Perhaps I'm too weak for the struggle,
Perhaps it's not equal fight,
Perhaps I imagine the trouble,
Perhaps I've to put it right.

At any rate, I'm wrung with anguish
With a soul too great for here,
At any rate, my spirits languish,
Depressed with a stupid fear.

UNTITLED

(Edinburgh, May 9, 1896)

Oh, my spirit's wild and my soul grows sad
With the power of these earnest dreams;
Let me go, let me go—I know they're glad
Who gaze on the deep broad stream.

Let me climb, let me climb, I'm sure I've time,
Ere the mist comes up from the sea;
Let me climb in time to the height sublime,
Let me reach where I long to be.

Oh, I'm tired and spent, but I seek the peak
In the sun glare, strong and wild—
Now I've reached the top—but the thing I seek
Is hid—and I cry like a child.

But I can't return, for the way is lost,
And the sun looms blurred and red;
If the dream was great, so I find's the cost,
Still I'll make me here my bed.

But all sleep has fled, and the night voice speaks,
And my soul's plunged deep in grief;
Oh, I feel it near—does the Spirit seek
To give my soul relief.

I stretch me back in the form of a cross
On the cold hill's barren head,
And I think of the greatness of my loss
And wish that my soul were dead.

Then I closed my eyes on the night's dull pain
And ne'er thought to see the light,
Till I ope'd my eyes in the falling rain
And straight saw a star shine bright.

As I gazed on that star, a new life moved
Through my frozen limbs apace,
And I rose me up and the new life proved,
And soon beheld before my face

A brighter day dawn with golden beam,
In the gloom of the night afar;
And I saw the stream of my earnest dream
Flow on 'neath the golden bar.

PRAYER

(Edinburgh, August 21, 1896)

O Master, hear our weeping,
For our souls are wrung with pain,
Because of our sinful seeking,
Because of our sordid speaking,
Because we are weak and vain.

O Master, aid our failings,
For our hearts are foolish things,
Because of the outward railings,
Because of the inward ailings,
Because of the sting sin brings.

O Master, make us holy,
For Thou art the Perfect One,
Because of Thy stooping lowly,
Because of Thy Passion solely,
Because Thou art God's own Son!

PRELUDE BY CHOPIN

(Perth, August 23, 1896)

O the wonder
Of that music in my ear!
How it touches—pains those fibres
Of my soul-life which I fear!
Fear because they wake emotions,
Whispers from another sphere.

Slow subdued a tender minor,
Constant, deep and wonder-ful;
Not a grief but something finer,
Something pure and spirit-ful
Underlies a great, strong yearning,
Weirdly strange yet power-ful,
Passionate, yet purely burning,
Disciplined, and prayer-ful.

IN PROCESS

(Edinburgh, August 25, 1896)

Through the darkness and the rain
Just the waiting and the pain,
In depression, just the same,
Is that all?

Through the stillness and the gloom
Just the quiet of this room,
Will the light come just as soon?
That is all.

Through the melancholy maze
Just this dazed and vacant gaze
With the brain a burning blaze,
Is that all?

Will tomorrow be the same,
Will the waiting be no blame,
Earning nothing, be no shame?
That is all.

Through the watches of the night
Just the angels out of sight,
I'll be sleeping till the light.
That is all.

SHADOWS
(Edinburgh, September 11, 1896)

The pale mists rise at the dying day
From the green fields under the sun,
But a warm red ray
Makes a rainbow way
Through the mist, when the day is done.

Through the pale white mists the shadows dream
From the night cloud under the star,
But a mystic sheen
Makes white angels seem
To be just where the shadows are.

THE CONSUMPTIVE
(Edinburgh, September 14, 1896)

"Waiting—wistful still?"
Yes, just for tonight,
Tomorrow, with the light,
I'm sure to be all right,
Don't you think I will?

"Waiting—wistful still?"
Yes, just for today,
Tomorrow, I'll away,
Just now I'm forced to stay,
For they say I'm ill.

"Waiting, wistful still?"
Yes, just for this year,
Because they say they fear
The cost will be too dear,
So I'm waiting—till!

"Waiting—wistful still?"
Yes! From the still white bed,
Came whispered from the dead,
"Till to God you're led,
Waiting, wistful still."

HOPELESS
(Edinburgh, September 15, 1896)

A grey, weird falling
  Dark and drear and dense,
With a soddened palling
  Over every sense.

In dull ease drifting
  Silent, slow, and still,
Just a steady shifting
  From life, hope, and will.

A sure, sad sinking,
  Scarce a gasp for breath,
After that no thinking
  But the mind in death.

BETTER MAIMED THAN LOST
(Edinburgh, November 15, 1896)

I descended into the fire of hell
And gazed until I burned;
I came, but how I came I cannot tell,
My vile heart led me being its own spell;
I looked and was marred and burned,
I entered on a heritage of woe
And never can return.
I broke the heart of God's own Son to go,
I spurned His Spirit who besought me so
And entered hell to burn.
And marvel ye that I must watch and pray
While ye are sweet asleep,
Lest haply His saving grace I stray,
Enticed by the things with which you play?
Sleep on—but I must weep.

MOODS
(Kirn, March 4, 1899)

Rain on, dark skies, through the night,
  The waters have burst their bound;
Destruction may rule till the light,
  But day follows night, ever round.

Scowl on, dark moods of the mind,
  Threaten, lower, and storm your way;
But the soul must bleed ere it find
  The good you are seeking to slay.

Moods pass away like the rain-clouds,
  Good is as day in the soul;
After the gloom of the earth-shrouds
  Cometh complete heaven's whole.

AFTERWARD

(Kirn, January 22, 1900)

O my beloved Jesus! Not Thy cross
Nor any portion of Thine earthly life
Revealed Thy love to me.
But when my heart broke in its first true love,
And all my feelings like a lash of pain
Recoiled and stung me, till my tortured nerves
Refused to aid my spirit—

Then, in that pain, I saw Thee, O my Christ!
And that my first love, which so hopeless seemed,
Was after all for Thee disguised indeed.
But I mistook the form assumed by Thee,
And now I love Thee, Jesus, with the love
That lovers think they have for those they love.
O rapture! where there was such pain before.

SIN IN PENITENCE

(Kirn, September 24, 1900)

Let me lay my life here
Where my sin is known,
  Where the rapture and the fear,
  Where the laughter and the tear
Isolate my heart, alone.

Jesus, here, my wandering heart
Turneth now to Thee,
  Till in all its inmost part
  Sweetly bitter is the smart
Of my sin in me.

Cowardly sorrow maketh plaint,
"This is hard to bear."
  Maketh shape at being saint,
  While the loathsome sin doth taint
All that others think so fair.

Jesus, Jesus, I can't pray,
For the horror of the thing
  Haunts my waking thoughts alway,
  And I have no word to say
For my wicked, wicked sin.

"STRIVE TO ENTER IN AT THE STRAIT GATE"

(Kirn, June 7, 1901)

"Cut it off." My heart is bleeding,
And my spirit's wrung with pain,
Yet I hear my Jesus pleading,
"Cut it off or all is vain."

So I've stopped my ears in terror
Lest self-pity make me quail,
Lest at last I take the error
And God's purpose thwart and fail.

I am bowed to death in sadness,
For the pain is all too great,
But the dear Lord must find pleasure
In the way He maketh straight.

ABIDE WITH ME

(Kirn, June 8, 1901)

Come from the hush of the midnight,
Come from the slumbering sky,
Soothe me to rest by the wayside
While Thou wouldst fain pass by.

Come from the mystery shrouding
Where Thou hast drawn out of sight;
Sorrow and sin are clouding
What Thou didst make for the light.

Come, Thou wast slain to redeem me,
Wrest me from sin and the grave;
Lift up my faith, till from out Thee
Cometh the grace to enslave.

GLEN MASSON

(Kirn, June 1901)

As I rested on a boulder
In a torrent's course midway
And the water o'er its shoulder
Made grand music and display,

As I gazed upon the hill's rise,
Blundering upward to the blue
Where the silver cirrus cloud lies
And the pure air wanders to,

I was rapt away from sadness,
And I left all inner grief
To the healing and the gladness
Of that hour and knew relief.

PEACE LIKE A RIVER

(Kirn)

Deep between the blundering masses
Roars the torrent's thundering might;
Through or round the rocks it passes,
Conquering what disputes its right.

Waters born far on the highlands
Gather volume towards the sea,
Till they reach the fruitful broadlands
Where all turmoils cease to be.

EARLY MORNING

(Kirn, July 2, 1901)

Two crimson poppies sway and swing
In the breeze at the day's sweet rise,
And the branches rustle and the birds they sing
O'er the dew on the grass that lies.

The daisies pure with a silver sheen
Spread around to the far away,
With yellow relief and emerald green
In the same old lavish way.

Far above in the great stretch of blue
Fly the fragments of the scattered night,
And the sun's old glory is bursting through
In a wondrous paean of light.

6TH PSALM ALLOA

(Kirn, July 13, 1901)

Rebuke me not nor chasten me,
O Lord of mercy great;
My soul is vexed, as unto Thee
My wounded soul I take.

O heal me, Lord, heal even me,
For I am wasting sore;
My soul is pained and what I see
Brings anguish more and more.

And thou, my Lord, how long, how long?
Return Thou unto me;
Thy lovingkindness it is strong,
Such kindness let me see.

In death, in death can ought bring back
Remembrances and fears?
All night my tortured spirit racks,
All night I spend in tears.

I waste away because of grief,
My body waxeth old,
Because I find out no relief
From sorrow's cruel hold.

Arise, my soul, the Lord is near,
My weeping voice He knows;
Depart from me each evil fear,
The Lord hath turned my woes.

Turn back, turn back, each wretched sin,
The Lord will answer me,
And His own peace shall reign within;
Turn back, ye sins, and flee!

HEALING

(Kirn, July 1901)

Whisper softly, gentle wind,
From the hills and flowers,
Waken in my heart and mind
Memories of love entwined
With visions of glad hours.

What though now the curlew's cry
Suits my sadder heart.
What though now a lonely sigh
Breaketh from me where I lie,
Breaketh from an inward smart.

It is worth the present pain,
Love of days gone by
In the sunshine and the rain
In the rapture I have lain
Yet suffered not to die.

Let the proving hours of time
Try me as they may;
Hope is 'twined with love of mine,
Pain is but a countersign,
Guiding on a sterner way.

SEA-BAY

(West Bay, August 1901)

Oh, the rush of the salt sea foam,
And the mass of clouds that roam
  O'er the sky and the hill
  At the wild wind's will
Have a wayward and wandering home.

Oh, the scream of the sea bird's cry
As it's blown across the sky
  Has a keeping sweet
  Where the strong waves meet
With the clouds' and winds' lullaby.

Oh, the toss and the heave and the sway
Of the sea in this old, old way
  As it dashing fights
  With the headland heights
Of the shores in our western bay.

Oh, I like the passionate sea,
For it longs like the soul of me
  With a conscious power
  And a gifted dower
For the thing that may ever be.

FRUITLESS SORROW

(Kirn, September 30, 1901)

I would rather the flood went o'er me,
  The flood of the great wild sea,
With its acres of secret waters
  Than mourn o'er the never-to-be.

Oh, the wounds of the martyred Master
  Are sweet to my mind of grief,
I would leap with joy at disaster
  Akin to the crucified thief.

But the sapping of hopeless sorrow
  Means death to a youthful life,
But the pain of each new day's morrow
  Serves as good to the new day's strife.

PRAYER PLEADING

(Kirn, September 30, 1901)

O take my heart, my Saviour,
  Move its inward springs for me,
Till Thy life in my behaviour
  Springs in actions constantly.

O my Saviour, I am mourning
  For a living touch with Thee;
Let Thy Spirit's pure adorning
  Mould Thy character in me.

O do hear me, O do hear me,
  Else I think my heart will break;
In its longing, be Thou near me,
  And my burning thirst—oh slake!

O Lord Jesus, hear my crying
  For a consecrated life,
For I bite the dust in trying
  For release from this dark strife.

NOTE ADDED NOVEMBER 1, 1906

In November 1901 by an entire consecration and acceptance of sanctification at the Lord's hands, I was baptised with the Holy Ghost, and unspeakable joy and peace have resulted, ever-deepening since. The desire to write poetry seems to have gone, perhaps in the desire to live poetry. Oswald Chambers

UNTITLED

(November 25, 1905)

Wilted flowers and faded leaves,
  Wailing wind and wistful light,
Barren fields and huddled sheaves,
There the wondering spirit grieves,
  Mourns the settled autumn night.

Wilderness waste and wild
Stretched around the Spirit's child
Seem a garden fair and mild;
For the Lord has weaved a lure,
Weaved it wide and weaved it sure,
Won that soul so lone, so poor,
Clasped it close and kissed it pure,
Wooed and won that heart to Him.

42ND PSALM (Modern Rendering)

(November 29, 1905)

The windy moor, the soaking sod,
  The curlew crying through the murk,
The daylight sweeping like a rod
  Of tired justice where some horrors lurk.

The East has gone from out the day,
  The West has cast away its light;
My heart has faltered on its way,
  A wayless way unused at night.

O shuddering air, O ghostly gleams,
  O lonely, isolating gloom,
Around me surge thy severing streams
  That moaning mourn a dirgeful doom.

Bend o'er me lower, soft and low,
  I find Thee greater than my loss;
A marvel masters, great and slow
  The pain, the sorrow of the Cross.

O draw me nearer, nearer, Lord,
  O greater than my lonely heart;
My Lord, my God, my all adored,
  Beloved and my better part.

ACKNOWLEDGMENTS

Without the help of every person listed here, this book could not have been written. I am deeply grateful for their unselfish, kind assistance.

UNITED KINGDOM

Kathleen Chambers—For her many hours of conversation, countless cups of tea, and most of all her willingness to share the life of her mother and father with me.

Council members, Oswald Chambers Publications Association, Ltd.—For their unflagging encouragement and support: Maurice Garton, Rev. Arthur Neil, Eric and Mary Pearson, Rev. David Holmwood, John Sanders, John Wood.

Lois Pulford—For freely sharing her mother's personal papers.

Mary Lambert—For materials from her father and grandfather.

Mr. S. M. Turner—For his hospitality and persevering help.

Mr. J. A. Harper, secretary, The League of Prayer, Rotherham—For many hours of personal assistance.

Colin Glennie—For an unlocked church door in Perth and a family meal in his home.

Rev. James Gordon, pastor, Crown Terrace Baptist Church, Aberdeen—For his generosity, insight, and the best fish and chips in Britain.

David and Beryl Littlehales, and the staff of the Foreign Missions Club, London—For a home away from home.

Dr. Donald Meek, University of Edinburgh—For his Highland perspective on places and people, especially Duncan MacGregor.

Dr. David Bebbington, University of Stirling—For helping set the historical stage of Oswald Chambers' life.

Mr. John Pollock—For a letter that showed the way.

Chris Almond—Rye Lane Baptist Chapel.

Heather Bell—Librarian, Nazarene Theological College, Manchester.

Mr. and Mrs. Eddie (Margaret) Bowes—Durrington.

Mr. J.M.Y. Briggs—Department of History, University of Keele.

Mr. Wilfred Burridge—Lydbury North.

Mr. and Mrs. Jack Chambers—Saffron Walden.

Mr. Leonard Chambers—Worcester.

Mr. and Mrs. Robert Chambers—Glasgow.

Jo Currie—Special Collections, University of Edinburgh.

Rev. Tim Dack—Clapham Junction Nazarene Church, London.

Mark Dever—Ph.D. candidate, Cambridge University.

Bill Downing—Eltham Park Baptist Church.

Dr. J. D. Douglas—St. Andrews.

Jeremy Duncan—Librarian, Sandeman Library, Perth.

Mrs. Irene East—Cheltenham.

Sam Johnston and Janet Wood—National Council of Y.M.C.A, London.

Rosemary Keen—Archivist, Church Missionary Society, London.

Mr. E. W. Lawrence—Woking.

Susan Mills—Angus Library, Regent's Park College, Oxford.

Mr. Geoffrey Palmer—Former Y.M.C.A. secretary, London.

Mrs. Margaret Payne—Belvedere Baptist Church.

Sue Payne—Museum and Art Gallery, Perth.

Miss Christine Penney—Special Collections, University of Birmingham.

Miss Betty Potts—Portinscale, Keswick.

Mrs. Judy Powles—Spurgeon's College, London.

Mrs. Helen Pugh—British Red Cross Archives, Guildford.

Miss Christine Reynolds—St. Leonard's-on-Sea.

Maurice Rowlandson—Former secretary, The Keswick Convention, London.

Rev. Alex Russell, George and Irene Newall—Dunoon Baptist Church.

Bill Scott—Local History Library, Dunoon.

Scottish Baptist College—Glasgow.

Mr. Peter Thompson—MECO, Tunbridge Wells.

Stephen Walton—Imperial War Museum, London.

Jean Wilson—The Office Ltd., London.

Dr. David Wright—University of Edinburgh.

EGYPT

Joe and Marilyn Spradley, Cairo—For gracious hospitality in their home and invaluable help.

Rev. Michael Shelley, pastor, St. Andrews Church, Cairo—For the visit to Oswald Chambers' grave.

Mr. Samy Armia and Mr. Aziz Hanna, Y.M.C.A., Cairo—For their time and interest.

AUSTRALIA

Dr. John Dearin—Tamworth, New South Wales.

UNITED STATES

Dr. Bob De Vries, Discovery House Publishers—For his interest and vision that fueled this biography from concept to completion.

Carol Holquist, Discovery House Publishers—For her faithful service behind the scenes.

Tim Beals, Discovery House Publishers—For his skillful editing and wise suggestions.

Rev. Glenn Black—Wesleyan Church, Lexington, KY.

Mr. Chad Boorsma—Joint Archives of Holland, Holland, MI.

Mrs. May Conklin—Binghamton, NY.

Dr. Stephen N. Dunning—The University of Pennsylvania.

Ed and Rachel Erny, OMS International, Greenwood, IN—For the hospitality of their home and many hours of help.

Mr. Robert D. Foster, Lost Valley Ranch, CO—For his loan of a book and his life of encouragement.

Mr. Larry Haise—Ft. Collins, CO.

Dr. George Harris—Denton, MD.

William Kostlevy—Asbury Seminary Library, Wilmore, KY.

Mr. James Lynch—American Baptist Historical Society, Rochester, NY.

David Malone—Wheaton College Archives and Special Collections, Wheaton, IL.

Mrs. Daisy Nakada and Mrs. June Sumida—Culver City, CA.

Scotti Oliver—The Talbot County Free Library, Easton, MD.

Staff of the Pikes Peak Library System—Colorado Springs, CO.

Mr. Walter Standley—Ft. Pierce, FL.

Mr. Robert Shuster—Billy Graham Center Archives, Wheaton, IL.

Valerie Taylor—Caroline County Public Library, Denton, MD.

Donna Watson—Wesleyan Church Archives, Indianapolis, IN.

Mrs. Alice Weingard, Mr. Kenneth Stettler—God's Bible School, Cincinnnati, OH.

Finally, for the many friends whose prayers undergirded the research and writing of this book.

BIBLIOGRAPHY

BOOKS

Barabas, Steven. *So Great Salvation: The History and Message of the Keswick Convention.* London: Marshall, Morgan & Scott, 1952.

Barbour, G. F. *The Life of Alexander Whyte, D.D.* London: Hodder and Stoughton Ltd., 1923.

Barrett, James W. *The War Work of the Y.M.C.A. in Egypt*. London: H. K. Lewis & Co. Ltd., 1919.

Barrett, James W. *A Vision of the Possible*. London: H. K. Lewis & Co. Ltd., 1919.

Barrett, James W. and P. E. Deane. *The Australian Army Medical Corps in Egypt*. London: H. K. Lewis, 1918.

Bean, C.E.W. *Official History of Australia in the War of 1914–1918*, Vol. I. Sydney: Angus and Robertson, 1929.

Bebbington, D. W. *Evangelicalism in Modern Britain*. London: Unwin Hyman, 1989.

Bebbington, D. W., editor. *The Baptists in Scotland*. Glasgow: The Baptist Union of Scotland, 1988.

Binfield, Clyde. *George Williams and the Y.M.C.A.* London: William Heinemann Ltd., 1973.

British Red Cross Society. *Reports By the Joint War Committee, Covering 1914–19.* London: His Majesty's Stationery Office, 1921.

Cadenhead, William G. *The Memoirs of an Ordinary Man*. Privately published, 1969. Courtesy of The Imperial War Museum, London.

Chambers, Gertrude H. (Biddy). *Oswald Chambers: His Life and Work.* London: Simpkin Marshall Ltd., 1933, 1938, 1959.

Cowman, Lettie B. *Charles E. Cowman: Missionary Warrior.* Los Angeles: The Oriental Missionary Society, 1928.

Day, Lloyd Raymond. *A History of God's Bible School in Cincinnati, 1900–1949*. Unpublished thesis, University of Cincinnati, 1949.

Erny, Edward and Esther. *No Guarantee But God: The Story of the Founders of the Oriental Missionary Society.* Greenwood, IN: The Oriental Missionary Society, 1969.

Evans, Eifion. *The Welsh Revival of 1904*. Bridgend: Evangelical Press of Wales, Bryntirion, 1969.

Findlay, W. H. *Heritage of Perth*. Perth: Photolog Press, 1984.

Ford, Jack. *In the Steps of John Wesley.* Kansas City: Nazarene Publishing House, 1968.

Frayling, Christopher. *The Royal College of Art*. London: Barrie and Jenkins Ltd., 1987.

Fullerton, W. Y. *F. B. Meyer: A Biography.* London: Marshall, Morgan & Scott, 1930.

Gammie, Alexander. *Preachers I Have Heard*. London: Pickering & Inglis Ltd., 1945.

Gammie, Alexander. *William Quarrier and the story of The Orphan Homes of Scotland*. London: Pickering & Inglis Ltd., nd.

Gordon, James M. *Evangelical Spirituality.* London: SPCK, 1991.

Grubb, Norman P. *C. T. Studd: Cricketer and Pioneer.* Ft. Washington, PA: Christian Literature Crusade, 1982. (First published in Britain, 1933.)

Harris, Frederick, managing editor. *Service With Fighting Men: An Account of the Work of the American Y.M.C.A.s in the World War*, Vols. I and II. New York: Association Press, 1922.

Hartley, Marie and Joan Ingilby. *Yorkshire Village*. Otley, UK: Smith Settle Ltd., 1989. First published by J. M. Dent and Sons Ltd, 1953.

Hooker, Mary R. *Adventures of an Agnostic: Life and Letters of Reader Harris.* London: Marshall, Morgan & Scott, 1959.

King, Harriet Eleanor Hamilton. *The Disciples*. London: Kegan, Paul, Trench, Trubner & Co., Ltd., 1907.

Lambert, David W. *Oswald Chambers: An Unbribed Soul.* Ft. Washington, PA: Christian Literature Crusade, 1968.

MacGregor, Duncan. *Lady Christ*. London: Arthur H. Stockwell, 1901.

Mott, John R. *For the Millions of Men Now Under Arms*, Vols. I and II. New York: Young Men's Christian Association International Committee, reports, 1915–19.

Padwick, Constance E. *Temple Gairdner of Cairo*. London: SPCK, 1929.

Patty, John C. *Lucius Bunyan Compton: The Mountaineer Evangelist*. Asheville, NC: Eliada Orphanage, 1914.

Pollock, J. C. *The Keswick Story.* London: Hodder and Stoughton, Ltd., 1964.

Porritt, Arthur. *John Henry Jowett*. London: Hodder and Stoughton, Ltd., 1924.

Rose, Delbert R. *A Theology of Christian Experience*. Minneapolis, MN: Bethany Fellowship, Inc., 1965.

Smart, Edward. *The History of Perth Academy.* Perth: Milne, Tannahill, & Methven, 1932.

Stalker, Charles H. *Twice Around The World With The Holy Ghost.* Cincinnati, OH: Privately published, 1906.

Standley, Meredith G. *My Life as I Have Lived It For Christ and Others.* Cincinnati, OH: Privately published, 1949.

Synan, Vinson. *The Holiness-Pentecostal Movement in the United States.* Grand Rapids, MI: William B. Eerdmans, 1971.

Thomas, Paul Westphal and Paul William Thomas. *The Days of Our Pilgrimage,* (The History of the Pilgrim Holiness Church). Marion, IN: The Wesley Press, 1976.

Wilson, J. Christy. *Flaming Prophet: The Story of Samuel Zwemer.* New York: Friendship Press, 1970.

Wood, Robert D. *In These Mortal Hands: The Story of the Oriental Missionary Society, the First 50 Years.* Greenwood, IN: OMS International, 1983.

Yapp, Arthur K. *In The Service Of Youth.* London: Nisbet & Co. Ltd., 1927.

Yoneda, Isamu. *Biography of Juji Nakada.* Tokyo: Fukuin Senkyo Kai, 1959. Excerpts (pp. 102–124) translated by June Sumida and Peter Sowa. Additional translation and summary by Arthur Shelton.

BOOKS BY OSWALD CHAMBERS

Approved Unto God
Baffled to Fight Better
Biblical Ethics
Biblical Psychology
Bringing Sons into Glory
Christian Disciplines
Conformed to His Image
Disciples Indeed
God's Workmanship
He Shall Glorify Me
The Highest Good
If Thou Wilt Be Perfect
If You Will Ask
A Little Book of Prayer

The Love of God
The Moral Foundations of Life
My Utmost for His Highest
Not Knowing Where
Our Brilliant Heritage
The Philosophy of Sin
The Place of Help
The Psychology of Redemption
The Servant and His Lord
Shade of His Hand
The Shadow of an Agony
So Send I You
Studies in The Sermon on The Mount
Workmen of God

PERIODICALS

Aberdeen Herald, Aberdeen, Scotland.

Aberdeen Journal and General Advertiser for the North of Scotland.

Blessed Be Egypt, Magazine of the Nile Mission Press, Cairo.

The Bond of Union, Journal of the Baptist Total Abstinence Association.

B.T.C. Monthly Journal.

The Cincinnati Enquirer, Cincinnati, OH.

The Cincinnati Post, Cincinnati, OH.

Denton Journal, Denton, MD.

The Dunoon Herald and Cowal Advertiser, Dunoon, Scotland.

The Dunoon Observer and Argyllshire Standard, Dunoon, Scotland.

Egypt General Mission News, London/Cairo.

The Egyptian Gazette, Cairo.

The Egyptian Mail, Cairo.

Electric Messages: A Monthly Holiness Missionary Journal, Oriental Missionary Society, Tokyo. 1903–10.

Eltham and District Times, Eltham, England.

God's Revivalist and Bible Advocate, published by God's Bible School, Cincinnati, Ohio.

The Holiness Mission Journal, London.

The Keswick Week, 1897–1915.

London Daily Telegraph.

The Perthshire Advertiser, Perth, Scotland.

The Red Cross Journal.

The Red Triangle, Y.M.C.A. Magazine, London.

The Red Triangle Bulletin, Weekly Supplement to The Red Triangle.

The Sphinx, weekly magazine, Cairo.

South London Times.

Tongues of Fire, from 1916 *Spiritual Life*, London.

PAMPHLETS AND PAPERS

"The American Holiness Movement: A Bibliographic Introduction" by Donald W. Dayton. Wilmore, KY: B. L. Fisher Library, Asbury Theological Seminary, 1971.

"The Baptists in Perth: 1650–1971" compiled by Jack Hunter, secretary, Perth Baptist Church.

"The Chocolate Soldier" by C. T. Studd. Ft. Washington, PA: Christian Literature Crusade. (First published in Britain in 1916.)

"F. B. Meyer in Britain and America" by Ian Randall. Paper presented at "Evangelicalism in Trans-Atlantic Perspective," Institute for the Study of American Evangelicalism, Wheaton College, April 1992.

"The League of Prayer: 1891–1991" by Maurice Winterburn. Rotherham, England: The League of Prayer.

"Prospectus for Session 1907–1908," Sharp's Institution, Perth.

ARTICLES

"Call to Holiness," by Geoffrey Hanks, *Christian Herald*, (Britain), 20 July 1991.

"The City of Cairo According to the Census of 1917," by Samuel M. Zwemer, *Moslem World*, July 1920.

"Juji Nakada: The Moody of Japan," by Arthur Shelton. *Japan Harvest,* Winter 1961.

"The Ministry of the Unnoticed," by Sherwood E. Wirt, *Decision,* July 1974.

"Oswald Chambers," by Delbert R. Rose, *The Herald,* October 17, 1973.

"Poured Out Wine," by Laura Petri, Ph.D., *Salvation Army War Cry,* Sweden.

"Their Utmost for His Highest," by Sherwood E. Wirt, *Christianity Today,* June 21, 1974.

INTERVIEWS

Dr. David Bebbington, University of Stirling, Scotland, March 1992.

Rev. Glenn Black, The Wesleyan Church, Lexington, KY, December 1991.

Mrs. Margaret Ofverberg Bowes, Durrington-on-Sea, England, March 1992.

Miss Kathleen Chambers, London, September 1991-October 1992.

Mr. and Mrs. Robert Chambers, Glasgow, Scotland, March 1992.

Mr. and Mrs. Jack Chambers, Saffron Walden, England, March 1992.

Mrs. Enid Clark, Bromley, England, May 1992.

Mrs. Mary Conklin—Binghamton, NY, January 1992.

Dr. Melvin Dieter, Lyndhurst, VA, January 1992.

Rev. Paul Dieter, Denton, MD, February 1992.

Miss Dorothy Docking, Santa Barbara, CA, April 1992.

Dr. Wesley Duewel, OMS, Greenwood, IN, December 1991.

Mrs. Elizabeth Stalker Earle, Sebring, OH, February 1992.

Ed Erny, OMS, Greenwood, IN, December 1991.

Mr. James Foster, Hawes, Yorkshire, England, June 1992.

Dr. George Harris, Denton, MD, February 1992.

Miss Katie Kent, Dunoon, Scotland, September 1991.

William Kostlevy, Special Collections Librarian, Asbury Theological Seminary, December 1991.

Miss Mary Lambert, South Chard, England, March 1992.

Mr. W. J. Lowles, Swanley, England, May 1992.

Dr. Donald Meek, University of Edinburgh, Scotland, March 1992.

Miss Etta Mitchell and Miss Etta Clough, Centreville, MD, February 1992.

Mr. J. R. Mitchell, Wilmore, KY, December 1991.

Mrs. Daisy Nakada & Mrs. June Sumida, Culver City, CA, November 1991.

Mrs. Eileen Page, Wimbledon, England, June 1992.

Miss Betty Potts, Portinscale, Keswick, October 1992.

Miss Lois Pulford, Ross-on-Wye, England, March and June 1992.

Miss Christine Reynolds, St. Leonard's-on-Sea, England, March 1992.

Mrs. Amaris Richardson, Tunbridge Wells, England, March 1992.

Mr. Maurice Rowlandson, London, September 1991.

Miss Martha Roy, Cairo, Egypt, June 1992.

Miss Grace Simpson, Oxford, England, March 1992.

Mr. Walter Standley, Ft. Pierce, FL, February 1992.

Mr. S. M. Turner, Tunbridge Wells, England, March 1992.

Mrs. Amy Ruth (Zwemer) Violette, July 1992.

LOCAL CHURCH MINUTE BOOKS, HISTORIES, AND RECORDS

Belvedere Baptist Church—Belvedere, England.

Chicago Baptist Association Annual Reports.

Crown Terrace Baptist Church—Aberdeen, Scotland.

Dunoon Baptist Church—Dunoon, Scotland.

Eltham Park Baptist Church—Eltham, England.

Perth Baptist Chapel—Perth, Scotland.

Rye Lane Baptist Church—Peckham, England.

PERSONAL LETTERS AND PAPERS

Oswald Chambers, Biddy Chambers, Kathleen Chambers.

Gladys Ingram Donnithorne.

William Jessop.

Eva Spink Pulford.
Elizabeth West, Class notes, God's Bible School, 1907.

OFFICIAL DOCUMENTS AND RECORDS

Birth/Death Certificates: Public Records Office, London.
Ships Passenger Lists: Public Records Office, Kew.
Census Records: Public Records Office, Chancery Lane, London.
Census Records: Register House, Edinburgh, Scotland.

INDEX

A

B

C

D

E

F

G

H

I

J

K

L

M

N

O

P

Q

R

S

T

W

Y

Z

Note to the Reader

The publisher invites you to share your response to the message of this book by writing Discovery House Publishers, P. O. Box 3566, Grand Rapids, MI 49501, U.S.A. or by calling 1-800-653-8333. For information about other Discovery House publications, contact us at the same address and phone number.